ENVIRONMENTAL ACTIVISM AND WORLD CIVIC POLITICS

SUNY SERIES IN INTERNATIONAL
ENVIRONMENTAL POLICY AND THEORY
SHELDON KAMIENIECKI, EDITOR

ENVIRONMENTAL ACTIVISM AND WORLD CIVIC POLITICS

PAUL WAPNER

State University of New York Press

Published by
State University of New York Press, Albany

© 1996 State University of New York

For information, address the State University of New York Press,
90 State Street, Suite 700, Albany, NY 12207

Production by E. Moore
Marketing by Fran Keneston

Library of Congress Cataloging-in-Publication Data

Wapner, Paul Kevin.
    Environmental activism and world civic politics / Paul Wapner.
        p. cm. — (SUNY series in international environmental policy
    and theory)
        Includes bibliographical references (p.   ) and index.
        ISBN 0–7914–2789–7 (acid-free paper). — ISBN 0–7914–2790–0 (pbk.
    acid-free paper)
        1. Environmentalism. 2. Non-governmental organizations—Political
    activity. I. Title. II. Series
    GE195.W37 1996
    363.7'057—dc20   95-12889
                                                            CIP

10 9 8 7 6 5 4

For my parents

Morton Bernard Wapner
Elinor Sandra Wapner

Contents

Acknowledgments

In writing about international environmental politics, I have had the good fortune to enjoy the support of many scholars, activists, friends, and a number of institutions. It is a pleasure to express my gratitude to them.

I began researching this book as a graduate student in the Department of Politics at Princeton University. Among my professors and colleagues, I wish to thank Daniel Deudney, Michael Doyle, Hal Feiveson, Robert Gilpin, David Jacobson, Kenneth Oye, Thomas Rochon, Natania Rosenfeld, and Sheldon Wolin. In their own way, each of these people forced me to think more carefully about the manuscript and inspired me to demand more of myself in writing it.

Three people stand out as having made an indelible mark on my thought and political orientation, and their help throughout the writing of this book was indispensable. Leslie Thiele provided true intellectual friendship. He holds the record for reading the manuscript and each time worked hard to make it reflect the best of my thinking. I appreciate his ability to genuinely engage the argument, his patience, and his humor. Michael Walzer read each chapter and provided valuable comments. Talking with him at length about the nature of social criticism and its relationship to environmentalism played a fundamental role in the way I conceptualized the manuscript. While my presentation is not "Walzerian," his thinking and scholarly attitude very much inform the way I wrestle with questions of environmental activism. I owe my deepest intellectual debt to Richard Falk. Richard served as my primary advisor on the dissertation and has been a source of encouragement over the years. His own ideas about social movements and world order provide the conceptual backdrop for the book, and his ability to be both critical and supportive is largely responsible for its quality.

Researching this book led me into the lives of countless activists who were kind enough to share with me their knowledge and resources regarding environmental politics. I am grateful to all of them and wish to extend a special thanks to Twelley Canon, Joshua Handler, Anne Leonard, Dave Malakoff, Karen Topakian, and Marike Torfs.

As an assistant professor in the School of International Service at The American University, I have benefitted from being part of an intellectual community that supports my work while concomitantly being critical of its excesses. This proved helpful in the editing process. Among my colleagues, I am grateful to Philip Brenner, Louis Goodman, James Mittelman, and especially Nicholas Onuf for their willingness to work through parts of the argument with me. Stanley Burgiel, Kathleen Farley, Thomas Johnson, Bryan Larson, Lori Lindburg, Jamie Moon, and Stephen Osgood provided valuable research assistance.

The John D. and Catherine T. MacArthur Foundation and the Center of International Studies at Princeton provided financial assistance for researching and revising the manuscript. I very much appreciate their generosity.

From a different corner of my life, I am indebted to family and friends. Ever since I began this project my grandmother, Anne Kaytes, has been asking the perennial question, "When?" This publication gives me the opportunity finally to answer her and to thank her and the rest of my family—Howard Wapner, Susan Thiele, Jacob Thiele, and Faye and Joseph Wapner—for years of unending enthusiasm and support. Through their generosity, in all senses of the word, they have made the effort more meaningful and enjoyable. Mordecai Morgenstern, Joanna Bottaro and John Bennett, dear old friends, provided constant kindness and for this I am grateful.

My wife and *beshert*, Diane Singerman, enabled me to finish the book with a sense of purpose and a lot of smiling. Her presence in my life is a constant source of enrichment. She recently gave birth to our daughter, Eliza, and together both of them provide a steady reminder of the importance of environmental activism.

Finally, my deepest thanks go to my parents. From day one, they wished only the best for me. I am very fortunate to dedicate this book to them.

1   Introduction

They are wrong who think that politics is like an ocean voyager or a military campaign, something to be done with some end in view, something which levels off as soon as that end is reached. It is not a public chore to be got over with; it is a way of life.

—Plutarch

There is now widespread agreement that environmental issues represent enduring challenges to the way people everywhere live their lives. We now know, "in our bones," as William Ophuls put it,[1] that we cannot continue using resources and producing wastes irrespective of the earth's carrying capacity but rather must bring our social and productive activities more into line with the biological limits of the earth. Indeed, almost any indicator one chooses to look at tells essentially the same story: unless human beings alter their activities on a widespread scale, the quality of life on earth will be greatly compromised, if not fundamentally threatened, due to environmental degradation.

Developing and sustaining an environmentally sound course, however, is no easy matter, especially recognizing that environmental dangers are the cumulative effects of practices taking place in diverse settings, animated by multifarious factors. Moreover, environmental protection is not the only aim of societies and thus must be balanced with other social goals, such as economic well-being, which, depending upon how one thinks about it, can conflict with environmentally sound measures. To reorient human activities on such a scale and order of complexity entails employing means of governance that can actually influence vast and diverse numbers of people. It requires finding ways to constrain and direct activities, in a feasible manner, away from environmentally harmful practices and toward more environmentally sound ones. To put it in ordinary language, environmental concern fundamentally involves politics.

Over the past few decades, national governments, public and private research institutions, and corporations have become involved in environmental politics. They have all worked, in one capacity or another, to shape widespread human behavior with regard to environmental issues. Over this same period of time, a host of citizen-organized activist groups have arisen—or greatly expanded their size and scope—with the aim of protecting the earth. While data are sketchy, it is estimated that presently there are over 100,000 nongovernmental organizations (NGOs) working, in some capacity, for environmental protection, and a majority of these are activist groups.[2] Perhaps more impressive than numbers, the scope and power of environmental activist organizations has dramatically increased. In recent years, a number of groups have become transnational. They are organized across state boundaries and work toward environmental protection at the global level. The budgets of the largest of these groups are greater than the amounts most countries spend on environmental issues and at least double what the United Nations Environment Programme (UNEP) spends annually for its work.[3] Furthermore, membership in these organizations has grown over the last two decades to a point where millions of people are currently members of transnational environmental groups.[4] The best known of these organizations include Greenpeace, Friends of the Earth (FOE), the Chipko Movement, Conservation International, and World Wildlife Fund (WWF).

This book is about transnational environmental activist groups. It describes and analyzes the strategies they employ to shape widespread behavior or, put differently, their politics. Despite the increasing presence of environmental activist groups in world environmental affairs, few studies exist that try to understand what, in fact, these organizations are doing.[5] This is unfortunate because as I hope to show transnational environmental activists are fashioning a type of politics that, while not an answer to contemporary environmental problems, greatly contributes to global environmental protection. In what follows, I bring this type of political practice into sharp relief and explore its meaning for both environmental affairs and the study of international relations. For reasons to be explained, I refer to this practice as world civic politics.

When most of us think about environmental politics, we tend to focus on nation-states. States are the main actors in world affairs and thus represent the primary mechanisms for addressing issues such as ozone depletion, global warming, and threats to biological diversity. It makes sense, then, to see transnational environmental activists foremost as pressure groups that try to persuade governments to work for environmental well-being. Activists, from this perspective, lobby government officials in diverse countries and try to influence state officials at international conferences and other forums to support environmental protection measures. Such a view would not be far off the mark. Transnational activists devote tremendous effort toward lobbying, and this has been crucial to advancing international environmental law and practice. Such effort has been formidable in, for example, strengthening the London Dumping Convention,[6] establishing an international ban on elephant ivory trading,[7] and enforcing the Convention on International Trade in Endangered Species (CITES).[8]

The point of departure for this book is that the governmental dimension of world politics, and thus the lobbying efforts of transnational environmental activist groups, represent only one element of world political activity and a focus on them exclusively constitutes an incomplete approach to and understanding of environmental protection. To be sure, nation-states are essential in addressing environmental issues and activist efforts to pressure them are significant in world environmental affairs. Additionally, however, there are other arenas for organizing and carrying out efforts that are separate from the realm of government. These other arenas can be found in what has been called global civil society,[9] and the attempt to use them for environmental protection purposes is a form of world civic politics. Transnational environmental groups practice world civic politics in addition to lobbying, and their work along these lines has become an important component of environmental politics more generally.

Public activity both within countries and beyond their borders is not completely organized by the institution of the state. The state's military, police, legal, administrative, and productive organs penetrate only certain domains of collective experience. Other spheres not only exist but greatly influence the character of public life. The most obvious is the economic realm insofar as it is independent of the state. Market forces, both domestically and internationally, shape the way vast numbers of people act in reference to issues of public concern and involvement. Additional mechanisms exist throughout and across societies in the form of social and cultural networks that structure collective behavior. Voluntary associations affiliated with science, trade, cultural expression, religion, and production influence widespread practices.

The underlying character of these nonstate arenas is that they take place in the civil dimension of world collective life. Civil society is understood to be that arena of social engagement existing above the individual yet below the state.[10] It is a complex network of economic, cultural, and social practices based on friendship, custom, the market, and voluntary affiliation.[11] Although the concept arose in the analysis of domestic societies, it is beginning to make sense on a global level.[12] The interpenetration of markets, the intermeshing of symbolic meaning systems, and the proliferation of transnational collective endeavors signal the formation of a thin, but nevertheless present, form of global civil society. Global civil society, as such, is that slice of associational life that exists above the individual and below the state, but also across national boundaries.

Like its domestic counterpart, global civil society consists of structures that define and shape public affairs. When people organize themselves across state boundaries they create institutional and ideational structures which lend predictability to their collective endeavors and partially shape wider patterns of transnational social practice. For environmental activists, this does not happen simply as a matter of course, but can be deliberately fashioned to further particular ends; actors can intentionally participate in the formation and manipulation of global civil society. The politicization of global civil society involves turning the realms of transnational social, cultural, and economic life into levers of power that can be used to affect world public affairs.

One can appreciate the idea of world civic politics by drawing an analogy between activist efforts at the domestic and international levels. According to Melucci, Habermas, Offe, and others, the myriad of contemporary domestic peace, human rights, women's, and human potential movements in the developed world both lobby their respective governments and work through their societies to affect change.[13] In this latter regard, movements identify and manipulate nonstate levers of power, institutions, and modes of action to alter the dynamics of domestic collective life. The French antinuclear movement, the early years of the German Green Party, and the feminist movement in the United Kingdom represent significant attempts to politicize various arenas to bring about change.[14] Likewise, present day grassroots organizations—from new populism in the United States to Christian-based communities in Latin America to alternative development organizations in India—are all targeting their governments and nurturing modes of political expression outside state control.[15] Finally, the early years of Solidarity in Poland and Charter 77 in former Czechoslovakia illustrate the multifaceted character of activist politics. Recognizing the limits of influencing their respective states directly, Solidarity and Charter 77 created and utilized horizontal, societal associations involving church activities, savings associations, literary ventures, and the like to help order public life and bring about widespread changes.[16] In each case, actors do not ignore the state but rather make a strategic decision to explore the political potential of unofficial realms of collective action. In each instance, groups target governmental officials when appropriate and when it appears efficacious. When this route of political expression fails or proves too dangerous, they seek other means of affecting widespread conditions and practices.

Moved up a political notch, this form of politics helps explain the efforts of transnational environmental groups. Greenpeace, Friends of the Earth, Earth Island Institute, and so forth target governments and try to change state behavior to further their aims. In fact, this type of activity consumes a tremendous amount of their efforts. When this route fails or proves less efficacious, however, they work through transnational economic, social, and cultural networks to achieve their ends. In this capacity they practice world civic politics.

CIVIL SOCIETY AND POLITICS

Contemporary understandings of civil society stem largely from Hegel and to a lesser extent Tocqueville. Hegel's main contribution is to define civil society in contrast to the state. For Hegel, civil society is a sphere or "moment" of political order wherein free association takes place between individuals. It is an arena of particular needs, private interests, and divisiveness but within which citizens can come together to realize joint aims.[17] Building upon Hegel's view, many contemporary theorists also understand civil society in contrast to the state. Civil society is the arena beyond the individual in which people engage in spontaneous, customary, and nonlegalistic forms of association with the intention of, as Tocqueville put it, pursuing "great aims in common."[18] The state, on the other hand, is a complex network of governmental institutions—including the military, bureaucracy, and executive offices—that constitute a legal or constitutional order. This order is animated by formal, official authority and aims to administer and control a given territory.[19]

The distinction between the state and civil society is crucial for developing a first-cut understanding of world civic politics. Analytically, the two realms circumscribe different types of activity and, when transnational environmental activists politicize global civil society, they are not engaged in directly manipulating or targeting formal, official offices. It is important to recognize, however, that civil society is not wholly autonomous or completely separate from the activities of states. As Gramsci and others have argued, state rule often permeates throughout civil society to consolidate power. In these instances, the state and civil society are practically indistinguishable as schools, councils, universities, churches, and even activist groups are regulated, monitored, or run by the state itself.[20] Moreover, even in societies that are not so saturated by the presence of the state—in which a robust civil society is thought to exist independent of the state—it is inaccurate to assume a sharp distinction. The boundaries of the state are always ill-defined and essentially amorphous, leaking into and overlapping with civil society itself.[21]

Following this line of thought, the elusive, porous and mobile boundaries between the state and civil society make clear that when actions take place in one realm—although they have a distinct quality of efficacy about them—they have consequences for the other realm.[22] The same is true at the global level. Global civil society does not exist in a vacuum but operates alongside of and constantly interacts with the state system. The actions of the states greatly structure the content and significance of economic, social, and cultural practices throughout the world; and these same practices, in turn, shape the character of state action. World civic politics, then, is not a practice that is immune from and unconcerned with state activity. Overlaps exist and, as will be shown, they are important to strategies of particular transnational environmental groups.[23]

Having said this, it is absolutely essential to emphasize that it is not the entanglements and overlaps with states and the state system that make efforts undertaken in global civil society "political." Just because overlaps exist does not mean that they are the *raison d'être* of politics; transnational activism does not simply become politically relevant when it intersects with state behavior. Rather, its political character consists in the ability to use the cultural, social, and economic networks of the world to alter and shape widespread behavior. That these networks happen to imbricate the domain of states reveals more about the contours and texture of the playing field within which activists and others operate than the character of politics itself.

There is a tendency in the study of international relations to see politics as a practice associated solely with national governments. There are good historical and intellectual reasons for this. Since roughly the Peace of Westphalia in 1648, states have emerged that hold a monopoly over the legitimate use of violence within given territories and constitute legal and constitutional orders. The state, as such, has become the primary institution capable of commanding widespread authority and thus able to direct large-scale human activity. Many scholars have, understandably, abstracted from the powerful presence of the state to conceive of this capability as the essence of politics itself. Politics, for them, consists in the practice of governance that is national in character and operative through the means of law or, more specifically, law backed by force. To use Lasswell's often-quoted definition, politics is about who gets what, when and how; and many see national governments as the sole authoritative mechanism that makes these decisions.

While governments are the main authoritative political institutions, politics as an activity or politically relevant behavior itself is not exhausted by them. In its broadest sense, politics has to do with the interface of power and what Cicero called, *res publica,* the public thing or public domain.[24] That is, politics is the employment of means to order, direct, and manage human behavior in matters of common concern and involvement. National governments, to be sure, are specific actors involved in politics. They are material entities with bureaucracies, personnel, equipment, and budgets that aim to govern affairs. They do not, however, monopolize the practice itself.

The idea of world civic politics signifies that embedded in the activities of transnational environmental groups is an understanding that states do not hold a monopoly over the instruments that govern human affairs but rather that nonstate forms of governance exist and can be used to effect widespread change.[25] To the extent that activists are successful at translating this understanding into an effective strategy of change—something to be demonstrated in the following pages—one must develop greater appreciation for a civic notion of governance and politics in a global context.

WORLD CIVIC POLITICS AND GLOBAL ENVIRONMENTAL GOVERNANCE

The practice of world civic politics not only raises questions about conventional understandings of politics but also introduces a fundamentally different approach to global environmental governance. As mentioned, most students of international relations—and, by extension, students of international environmental politics—privilege the state in their analyses. In the context of global environmental governance, this consists of a view that could be called *statism*. Statism is the position that environmental problems can best be addressed by existing nation-states under the rubric of the contemporary state system. States, as the main actors in international affairs, are the primary mechanisms able to reach into and influence the lives of vast numbers of people and, as such, represent *the* entity for undertaking environmental protection. (To be sure, nongovernmental organizations play a role in international politics, according to statists, but, as mentioned, do so by influencing states.) Statists point to agreements such as CITES and the Montreal Protocol on Substances that Deplete the Ozone Layer as instances of successful multilateral accords and use them as models to argue that states, themselves, can and will address transboundary and global environmental problems.

Notwithstanding a respectable record of international cooperation on environmental issues, a sizeable number of scholars express disappointment with the ability of states to address successfully environmental dangers. For these thinkers, states will never be able to secure environmental well-being as long as they operate in the context of the state system. Rather, promising environmental action will only come about in a reformed world order—where the size, scope, and character of existing states are radically changed. For these thinkers, international regimes like CITES and so forth are mere window dressing for problems that require greater coordination between states than is possible in the present system and that, at times, defy state capabilities altogether. While a diverse group, there are essentially two schools of thought promoting a radical restructuring of the state system: supra-statism and sub-statism.[26]

Supra-statism maintains that the problematic character of the state system can only be overcome by creating a world government to generate, legislate, and enforce environmental regulations. Supra-statists argue that the mismatch between the unitary character of environmental issues and the fragmentary structure of the state system will always lead to insufficient environmental protection as states undertake inadequate domestic measures, negotiate weak accords, or capriciously comply with international mandates when this best serves their interests. A world government, according to supra-statists, would transcend the narrow aspirations of independent states and protect the entire earth by enacting consistent and comprehensive environmental measures worldwide.

Sub-statists, on the other hand, also feel the state system is at the core of environmental degradation but argue for a different type of remedy. Instead of building a supra-state to address environmental issues, this second school of thought calls for breaking up existing ones. For sub-statists, environmental dilemmas arise because of the increasing scale of human organization and practices throughout the world. Large-scale enterprises necessitate concentrating power which involves using technologies and pursuing forms of economic activity that are insensitive to local and regional dimensions of environmental issues. What is needed, according to sub-statism, is to decentralize power and fashion governing units that correspond and are responsive to on-the-ground practices that damage the environment. In one formulation, governing units would coincide with natural bioregions, which constitute semicontained ecosystems that have their own ecological imperatives.

While supra-statism and sub-statism present themselves as radical perspectives on global environmental governance, it is curious that, analytically, they do not represent fundamental departures from statism. All three emphasize that the institutional make-up of world affairs is central to environmental protection; all three approaches see the institution of the modern state playing a pivotal role as either the only route to effective environmental protection or the foil against which alternative routes must be explored. All three end up, in other words, reifying the governmental dimension of politics and thereby discounting other avenues for addressing environmental dangers. This is unfortunate because such a focus unduly constrains environmental political thought and action.

World civic politics does not privilege the state and is thus fundamentally different from statism, supra-statism, and sub-statism. The state is the central, but by no means the only, fact of global political life. World civic politics works underneath, above, and around the state to bring about widespread change. Its approach to global environmental governance rests on the view that the state system alone cannot solve our environmental woes nor will substituting it with some other institutional form do the trick. The dynamics of environmental harm exceed the workings of the state system and thus relying solely on it or proposing alternative arrangements in its place are incomplete enterprises. Additionally, political effort must enlist nonstate mechanisms which operate in tandem with state activities and at the level, but not of the instrumental quality, of supra-statism and sub-statism. That is, environmental politics must work above, below, and at the level of interstate relations to advance environmental protection but do so in ways that do not simply focus on the governmental dimension available or proposed at each level of political activity. World civic politics, then, augments a governmental approach to politics and, as such, complements the politics of the state system and enlarges the political imagination as it reflects upon global environmental governance.[27]

NONGOVERNMENTAL ORGANIZATIONS AND THE STUDY OF WORLD POLITICS

While this book analyzes the politics of transnational environmental activist groups, at a higher level of abstraction it seeks to shift the terms of debate among students of international relations regarding the role of nongovernmental organizations. For decades, scholars have assumed that the conception and meaning of NGOs has been settled. NGOs, according to this assumption, are best understood as transnational pressure groups which gain political relevance to the degree they influence state action. That is, NGOs matter in world politics to the extent that they change states' policies or create conditions in the international system that enhance or diminish interstate cooperation. As a result, most studies of NGOs aim to demonstrate and measure NGO influence on state behavior.[28]

The premise of this book is that the conception and meaning of NGOs in world affairs is not settled and will remain problematic as long as scholars remain focused on the relations between NGOs and the state, and ignore the civic dimension of NGO efforts. NGO activities within and across societies are a proper object of study and only by including them can one render an accurate understanding of NGOs and, by extension, world politics. By highlighting the world civic politics practiced by transnational environmental activists—a subset of NGOs—this book assumes a critical stance toward contemporary NGO research and, to the degree the book's conclusions are persuasive, calls for recasting the role of NGOs in world affairs.

Sustained debate about NGOs began in the 1960s and early 1970s. At the time, many scholars argued that nonstate actors were growing in number and power and, as a consequence, students of world politics would be better served paying attention to NGOs as well as, if not instead of, nation-states. For example, a substantial number of multinational corporations (MNCs) had assets that exceeded the gross national product (GNP) of certain states and had projects taking place in a host of countries;[29] as a result, many scholars claimed that MNCs were curtailing state action and represented an independent variable for explaining world events.[30] Likewise, advances in communication technology were allowing nonstate actors such as revolutionary groups, the Catholic Church, and political parties to play a greater role in world politics. Innovations in overseas travel, international wire services, computer networks, and telecommunications were enabling these actors to influence the ideas, values, and political persuasions of people across the globe. Scholars argued that they were having a significant impact on questions of peace, international morality, and the salience of political issues.[31] In short, the surge in transnational activity suggested that the state might not be the most important variable to study when trying to understand world events.[32]

The debate over the relative importance of the state in world affairs had an impact in the field insofar as it convinced political realists—those who most explicitly privileged the state in the 1960s and 1970s—that NGOs matter.[33] To be sure, this took some effort. Defenders of the strictly state-centric model argued, for example, that the proliferation of NGOs was a function of hegemonic stability and thus derivative of interstate behavior.[34] Others claimed that transnationalism was not increasing interdependence between states, and hence restricting states' ability to control events, but that the amount of interdependence had actually been decreasing compared to earlier times.[35] Furthermore, many claimed that while the number of nonstate actors was rising significantly, NGOs were not involved in the most consequential world events at the time. Compared to nation-states, nonstate actors were marginal in political importance.[36] Notwithstanding these arguments, by the 1980s,

NGOs had won significance and scholars began to take them seriously. They became a legitimate object of study.

The debate about NGOs, while important, suffered premature closure. This is because scholars saw NGO significance, ultimately, in terms of state power. That is, in most subsequent studies NGOs gained prominence only to the degree that they affected state policies; their influence on world affairs apart from this role was neglected.[37] One of the reasons for this is that the debate itself was formulated in a way that could only have had this result. Scholars saw the controversy as a "unit of analysis" problem. They argued over which variable should be the proper object of research in world politics. Should one study, for instance, MNCs, the state, revolutionary groups or transnational political parties to understand world affairs? Stated as such, transnationalists were associated with a "sovereignty at bay" model of world politics, which claimed that NGOs were eclipsing states as the key independent actors in world affairs.[38] Unfortunately, this set up the debate as an either/or proposition: either the state was the primary mover and shaker of world affairs or it was not. As a result critics had only to demonstrate the superior causal agency of the state to dismiss or greatly deflate the transnationalist challenge, which is exactly what occurred.[39]

More recently, a resurgence of interest in NGOs has led to efforts to conceptualize them outside the unit of analysis problem. Most of this work is part of a broader set of concerns loosely associated with the so-called third debate, the argument over the proper paradigm for studying international relations. The third debate's origins lie in the questioning of the state-centric model of the 1970s and 1980s but it has since expanded to include epistemological, ontological, and axiological concerns.[40] Interest in NGOs has emerged under the rubric of the third debate insofar as scholars have advanced a number of propositions regarding how, why and to what extent NGOs matter in world affairs based on sophisticated understandings of power, knowledge and agency. Notable here is Rosenau's notion of sovereignty-free actors and the influence of micro-processes on macro-phenomena.[41] Walker's insights concerning the critical component of social movements[42] and Falk's understanding of the anti-statist logic of activist groups.[43] My work uses these propositions as a point of departure but seeks to situate them within a broader frame of reference. In my view the analytic significance of these and similar efforts can be advanced by encompassing them within a larger investigation into the nature of world politics.[41]

Throughout the earlier transnationalist debate, scholars never questioned the essential quality of world political activity. Having lost part of the argument, after being forced to acknowledge the centrality of the state, they failed to ask what constitutes relevant political behavior, what power is, and which dimensions of collective life are most significant for bringing about changes in human practices. Students of international relations fell back on the traditional notion that genuine political activity is the interaction of nation-states, that power consists in the means available to states, and that the state system is *the* arena for affecting human behavior throughout the world. Thus, NGOs became important, but only because they influenced state behavior; they did not affect world affairs in their own right.[44] Current research can fall into this same trap if not understood to be part of a more fundamental type of examination.

This book studies NGOs with a particular focus on the meaning of world politics. It eschews an understanding in which the multifarious activities of actors gain relevance only insofar as they affect states and, concentrates instead, on articulating NGO activity which orders, directs, and manages widespread behavior throughout the world. One can get a sense of this through a study of transnational environmental activist groups. In doing so, however, one must focus on the political action of these organizations itself and trace its world significance and interpret its meaning independent of the argument about relative causal weight. That is, one must be more interested in understanding the nature of certain types of political action than in ranking different agents that engage in politics. By doing so, scholars will be able to recognize that NGOs are significant in world affairs not only because they influence states but also because they affect the behavior of larger collectivities throughout the world. They do so by manipulating governing structures of global civil society or, put differently, engaging in world civic politics.

Presentation of the Argument

This book is organized along the following lines. Having introduced the theoretical argument, the next chapter justifies the reason activists work in the civic dimension of collective life and sets up an analytical framework for understanding how they do so. It begins by examining and then critically assessing the way the contemporary state system addresses environmental issues. This includes a review of state activities at the domestic, international, and global levels, and theoretical and empirical accounts of why such efforts, while essential, are insufficient. The chapter goes on to describe and critically analyze the two most prominent conceptual alternatives to the state system: supra-statism and sub-statism. These schools of thought are placed in the context of international relations scholarship more generally and analyzed regarding the contribution they can make to global environmental protection. The chapter argues that, although they offer valuable insights—insights around which activists organize their efforts and thus significant for the overall argument of the book—ultimately, they place too much emphasis on the governmental dimension of politics and neglect other arenas for global environmental political action. Each sees the institution of the modern state and the system within which it is situated as the central facts of world environmental politics. This greatly biases thinking and acting with reference to environmental politics. The chapter concludes by introducing transnational environmental activist groups and making a preliminary case for turning to them to learn about nonstate forms of world environmental politics.

In the following three chapters, I present case studies of the way Greenpeace, Friends of the Earth, and World Wildlife Fund, respectively, undertake their efforts. These chapters aim to explicate the nature of world civic politics by depicting the world civic dimension of each of these group's activities. Each chapter consists of two parts. The first is an empirical discussion which outlines the origins, organizational structure, and political strategies of a single group. This introduces readers to the organization under consideration and describes the nonstatist dimension of its politics. The second part interprets this dimension in the context of world politics more generally. This latter discussion is more theoretical and explains the genuine political character of activists' nonstate-oriented efforts. It aims to speak to the question of accurately conceptualizing world politics.

The first group I study is Greenpeace. While Greenpeace engages in numerous political activities, I pay particular attention to the way it disseminates an ecological sensibility. Greenpeace's work entails persuading all types of people to care about environmental conditions and to take actions to protect the earth. To do this, Greenpeace targets the global cultural realm. It clues into internationally shared modes of discourse, such as moral norms, symbols, and scientific argument, and it manipulates them to induce people to pursue, what Greenpeace assumes are, environmentally sound practices. My aim is to convince the reader that this is a significant form of world politics even though it is not a matter of state activity.

The second group I study is World Wildlife Fund. Among its many activities, World Wildlife Fund devotes much effort to actual environmental restoration and protection. World Wildlife Fund works in environmentally stressed regions and engages local residents in programs of environmental renewal. Its intention is to empower local people so they can maintain the environmental integrity of their own environments. This is part of a broader strategy of strengthening civil societies throughout the world. My aim in this chapter is to demonstrate that actual local environmental–rescue work is a significant form of world politics.

The last group I examine is Friends of the Earth. Among its many activities, Friends of the Earth works directly at the interface between states and global civil society. States are enmeshed in networks of economic, social, and cultural processes that are not derivative of interstate relations. Friends of the Earth focuses on these processes and alters them so they will reflect a concern for the global environment. To the degree that governments interact with these processes, they become more accountable to environmental protection. What is key to recognize in this chapter is that while Friends of the Earth directs its efforts, in large part, to the activities of states, again, the emphasis is on politicizing global civil society. My intention is to persuade the reader that this is a genuinely important form of world politics even though the dynamics at work are not statist in nature.

After presenting the case studies, I return to the issue of worldwide forms of governance. Using the empirical and interpretive material presented in previous chapters, I argue in theoretical terms for the efficacy of world civic politics. Elaborating on the nature of disseminating an ecological sensibility, empowering local residents, and manipulating the interdependencies of world affairs, I emphasize how these nonstatist mechanisms actually alter the way people around the globe live their lives. In this last chapter, I describe in detail the notion of world civic politics and reflect upon its meaning for scholarship in international relations. I conclude that, when scholars duly appreciate the element of governance inherent in world civic politics, they are better able to understand the nature of world politics itself.

Before proceeding, it is necessary to make three caveats regarding this study. First, although I refer to transnational environmental activist groups in general, this work focuses predominantly on northern organizations. Greenpeace, World Wildlife Fund, and Friends of the Earth originated and maintain central headquarters in the developed world.[45] By focusing on these organizations, then, I am assuming that an understanding of northern organizations will shed light upon all transnational groups. This premise may, of course, turn out to be false.[46]

Second, although this book examines transnational environmental groups, it does not suggest that such organizations have a monopoly on ecological wisdom, are the harbingers of an environmentally sound future, or stand beyond justifiable criticism. Activists, like all political actors, have their own problems. Important questions need to be asked, for example, about their use, and at times misuse, of scientific evidence; their accountability (they are not elected officials); and the often antagonistic relations between groups. I do not address these dimensions of activist groups in great detail in the book, although in quite a few places I refer to points of contestation about particular issues. I do this not to overlook the problems associated with transnational activist groups so much as to maintain a focus on the type of politics they employ to further their goals. In other words, one need not necessarily support the work of transnational environmental groups to understand how they operate in the international arena.

Finally, although I present a sympathetic reading of activist groups, I do not believe they represent an answer to global environmental problems. Indeed, there is no answer per se. There is a long history of anthropogenic environmental abuse; living on the earth in ways that do not disrupt its ecological integrity has always been—and seemingly will always be—an unending challenge.[47] Part of the reason for this is that environmental issues are not puzzles in search of solutions but rather perennial challenges that successive generations must persistently confront anew. These challenges involve constantly searching for more sensitive and sustainable ways of interacting with the natural environment not discovering some single answer to environmental protection. Transnational environmental groups are very much a part of that search, and one can learn much by studying their politics. One cannot look to activists, however, for a so-called solution to humanity's environmental woes.

2 The State and Environmental Challenges

In a social evolutionary perspective, the people pre-existed the state and will be very much there after this particular form of socio-economic and political management has been transcended by better arrangements.
—Kishmore Saint

There is a Sufi story of Mulla Nasrudin who comes back from the marketplace with a basket full of hot chili peppers. While he is sitting in his room eating one after the other, a student enters and inquires why he is eating what are obviously burning hot peppers. Nasrudin's eyes are tearing, his lips are chapped, his nose is red, and his tongue is swollen inside his mouth. "How can you do that to yourself?" asks the student. "How can you continue to eat one awful pepper after another?" Nasrudin replies, "I keep thinking that eventually I will find a sweet one."[1]

Nasrudin's stubborn persistence is emblematic of how most of us approach global environmental problems. We keep focusing on a single political form with the belief that if we just concentrate hard enough or learn to exploit masterfully its capabilities, it will yield up solutions to our ecological woes. Our fixation, however, like Nasrudin's, has its dangers: not only will our lips chap and our eyes tear as we experience advanced stages of, for example, the greenhouse effect or ozone depletion, our very survival will be at risk. It is folly to remain politically narrow-minded.

We are politically preoccupied with the modern state. This, of course, is no surprise. Since at least the seventeenth century the state has progressively become *the* predominant form of political organization on the planet. Currently, all people live within the jurisdiction of a state, and the actions between states are clearly the most important in world politics. This has led many to look to the state as the single most effective mechanism for influencing people's lives and, by extension, the only route to genuine environmental protection. Most environmental protection efforts involve the state, and the vast majority of scholarship focuses on state activities.

What is curious is that our preoccupation with the state runs so deep that it not only organizes our practices and informs our studies, but also infects our political imaginations. There are a number of scholars who doubt the ability of the state to sufficiently address environmental issues. These people feel that the state, as an institution, is ill-equipped to regulate the multifarious practices that contribute to environmental harm and that the state system, as the context within which states operate, imposes constraints that render states incapable of working for genuine global well-being. As a result, these thinkers envision alternative arrangements; they conceptualize what a transformed state and state system would look like if such institutions were fashioned in the service of environmental protection. The problem with much of this thought, however, is that, while it presents itself as incisively critical and understands itself as radical—to the degree it questions the foundational structure of contemporary world politics—it nevertheless still privileges the state. It locates the state system at the core of environmental politics—either as the cause of environmental harm or the obstacle to environmental protection—and thus the structure against which alternatives must be explored. As a result, it tends to prescribe governmental changes as a route to environmental well-being rather than other types of political activity.

While a diverse lot, radical perspectives on global environmental politics tend to fall into one of two schools of thought: supra-statism and sub-statism. The first calls for establishing some form of world government. It argues that the fragmentary nature of the current system inspires states to be too parochial and that this precludes genuinely cooperative and forward-looking initiatives for global environmental protection. The second claims that power is too concentrated in existing states and is therefore too insensitive to the actual dynamics of environmental degradation. It calls for breaking up states and decentralizing the mechanisms that monitor and regulate activities that affect the environment. While innovative, both supra-statism and sub-statism maintain a focus on the state insofar as they wish to reconstitute political authority either above or below it as an answer to environmental issues. That is, the political challenge for both is to reconfigure the size, scope, or character of government so that it will be more responsive to environmental problems. Such a project privileges the state insofar as government, in an international context, usually refers to the nation-state. Thus, finding the right fit between the institution of government and environmental issues is still a matter of placing the state at the center of political inquiry and analysis.

The purpose of this chapter is to illustrate and critically analyze the state-centric nature of contemporary environmental politics and the central role the state plays in supra-statism and sub-statism. In doing so, the chapter serves two functions within the overall scheme of the book. On the one hand, it provides justification for exploring a politics that takes place in global civil society rather than simply and exclusively within the sphere of nation-states. To the degree contemporary statist, that is, state-to-state efforts, fail to address environmental issues, and supra-statist and sub-statist orientations are found wanting, it makes sense to expand political action beyond the state. The first function of this chapter, then, is to explain why transnational environmental activists work beyond the state and engage in world civic politics. On the other hand, an analysis of statism, supra-statism, and sub-statism sets the stage for elaborating the nature of world civic politics. While, in themselves, problematic—insofar as they focus too much on the institution of the modern state—statism, supra-statism, and sub-statism work at levels of politics that can be engaged but not necessarily in an institutional manner. As will become clear over the course of the next few chapters, transnational environmental groups work in ways that parallel statism, supra-statism and sub-statism, and yet avoid institutional reification. They invest themselves at each level of political engagement—at the state, supranational, and subnational levels—but do so in ways that activate unofficial, non-state-constituted types of governance. Activists pursue, what I call, *localist, globalist* and *internationalist* types of actions that aim not to establish governmental institutions nor to dismantle existing ones but to enlist the governing capabilities of instruments available below, above, and at the level of the state. These instruments are part of global civil society, and by employing them activists engage in world civic politics.

STATISM AND ITS CRITICS

The state system has done much to address environmental issues. Over the past two decades, many national governments have increased their commitment to environmental protection and have devised policies and undertaken specific actions to translate that commitment into practice. One indication of this is the growth of environmental ministries throughout the world. In 1972 only 25 countries possessed national environmental agencies, with only 11 in the developing world. In contrast, at present there are over 140 national environmental agencies with 110 of them in the developing world.[2] These ministries have been essential in promoting environmental legislation within and among various states. At the national level, for instance, there is now a robust body of environmental law operative in many countries.

The state system has also shown an ability to address international and global environmental problems.[3] The United Nations Conference on the Human Environment (UNCHE), held in Stockholm in 1972, placed environmental issues on the international agenda for the first time and, among its achievements, established the United Nations Environment Programme as a permanent body to oversee the earth's environmental well-being.[4] Since UNCHE, environmental issues have become standard fare in international diplomacy, and governments have signed numerous agreements that seek to minimize transboundary environmental harm. Of the roughly 170 international environmental treaties on record, two thirds of them have been signed since 1972 and address issues ranging from stratospheric ozone depletion to toxic waste exports.[5]

Such international efforts were given an additional boost at the United Nations Conference on Environment and Development (UNCED), held in 1992 in Rio de Janeiro. At UNCED, governments signed conventions focusing on biological diversity and climate change, and crafted a number of documents acknowledging and committing themselves to address the relationship between environment and development issues. Further, they established the Commission on Sustainable Development (CSD) to monitor compliance with the Rio agreements and further institutionalized the Global Environmental Facility (GEF) to finance sustainable development projects throughout the world.[6]

According to many observers, these efforts are admirable and indicate that the state system can do much to address environmental issues. Nonetheless, a sizeable number of critics point out that when such efforts are taken as a whole, they do not reflect a strong record of protection nor represent an overall strategy toward environmental well-being.[7] This evaluation stems, at first, from empirical evidence that despite significant national and international efforts, the forces that cause environmental degradation continue unabated and have in fact gained momentum over the past twenty-five years—the period marking the heyday of international environmental efforts.

Using 1972 as a benchmark, almost all indicators of environmental well-being suggest accelerated decline in the overall quality of air, water, and soil throughout the world. To cite just three examples: in the early 1970s, species extinction was taking place at a rate of one species per day.[8] In the 1990s, after many international agreements and much national effort, estimates now predict that approximately 140 species become extinct daily.[9] Additionally, atmospheric concentrations of carbon dioxide, the principal greenhouse gas, have increased 35 percent since UNCHE, with carbon emissions rising from 4.32 billion metric tons in 1972 to 5.83 in 1990.[10] Finally, in the twenty years immediately following UNCHE, approximately 1.6 billion people were added to the earth's population. While the relationship between population and environmental harm is complex, it is important to note that this increase is more than the total number of inhabitants living on the planet in 1900.[11]

To be sure, there have been some achievements and some good news. Air quality in certain regions has improved due to curbs on the burning of particular substances; water pollution has diminished in places like the Great Lakes and the Mediterranean Sea because of sewage treatment and waste reduction; and sections of the earth's forests have been preserved as a result of environmental protection legislation. Nonetheless, these achievements have been, from a global perspective, small-scale and piecemeal. The forces and pace of environmental degradation are outstripping efforts to protect and restore the earth's ecosystem.[12]

Critics explain the losing battle in terms of the state system's inability to confront environmental issues in a unified and committed way. On the domestic level, for instance, they point out that although states have passed much national legislation, effective enforcement has been far more elusive. Jancar-Webster states, for example, that the countries of Eastern Europe and the former Soviet Union are unable or unwilling to enforce the hundreds of regulations and state promulgations aimed at environmental protection because of administrative irresponsibility and the seeming need for unbridled economic production.[13] Additionally, Schubert claims that although many Asian countries have written environmental protection policies into their constitutions and fundamental laws, enforcement is lax due to government incompetence and state commitments to high rates of economic growth.[14] More generally, Lynton Caldwell, author of the most comprehensive book on environmental policy to date, argues that notwithstanding significant efforts, no nation is doing better than simply "retarding the deterioration of its environment."[15] This stems in large measure, according to Caldwell, from the lack of concern at both the individual and government levels, which is necessary to bring issues of environmental management and protection to the forefront of public policy, and from the inability of many states—especially those most severely affected—to marshall adequate resources for appropriate responses to environmental dangers. To paraphrase Caldwell, no state is adequately protecting its environment in a systematic and promising way.[16]

On the international side, critics point out that although states have signed many agreements, compliance is far from perfect and violations abound.[17] For years, Iceland violated the International Whaling Commission (IWC) moratorium by engaging in commercial whaling under the guise of scientific research. (In 1992, Iceland quit the IWC.) In 1993, Norway openly defied the IWC ban, commercially killing 226 minke whales in the northeastern Atlantic and in 1994 repeated its intention to breach the ban.[18] The Cayman Islands have been in violation of the Convention on International Trade in Endangered Species for exporting endangered turtle skins to CITES signatories England, France, and Australia,[19] and Mexico has been cited in violation of CITES also for exporting endangered sea turtles to a number of other countries.[20] These represent only the most flagrant infractions. Noncompliance is a broader issue in that many states lack the resources to implement accords or choose not to abide by them because the international system lacks a strong mechanism of enforcement.[21]

Aside from compliance, critics also claim that existing treaties, even if complied with, are often inadequate to the task at hand. International treaties tend to represent the lowest common acceptable standards for environmental quality, and thus their restrictions and prohibitions tend to be weak. The Convention on

Climate Change agreed upon in Rio, for example, calls for partial measures and sets only voluntary deadlines (many of which are ignored); moreover, it fails to commit sufficient financial resources for implementation.[22] This represents a broader trend of avoiding measurable objectives in treaties that leads to varied and often inadequate forms of response.[23]

Finally, the effectiveness of international agreements is qualified by the fact that monitoring and verification of domestic implementation of international accords are carried out predominantly by states themselves. Self-monitoring and verification is a problem because it creates the possibility of lax implementation with no verifiable way to gauge effectiveness. According to separate studies carried out by the United Nations, the U.S. General Accounting Office, and World Resources Institute, most signatories to most international agreements fail to submit timely, accurate reports on their relevant activities. For example, only 30 percent of signatories to the MARPOL Convention for the Prevention of Pollution from Ships have ever submitted monitoring reports, and only 60 percent of parties to the 1972 London Dumping Convention have submitted reports on their dumping activities. Additionally, of the forty-six parties to the International Tropical Timber Agreement, only fifteen provided required data on their harvesting and trading of timber in 1990.[24] Finally, as of May 1991, only half of the countries required under the Montreal Protocol reported data on activities that affect the ozone layer.[25]

For critics of the state system, these drawbacks point to an inability of states to respond to environmental issues in an adequate fashion. The partial, nonbinding, and unenforceable quality of international agreements support the assessment of Lynton Caldwell, that "[t]he record of organized international cooperation in environmental affairs is superficially impressive. Tangible results of international environmental cooperation, although significant, fall far behind the destructive advance of deforestation, desertification, and environmental contamination, the declining quality of air and water, the degrading of soils and accessible minerals, the loss of species and unique ecosystems, and the seemingly inexorable demands of human populations upon the capabilities of the environment for self-renewal."[26] Such assessment has led many to analyze the structural impediments toward environmental protection inherent in the state system and to prescribe alternative world orders. One school of thought along these lines is supra-statism.

SUPRA-STATISM

Building a World Government

The supra-statist critique begins with the insight that there is a fundamental mismatch between the quality of environmental issues and the structure of the state system. As the authors of *Our Common Future* put it, "The Earth is one but the world is not. We all depend on one biosphere for sustaining our lives. Yet each community, each country, strives for survival and prosperity with little regard for its impact on others."[27] Their point is that there is an incongruence between the character of the threat and the nature of the political mechanisms able to respond. Environmental issues are unitary in character, while the state system is fragmentary.

The state system is fragmentary and anarchic in that there exists no legal authority to govern relations at a level higher than the state itself. There is no central mechanism to coordinate practices between individual states, oversee global affairs, or regulate state activities that are harmful to the collective or the earth itself.[28] In this situation, states act to promote their *national interests*. This can refer to the interests of a state's elite, a majority of its citizens, or even—at least theoretically—the well-being of its entire people. It does not, however, refer to the well-being of the human species as a whole or the planet in its entirety.[29] This was demonstrated poignantly at UNCED when, for example, oil-rich states rejected all references to petroleum as environmentally harmful. The United Arab Emirates, for instance, claimed that oil was a "clean" resource because it produces less carbon dioxide than coal.[30] Malaysia, Indonesia, and Brazil, key timber-producing states, opposed any regulations that would have curtailed their right to cut their forests at current, unsustainable rates. Their opposition contributed to downgrading a proposed forest treaty to a set of nonbinding principles. Finally, the United States opposed all references to lifestyle changes and worked to minimize the link between consumption and environmental destruction. At Rio, former President Bush said that he was "President of the United States, not president of the world and [that he would] do what [was] best to defend U.S. interests."[31] These positions represent the dilemma of national leadership within a sovereign state system. "When it's most successful at solving problems to the benefit of its own people," writes Robert Tucker, "it works against the requirements of global life."[32] This captures, in a nutshell, the fundamental mismatch between the nature of global problems and the character of existing political structures.[33] As George Modelski put it years ago, "[a]nyone who gives a moment's reflection to the matter must come to the conclusion that states, being devices for governing partial or limited portions of the globe, and being responsible at best only to partial and limited constituencies, are hardly the most efficient organizations for giving attention to world problems. . . ."[34]

According to supra-statism, if a major obstacle to solving global problems is fragmentation of the units, then an obvious alternative would be to unify them, that is, create a supra-state that can transcend the narrow aspirations of diverse states and promote a global one. The thought is to move up a political notch, to move from nation-states to a single world state. This would relieve the bickering between sovereign units and unite humanity against common dangers that threaten its overall well-being. To put it slightly differently, if the key problem with the state system is that the individual state is too small to engender universalist solidarity and coordinate environmental efforts worldwide, then there needs to be a world state to bring the political mechanisms of the world in line with the character of global problems. The standard version of such unification is usually a form of world government.

The vast majority of world government schemes address issues of war and peace. The classic argument for world government is that order among states is best established by the same means that preserve order within them, viz. by a supreme, sovereign authority. The logic involved suggests that states currently exist in a Hobbesian 'state of nature.' This consists of a perpetual struggle for power in a war of all against all wherein life is 'nasty, brutish and short.' To escape from this, states must subordinate themselves to a common government. This sovereign authority would resolve conflicts and prescribe laws that would be backed by force. The governmental presence that would result is similar to that which exists on the national level of a well-organized state.

There is a long history of proposals for world government. Confucius, the Stoics, Rousseau, and Kant can be counted among its most famous theoretical advocates. Debate about world government reached its peak, however, shortly after the Second World War. The impetus for such thinking was to prevent the outbreak of another worldwide conflict and to avoid nuclear war. Aside from the host of theoretical schemes, there was also widespread popular interest in concretely establishing a world state; in the late 1940s, there were roughly seventy organizations around the world, with memberships totaling hundreds of thousands of people, who were committed to creating a world government. Additionally, close to a quarter of the members of the British Parliament and the U.S. Congress supported resolutions that, in principle, favored a world federal government.[35]

The most popular arguments and schemes for world government were put forward by the world federalists.[36] These people saw world government coming about not by conquest or treason (bypassing the political authority of states) but by a contract among existing states. Thus, they proposed a federation rather than an empire or a single world state. Within this camp, lines were drawn between those who saw the need for a complete and comprehensive form of government, the *maximalists*, and those who sought a form of governance that simply kept the peace between states, the *minimalists*.

For maximalists, the world needed a mechanism that could supervise and regulate all the chores of a national government on a global scale. The most famous and detailed of these schemes was that put forward by Robert Hutchins and the Committee to Frame a World Constitution. Under the Hutchins proposal, a world government would enjoy numerous powers including the settlement of disputes, the levying and collection of taxes, the coordination of transportation, and the issuance of a world currency. There would be an executive, judiciary, legislature, and armed forces. The Committee also proposed the creation of a federal capital and an official world language, calendar, and system of measurement. The idea was simply to create a sovereign body at the global level.[37]

The minimalists believed that such schemes went too far. There was no need for a comprehensive system of government at the global level. This would be cumbersome, redundant, and thus lower the prospects of it ever coming to be. Minimalists sought governance only over the instruments of war in order to prevent large-scale military conflict. If the elements of world governance proved successful in this respect, then it would be possible to extend the mandate to other areas. To do so prematurely, however, would be fatal to the entire enterprise.

The most popular proposal coming out of the minimalist camp was Grenville Clark and Louis Sohn's *World Peace Through World Law*. The strength of this work was that it did not seek to set up a whole new form of world government to address issues of war and peace, but rather sought only to strengthen the existing United Nations Charter. The proposal rested on modifying voting procedures, creating a world police force, strengthening the powers of the General Assembly and restricting the right of veto in the Security Council. Furthermore, Clark and Sohn suggested expanding agencies, especially in the sphere of economic development, to alleviate sources of instability and conflict throughout the world. If not the most famous, *World Peace Through World Law* is certainly the most detailed proposal for the reconstruction of the UN.[38]

A different but related approach to match political mechanisms to global problems is functionalism. While not strictly a form of world government, it represents a move upwards, away from the sovereign state, with the intention of creating a set of supra-state authorities to address problems confronting the whole world. The functionalist approach is most closely associated with the work of David Mitrany. For Mitrany, the problem with past schemes of integration is that they tried to use political means—that is, writing constitutions—to bridge the fragmentation of states. As the word functionalism makes clear, the road to unity is not through political but functional means. Many pragmatic problems that are not intrinsically political in nature arise in a world of sovereign states. International postal services, scientific collaboration on common problems, international labor conditions, and so forth represent dilemmas that are amenable to technical or logistical solutions and do not need the attention of formal governments. Mitrany suggests that the steady growth in activity by specialized agencies to address these functional dilemmas will generate a network of institutions that will enmesh and eventually supersede the nation-state system. As technical cooperation grows in significance, it will eclipse the loyalty to and political efficacy of individual states. States will be bound together not under the formal rubric of world government but intertwined by a proliferating network of international, functionally specific organizations.[39]

Ernst Haas puts forth a variant of functionalism that supports the notion that international agencies can create networks of cooperation and thus integrate the world in significant ways, but he parts with Mitrany on the way such networks encroach on the political sphere of nation-states. While Mitrany emphasizes the technical, nonpolitical dimension of international organizations, Haas contends that it is the extension of these agencies into the realm of politics that accounts for significant compromises of state sovereignty.

Through an exhaustive study of the International Labour Organization (ILO), Haas demonstrates that the politicization of the ILO was responsible for establishing international standards that became generalized rules of conduct for peoples and states around the world.[40] In both variations of functionalism, the key idea is that the fragmented character of the state system will be overcome by the proliferation of international agencies performing specific functions. Thus, the concept is not to draft a world constitution and find parties to sign it; world governance comes about as an indirect result of inroads made on state sovereignty in, at least initially, non-political areas.

Building a World State for the Environment

Environmental dangers are transboundary in character and, in the extreme, threaten the well-being of everyone on earth. Many thinkers attempting to come to terms with these dangers recognize several of the shortcomings associated with the state system mentioned in the previous section and have devised alternate schemes for confronting global dilemmas through world government. For these theorists, there must be a central guidance system to undertake environmental management on the globe. This will establish uniform policies and restrictions to preserve the earth's stock of renewable and nonrenewable resources and guard against dangers that threaten the planet's overall ecosystem.

The main arguments supporting world government as a way to address global environmental problems rest on the view that, left to their own designs, states will continue to ignore the ecological limits of the planet and forego necessary actions in defending the earth from decay. In the present state system there is little incentive for states to do otherwise. In fact, because we live in a competitive world—among individuals as well as states—there is an incentive to *exploit* resources. To the degree that the air, land, and water are common property, it is in people's personal—and states' national—interests to use scarce resources before their competitors do.

Garrett Hardin presents a theoretical explanation for this phenomenon in his now-famous essay, "The Tragedy of the Commons." He claims that most ecological resources—watersheds, oceans, atmosphere, biological cycles, and the biosphere itself—are part of the global commons. They are beyond the jurisdiction of individual states and are thus exploitable by anyone. Moreover, because such resources are limited, there is an incentive for states to use them before their counterparts do so. In such a situation, it is folly to allow individuals to make their own decisions about using resources. According to Hardin: "It is the essence of the system of the commons that the members are free to make their own decisions. It is also crystal clear that in a limited world—the only world we will ever know—freedom in the commons brings ruin to all."[41]

Hardin thus advocates the creation of new social arrangements to protect the commons and to make certain that people do not overuse the earth's resources. The logic here is that we cannot rely on volunteerism or conscience to protect the environment but are forced to resort to constraint: "Seeing the counterproductive results of voluntary compliance with guidelines, we finally admit the necessity of coercion for all—*mutual coercion, mutually agreed upon.*"[42] In his discussion of the use of the oceans, for example, Hardin recommends the creation of an international organization (including an international navy) to establish guidelines and enforce the regulated use of the oceans. "It is doubtful if we can create territories in the ocean by fencing [privatization]. If not, we must—if we have the will to do it—adopt the other alternative and socialize the oceans: create an international agency *with teeth.* Such an agency must issue not recommendations but directives; and enforce them."[43] Hardin never explicitly states that he favors a specific form of world government and is ambivalent about the precise means of institutionalizing global coercion. Nonetheless, this does not relieve the necessity of a worldwide force to keep the "ecological peace." For Hardin, the only solution to the tragedy of the commons is some form of world authority.

Robert Heilbroner is another theorist who sees the need for a sovereign authority to confront global environmental problems. He agrees with Hardin that individual conscience and volunteerism is far from enough to save humanity from large-scale eco-catastrophe. Such measures simply spell complacency and blindness. In his book, *An Inquiry into the Human Prospect,* Heilbroner argues additionally that neither capitalism nor socialism is able to address environmental problems sufficiently and thus the world faces difficult political choices in order to respond to environmental issues.

While Heilbroner is pessimistic about ever genuinely solving environmental dilemmas, he reluctantly suggests that the best hope we have in the long term is the creation of authoritarian-type regimes around the world, and possibly, global authoritarian governance. "The human prospect," he writes, "is not an irrevocable death sentence. It is not an inevitable doomsday toward which we are headed, although the risks of enormous catastrophes exist. . . . The death sentence is therefore better viewed as a contingent life sentence—one that will permit the continuation of human society, but only on a basis very different from that of the present, and probably only after much suffering during the period of transition."[44] He makes clear what this transition and the requirements for preserving life entail: "I do not see how one can avoid the conclusion," writes Heilbroner, "that the required transformation will be likely to exceed the capabilities of representative democracy."[45] In other words, "iron governments" are needed to address environmental threats. Heilbroner goes on to prescribe "a centralization of power as the only means by which our threatened and dangerous civilization will make way for its successor."[46] Put differently, for Heilbroner the only way to address environmental threats is through authoritarian rule with the greatest degree of centralization possible, that is, something above and beyond the current state system.

While both Hardin and Heilbroner call for centralized forms of governance, both carefully avoid the phrase *world government*.[47] Two such thinkers who do not mince words are William Ophuls and A. Stephen Boyan. Ophuls and Boyan depict the international arena as the "epitome of the Hobbesian state of nature." Left on their own, individual states will extract and destroy resources in a race against their counterparts. The authors resolve that the only way to defend the planetary ecosystem is to implement an authoritarian form of government on a global scale. "Without some kind of international machinery with enough authority and coercive power over sovereign states to keep them within the bounds of the environmental common interest of all on the planet, the world must suffer the ever-greater environmental ills ordained by the global tragedy of the commons."[48] For Ophuls and Boyan, then, world government is the only appropriate response to global environmental threats. Indeed, they conclude: "The need for a world government with enough coercive power over fractious nation states to achieve what reasonable people would regard as the planetary common interest has become overwhelming."[49]

World government has been part of the human imagination ever since people began to think about politics. It sits in the mind's eye like a solution to the perennial riddle of how human beings can live peacefully and harmoniously together on one earth. It answers the environmental threat because it seeks to rule out factionalism.

With the establishment of a world government all environmental problems could be viewed as external threats to the entire system or as common enemies of all who live on earth. The world could unify behind such a government to fight environmental abuse the way science fiction writers suggest the world would unite against an invasion from Mars. There would finally be one world to confront problems that face a single earth.

While world government looks appealing, it is also rife with problems. Critics point out, for example, that most concrete proposals for world government do not reflect a transcendence of the state system but simply an extension of it. Whatever kind of supra-state that is established would be organizationally and administratively based, at least initially, on the existing configuration of sovereign states. States are not about to disappear tomorrow. Thus, world government may simply be the worldwide legitimation and further codification of the state system. Critics also point out its infeasibility. Any preferred world government would come about through consent, through a social contract among existing states. To assume, however, that state officials, who benefit from the present hierarchical structure of statist politics would relinquish sovereign authority is foolhardy. State officials within Europe, for instance, who share a fairly common cultural background, are having difficulty compromising authority over economic affairs within a regional context. It is naive to think that governments all over the world would give up control in other, more intrusive areas.

Furthermore, notwithstanding its infeasibility, world government may not even be desirable. A world state could be a global Frankenstein: an organization capable of imposing tyrannical rule over the entire world. There is no reason to believe that a world government would necessarily be more benign than existing state governments. And, were it not, there would be no alternative governments to provide shelter, asylum, or protection. More importantly, there is nothing intrinsic to world government that precludes further ecological decay. It is the hope of people such as Hardin, Heilbroner, and Ophuls and Boyan that a world government would be committed to environmental protection, but this cannot be assured. Why should the creation of a world government necessitate governmental environmental commitment? Additionally, there is the generalized sense that large-scale structures would be ineffectual to the tasks at hand. As shown, most states cannot handle their own environmental dilemmas. Creating a world state may not be a solution so much as a further exacerbation of the problem. Finally, world government does not solve the problem of governance itself. Insofar as a world state would be a government, it would project power predominantly through law backed by force. As mentioned previously and discussed later, there are limitations to the degree to which this can actually affect human behavior.[50]

SUB-STATISM

Decentralizing the State

Proponents of world government claim that the state is too small to confront effectively environmental challenges. It does not enjoy the breadth of insight and concern, nor the capability, to address properly global environmental problems. For sub-statists, this notion is terribly misguided. Individual national governments—let alone world government—are not too small, but rather too large to address their own environmental threats. Such concentrations of power preclude a sensitivity to the actual dynamics of ecological decay and distort capabilities for swift and intelligent response. For sub-statists, the proper response is not to create a supra-state or even to work with existing ones to solve environmental dilemmas. Solutions lie in breaking up contemporary states, that is, in decentralizing political authority.

The sub-statist position rests on the notion that the world faces large-scale environmental problems because of the increased scale of human organization and practices on the globe. According to sub-statists, much of history illustrates a continual transfer of power, wealth, and authority from small units to larger ones. Villages grew into towns, cities, and eventually, nation-states; craftsmen joined guilds, built companies, and established national and multinational corporations. Centralization is responsible, in great measure, for current environmental problems because such concentrations of capabilities necessitate the use of advanced technologies that frequently precipitate massive disruptions of ecological processes. In addition, greater degrees of scale and power overwhelm the human ability to understand and control economic, political, and social processes. Large-scale technology takes the decision-making process away from individual human beings. The forces that determine the quality and quantity of housing, food, education, and work are out of reach of most individuals, thus making it difficult to regulate those activities that abuse the environment. Finally, sub-statists suggest that governments, at the state or supra-state level, are inherently hierarchical, precluding any meaningful participation in political processes. As a result, the political mechanism for response is too bulky and blunt to address the environmental problems at hand.[51]

The sub-statist position finds its conceptual roots in a wide range of sources. One source is anarchistic thought. The tradition of anarchism is characterized mainly by its opposition to forms of governance that interfere with spontaneous human expression and community. Most governments are hierarchically and bureaucratically ordered. This, according to anarchism, stifles voluntary patterns of cooperation and perverts innate human impulses. Anarchism prefers no structures of government and seeks to abolish all forms of authority so that human beings can control their own lives and work cooperatively to realize virtues that are possible within human community. Another way to say this is that anarchism rejects impersonal institutions in its assertion that voluntary patterns of cooperation, if able to flourish, would be sufficient to sustain political order. In such a situation, material needs and collective responsibilities would be met spontaneously, without coercion. Central to anarchist thought is a rejection of Hobbes's notion that life outside the protection of a sovereign is "nasty, brutish and short." In fact, it is quite the opposite. The true state of nature finds human beings cooperative, caring, and socially conscious. Living under the reins of a sovereign perverts these inclinations. Thus, for anarchists, the answer to common problems is certainly not larger, more coercive forms of government, like a world state, but rather, smaller units of organization within which human society could flourish on its own.

While nineteenth and early twentieth century anarchism focused predominantly on economic arrangements, a number of its thinkers had environmental concerns. Kropotkin, for instance, prescribed decentralization because this seemed the most appropriate political form for integrating nature and society. Indeed, he recognized humanity's responsibility to the natural world and noticed how natural surroundings determined, in part, the type and scale of the most desirable communities.[52] Such inclinations have led some to call Kropotkin and other anarchists, notably Elisee Reclus, "anarchist geographers."[53]

Aside from anarchism, sub-statism finds a conceptual grounding in the work of Leopold Kohr.[54] In his book, *The Breakdown of Nations*, Kohr claims that "there seems only one cause behind all forms of social misery: bigness. . . . Wherever something is wrong, something is too big."[55] Taking such an extreme position, Kohr maintains that all philosophical, political, cultural, economic, and administrative problems stem from the increasing scale of human endeavor. Their solution thus lies in the break-up of human organizations and practices. Since decentralization and disunion constitute the most basic organizing device of nature, Kohr proposes applying this principle to political affairs. "Instead of union," writes Kohr discussing plans for larger scales of governance, "let us have disunion now. Instead of fusing the small, let us create more and smaller ones."[56] For Kohr, existing nation-states are already too large to facilitate human problem solving. In fact, their scale alone is responsible for the emergence of such problems in the first place.

Decentralization to Protect the Environment

Sub-statism has found subscribers in environmental circles. To be sure, as Robyn Eckersley points out, the so-called eco-anarchists are a mixed group with predictably diverse views on environmental affairs.[57] What they share, however, is the belief that large social structures pervert human relations and experience and are the root cause of contemporary environmental problems.[58] Theodore Roszak, for example, believes that the sheer size of contemporary political, economic, and social organizations is responsible for present environmental dangers because large impersonal constructs diminish personal dignity and engender human dependence. In other words, they are too big to be sensitive to human understanding and control. Roszak sees a connection between the appropriate scale of things for individual persons and the needs of the planet, hence the title of his book, *Person/Planet*. "I believe there is a connection [between personhood and the planet]," he writes, "one that becomes visible when we realize that both person and planet are threatened by the same enemy. *The bigness of things.* The bigness of industrial structures, world markets, financial networks, mass political organizations, public institutions, military establishments, cities, bureaucracies. It is the insensitive colossalism of these systems that endangers the rights of the person and the rights of the planet."[59] According to Roszak, the answer to the environmental threat, as well as the solution to many of the problems that lead to personal dissatisfaction, is to reject large-scale organization and practices. World government, national governments, multinational corporations, and even large public schools are too big for the present needs of the planet. For Roszak, the opposite of big is not small, but personal. "[A]ll systems and institutions," he writes, "that become large enough to inhibit our [personal] growth endanger the planet as well."[60] Only a 'politics of the person' can solve our environmental dilemmas: "In seeking to save our personhood, we assert the human scale. In asserting the human scale, we subvert the regime of bigness. In subverting bigness, we save the planet."[61]

Roszak's thought, which links small-scale endeavors with environmental well-being, is shared by people such as E. F. Schumacher. Schumacher suggests that the world must adopt a form of "Buddhist economics," or an "economics of permanence," to protect the earth's ecosystem. This entails moving toward smaller-scale economic organizations and practicing a sensitivity toward the human subject when devising economic plans. This is necessary for human development, broadly defined, as well as ecological stability.[62]

The most comprehensive and directly environmental version of sub-statism is put forward by those associated with the concept of bioregionalism. As originally formulated by Peter Berg, bioregionalism is the notion that human beings must learn to "live-in-place." This entails getting to know the natural attributes that constitute one's immediate surroundings. Ideally one should be familiar with the rocks, plants, animals, cycles of seasons, and so forth that make up one's environment. Moreover, one should have a sense of the carrying capacity of the area, a sensitivity to the places that should not be stressed, and an appreciation for those spots where the land's bounties can best be developed.[63] As Berg puts it, bioregionalism is "a kind of spiritual identification with a particular kind of country and its wild nature [that is] the basis for the kind of land care the world so definitely needs."[64]

A bioregion is any part of the earth that enjoys boundaries that are determined predominantly by natural characteristics. It can be circumscribed by rivers, watersheds, valleys, and mountains which distinguish it from surrounding regions. One can identify a bioregion, then, by noticing the distinct formations and processes of flora, fauna, waterways, climate, land, and, to a degree, human cultures to which the area gives rise.

The key political component of bioregionalism is that the contemporary state system is ill-equipped to address environmental problems because it is organized around political territories rather than ecological ones. That is, the world is unable to confront environmental dilemmas successfully because it is not organized into bioregions.

The reasons for pursuing a bioregionalist perspective are similar to those for proposing world government. Hardin, Heilbroner, and Ophuls and Boyan reach their conclusions because they believe that human volunteerism and altruism are not enough to defend the planet. One simply cannot count on human beings to be good, ecologically sensitive persons. Bioregionalists agree with this view, but solve the problem not by creating a supra-state to enforce uniform behavior but by breaking up nation-states in an effort to get people in touch with and responsive to the land, water, and air that support them. Kirkpatrick Sale, for example, claims that the trick is to create systems that will work even if the people in them are not "good." This can be done only within a bioregion. In a bioregion, "people will do the environmentally 'correct' thing not because it is thought to be the *moral*, but rather the *practical*, thing to do. That cannot be done on a global scale, nor a continental, nor even a national one, because the human animal, being small and limited, has only a small view of the world and limited comprehension of how to act within it."[65] "By being continually in touch with the natural world," he writes, "every citizen, even the tiniest child, would realize that water does not come from a pipe in the basement, and tomatoes do not grow on supermarket shelves, and you can't throw anything away because there is no 'away'."[66] The idea is that neither altruism nor coercion is necessary to get people to act in an ecologically sound manner. Rather, simple common sense will tell people that to pollute the earth or to wreck its natural wonders is "wrong" because they will experience that wrong in a direct, personal way.[67]

The two key phrases of bioregionalism are: "know where your water comes from" and "saving the whole by saving the parts."[68] They suggest a scaling down of perspective, lifestyle, and community. One no longer looks across the globe for models of appropriate action or even for circumstances to pique active concern. One pays attention to one's place. This is the best contribution one can make to the well-being of the entire planet.

The sub-statist approach to environmental problems has much to recommend. There are, however, problems with it as a strategy

for approaching global environmental problems. First, it assumes
that all global threats stem from local instances of environmental
abuse and that by confronting them at the local level they will disappear. Prima facie, this makes much sense. All forms of environmental abuse start somewhere, and thus to attack the problem at
those "somewheres" appears as a logical approach to their alleviation. But this assumes the problems involved are not acute. It
implies that humanity has decades, or more realistically centuries,
to split itself up into small communities and to begin to tackle the
causes of environmental decay. According to most environmental
scientists and concerned citizens, this is not the case. Ozone depletion, global warming, threats to biodiversity, and so forth are problems that rest on the immediate horizon. There simply is not
enough time to create alternative communities and count on this to
imbue a sense of environmental concern among all citizens.

Another problem with sub-statism stems from its relative
strength. There is much to be said for concentrating on one's immediate environment and working to sustain it. Nonetheless, while
this will certainly create a hands-on concern for parts of the land,
who will look out for the whole? Who will act as custodians of the
entire planet? Many threats to the environment are due to the interaction between different ecological processes. There are connections, for example, between deforestation and global warming, and
between habitat destruction and threats to biodiversity. In any
future world, local deforestation and habitat destruction will take
place, if only in small doses. If one's ecological perspective is
directed solely at one's bioregion (or garden), what is going to ensure
that the host of local instances of environmental management
(which can include controlled burning of forests, limited mining of
the earth, and so on) will not eventuate in planetary abuse? Granted,
humanity may be in a much better position ecologically than it is at
present, but sub-statism does not appear to be the most appropriate
answer to specifically global environmental problems.

A third dilemma with sub-statist strategies is that human
activity is becoming more global and less local in scope. The average
U.S. meal travels 1,300 miles before it is eaten.[69] The clothes we
wear are more likely to come from across the ocean than from across
the street. Many of our friends live in other cities, not down the
block. The sub-statist vision, for many good reasons, wants to
change that. While trend is not destiny, present circumstances point
toward increasing, not diminishing, magnitudes of scale and scope.

Fourth, sub-statism appears unfeasible for the same reason world government appears unlikely. Present nation-states would have to relinquish their authority over their territories, something that will never happen. In a chapter titled, "Will States Dismember Themselves [to bring about smaller political units]?" Leopold Kohr offers one word: "No."[70] According to Kohr, "to believe in the willingness of the great powers to preside over their own liquidation . . . would not be a sign of faith, in the first place, but of lunacy."[71]

Finally, sub-statism suffers insofar as it assumes that people are essentially cooperative and ecologically mindful but become corrupted by the experience of living within large social structures. According to this assumption, if social life could simply be organized on a small scale, the inherent "goodness" of humans could naturally flourish. As Robyn Eckersley points out, however, the problem with this assumption is that it confuses the *potential* nature of humans with their *essential* nature. This conflation is simplistic and, to the degree that it underpins sub-statism, it places the entire perspective on theoretically shaky ground.[72]

THE STATE, GLOBAL ENVIRONMENTAL PROBLEMS, AND TRANSNATIONAL ACTIVIST GROUPS

The key characteristic of statism, supra-statism, and sub-statism is that all three orientations conceptualize environmental problems in the context of the modern state. The state system is either the answer to environmental challenges or the root cause of them. Put differently, the orienting principle of statism, supra-statism and sub-statism is that the size, scope, or quality of formal political institutions lie at the center of world environmental politics. Environmental politics is about finding the proper fit between the dynamics of environmental harm and an institutional form that can best respond. In the case of statism and supra-statism, this translates into not questioning the state as an institution per se but rather assuming its political efficacy and simply wanting to change its size, scope, or activities to address environmental problems. Statists, for instance, see the present system of sovereign units capable of addressing global problems through international cooperation, regional agreements, and the United Nations. The state, as such, is structurally amenable to solving environmental dilemmas—at most, small modifications should be made in the way individual states relate to each other.

Supra-statists also refuse to question the political efficacy of the state. For them, problems arise solely because existing states govern only segments of the planet. The idea is not to get rid of the state per se, but to create a single world state.

Of the three approaches, only the sub-statist position comes closest to questioning the ability of the state as an institution to confront environmental dilemmas. But, even here, the fundamental starting point is that the size of contemporary states is too big to respond to environmental issues, and thus states need to be broken up and power decentralized for genuine environmental protection. Indeed, in some cases of sub-statism there is nothing wrong with the institution of the modern state per se; it simply must be scaled down to a more ecologically beneficial size. For others, the state's bureaucratic and hierarchical character prevent it from pursuing successful environmental protection, and new forms of political association must be sought. But even in these latter formulations, the modern state serves as the foil against which notions of political community, governance, and environmental consciousness are developed. In short, each perspective orients its analysis around the state and assumes it is *the* political category for grounding reflection and practice.

There is nothing wrong with being state-centric per se. The state is the predominant political institution on the planet and deserves significant attention and scholarly analysis. Moreover, insofar as the state, as the institution under which societies are organized, is unable to address global environmental challenges in a successful way, it is fruitful to conceptualize alternative political structures and institutions. Nonetheless, if one takes seriously the criticisms regarding statism, supra-statism, and sub-statism out-lined above, such emphasis on the institution of the state restricts current environmental efforts rather than enlarging them and fails to do justice to the power of the political imagination as it reflects upon environmental issues

While a state-centric perspective has been dominant for the past few hundred years, it is becoming clear to many politically minded individuals that a state-centered notion of world politics is far from the only legitimate one, and, at this time, it may not even be the most insightful. Indeed, when it comes to environmental issues it actually prejudges and therefore limits, in detrimental ways, appropriate responses to global environmental problems. Within political science departments and out on the street many have been recognizing shortcomings and have been exploring alternative types of actions. Key to these efforts is the understanding that politics is not simply officially sanctioned activity associated with a government. In its most general sense, politics is about directing and ordering collective life in matters of common concern and involvement. It is about governance of public affairs. It has nothing to do, at least a priori, with the institution of the modern state. Such a general definition does not narrow the focus of what counts as political; it does not conflate all political activity to state action.

When it comes to environmental issues, no one expresses this view of politics more clearly than contemporary transnational environmental activist groups. Transnational groups want to affect world politics in whatever ways they can; they are not oriented toward merely influencing states. According to transnational environmental groups, when statists, supra-statists, and sub-statists engage in the project of getting the size, scope, and duties of the state "right," they are putting the cart before the horse, as it were. They start their analysis with the state and then simply question its appropriate size, scope, and tasks. In contrast, transnational environmental groups start with the issue of global environmental decay and engage in traditional state-oriented politics only to the degree and extent necessary to address the dilemmas at hand.

In the following chapters I describe and analyze the nonstate activities of transnational environmental activist groups. I do so paradoxically by using the schema of supra-statism, sub-statism, and statism to highlight the significance of their work. Instead of constructing a world government at the global level, or decentralizing governmental powers below states, or simply enhancing international cooperation at the interstate level, transnational environmental groups activate means of governance that operate at these levels of collective life but that do so without necessarily enlisting the governing mechanisms of the institution of the state itself. Transnational environmental activist groups work globally, locally, and at the state level, as it were, to change widespread behavior through enlisting mechanisms within global civil society rather than the governing instrumentalities of states. In this manner, they engage in world civic politics. In the following three chapters, I describe and analyze this type of political practice.

3 Greenpeace and Political Globalism

There are forces in the world which work, not in an arith-
metical, but in a geometrical ratio of increase. Educa-
tion, to use the expression of Plato, moves like a wheel
with an ever multiplying rapidity. Nor can we say how
great may be its influence, when it becomes universal.
                                              —Benjamin Jowett

Nonstate-oriented politics is nothing new. Since the dawn of
social life, human beings have worked to shape and direct collective
affairs independent of formal government. In recent years, however,
scholars have begun thinking theoretically about this type of activity and, in so doing, have provided a degree of conceptual clarity to
it. In particular, the contributions of social movement theory, post-
structuralism, feminism, and critical thought have broadened
understandings of power and thus have heightened our sensitivity
to how politics takes place in the home, office, and marketplace, as
well as in the halls of congresses and parliaments. Politics, in this
sense, is much more subtle to notice than the conduct of governments but, according to proponents of these orientations, no less
significant for political affairs.

It is with a more comprehensive notion of power that I wish to
begin investigating the ways in which transnational environmental
groups engage in world civic politics. By suspending judgment about
what constitutes real politics, one can focus on diverse forms of
agency that actually shape world environmental affairs. In this
chapter and the two that follow, I describe in detail the ways in
which activists work outside of, around, or at the margins of governmental activity in their efforts to alleviate global environmental
problems. This descriptive element will sensitize readers to genuinely alternative forms of political activism.

In addition to describing forms of nonstate environmental politics, one must still ask the political question about them: namely,

do they make a difference? Does all the time, money, and human energy involved actually contribute to addressing and partly alleviating environmental problems? Specifically, in what ways does a nonstate-oriented type of political action actually affect world environmental affairs? That activists employ such a politics is, as I will demonstrate, true; but does it really matter in terms of world politics? In this chapter, and in the two succeeding ones, in addition to describing the work of transnational activists, I furnish evidence to suggest that their efforts actually do matter in world political events. They create conditions that direct the actions of others within a world context.

To begin, I want to draw attention to a level of analysis that has a long history in the study of world politics but which is, at present, still underdeveloped and underappreciated. This is the level at which norms, values, and discourse operate in the global arena outside the domain of states.[1] It is that dimension of world experience where widespread, shared understandings among people throughout the globe act as determinants for present conditions on the planet. It is part of, for want of a better phrase, the *cultural* school of thought which believes that ideas within societies at large structure human collective life.[2] Working within this tradition, the key argument of this chapter is that transnational environmental groups contribute to addressing global environmental problems by heightening worldwide concern for the environment. They persuade vast numbers of people to care about and take actions to protect the earth's ecosystem. In short, they disseminate what I call an *ecological sensibility*. This serves an important political function in coming to terms with the environmental threat.

A sensibility operates as a political force insofar as it constrains and directs widespread behavior. It works at the ideational level to animate practices and is considered a form of *soft law* in contrast to the *hard law* of government directives, policies, and so forth. Scholars make it a habit of differentiating between hard and soft law insofar as they distinguish legal and cultural factors in their understanding of social change. On the one hand, there are those who claim that governmental action is the key to social change. Laws, policies, and directives drive social norms, and thus as they change, the entire configuration of social life will shift. Those who share this perspective see governmental action as the 'base' with cultural and social life being the 'superstructure.' On the other hand, there are those who claim that social norms are central to social change. Governmental decrees, from this perspective, are not the source of change but merely reflections of it. Laws and policies arise out of, or give authoritative expression to, norms that already enjoy widespread acceptance. Scholars sharing this view see social norms as the 'base' and governmental directives as the 'superstructure.'

Differentiating legal and cultural factors, while analytically helpful, is misguided when it forces a thinker to choose between them. When it comes to such large categories of social analysis, it is a mistake to assume that one dimension of social change is definitively more significant than the other. The obvious response to such differentiation is that both factors are important. Indeed, some argue that they are in dialectical relation to each other. As Christopher Stone writes, "in general, laws and cultural norms are mutually reinforcing. Formal laws arise from cultures, and command obedience in proportion to their coherence with the fundamental beliefs of the culture. Cultures, however, are not static. Law, and especially the activities of law making and legal reform, are among the forces that contribute to cultural evolution."[3]

In this chapter, I do not weigh in on the ideational side and argue for its primacy nor celebrate the dialectical relationship. Rather, I simply emphasize the degree to which widely held conceptualizations animate large-scale practices and use this to show how efforts to disseminate an ecological sensibility have world political significance. What makes such efforts political, it should be clear, is not that they are ultimately codified into law or governmental decree but that they represent the use of power to influence and guide widespread behavior. An ecological sensibility, then, is not itself an answer to global environmental threats nor *the* agent for shifting one state of affairs to another. It is, however, an important part of any genuine response to environmental harm. Put simplistically for the moment, it creates an ideational context which inspires and motivates people to act in the service of environmental well-being and thus constitutes the milieu within which environmentally sound actions can arise and be undertaken. While not solely responsible for the *existence* of this sensibility, transnational environmental groups deserve substantial credit for *spreading* it throughout the world.[4] Unfortunately, due to the centrality of the state in international relations and the underemphasis on the role of norms, values, and discourse among societies themselves, most studies of global environmental politics fail to notice this aspect of activists' work. They do not acknowledge this activity as a type of world politics.

In this chapter I explain how transnational environmental groups deliberately work to heighten concern for the environment throughout the world. I do so by focusing on how one group in particular, Greenpeace, deliberately disseminates an ecological sensibility. The presentation of my analysis is divided into two parts. First, I describe the origins, organizational structure, and specific strategies Greenpeace uses to persuade vast numbers of people to care about and take actions to protect the global environment. This serves as an empirical base from which to argue, in the second part of the chapter, that disseminating an ecological sensibility is a genuinely important *political* act. This argument is part of a larger endeavor to demonstrate that changing people's understandings of the world—independent from creating institutions associated with governments—is a significant dimension of world politics. The chapter ends by interpreting Greenpeace's activities in light of supra-statism and shows how Greenpeace works at a similar level of activity, but does so without trying simply to enlist the governing ability of state instrumentalities.

PART ONE

Origins of Greenpeace International

On October 1, 1969, there was a demonstration on the Canadian–United States border protesting the United States testing of nuclear weapons on Amchitka Island. Amchitka is a large rock formation at the tip of the Aleautian Islands in Alaska. Demonstrators blocked the main highway between British Columbia and the state of Washington in an effort to stop a U.S. test scheduled for early October. Their concern was that such an explosion would create tidal waves or cause an earthquake. Amchitka lies close to a fault line that runs down the Pacific coast near Vancouver and emerges as the San Andreas fault in California.

Two days after the demonstration, the U.S. tests went off as scheduled. There were no tidal waves or earthquakes. There were, however, stronger feelings against nuclear testing in general and the U.S. tests in particular. In Vancouver, a handful of people wanted to maintain the momentum of these feelings and direct them toward sustained opposition to U.S. nuclear testing. These people, consist-

ing of a small coterie of environmentalists and peace activists, organized themselves as the Don't Make a Wave Committee (DMWC)—
referring to possible effects of the tests.

Four future U.S. tests were scheduled for Amchitka, with the
first one planned for November 1971. In an attempt to stop these,
DMWC organized opposition and continuously brainstormed about
how to get the most powerful country on earth to change its mind.
After one of its notoriously long meetings, member Marie Bohlen
said, "Why the hell doesn't somebody just sail a boat up there and
park right next to the bomb? That's something everybody can
understand." According to Robert Hunter, one of the first members
of Greenpeace, people were sitting around considering the idea
when the telephone rang and a television station wanted to know
the Committee's plans concerning Amchitka. Jim Bohlen answered,
"Well, as a matter of fact, we're going to sail a ship up to Amchitka."
A few days later, the DMWC endorsed the idea. At the end of the
meeting Irving Stowe, another early member, held his hand up in a
"V" and said "peace." Another member responded, "Make it a *green*
peace." With this move, it is fair to say, Greenpeace was born.[5]

The first DMWC boat, the *Phyllis Cormack* (also called *Greenpeace*), left Vancouver Harbor for Amchitka in September 1971.
This was not the first time a ship sailed toward the tests. Quakers
from the U.S. had sent two boats toward Amchitka earlier although
both times they were seized before coming close to the test site. The
reason for this was that the *Phoenix* and the *Golden Rule* were operated by U.S. citizens and therefore were vulnerable to arrests by U.S.
officials. Sending the *Phyllis Cormack* would scramble the nation-
alistic character of the challenge. The *Phyllis Cormack* was registered as a Canadian ship and carried mostly Canadian citizens. It
could sail into the test zone and, as long as it remained in international waters, could not be seized by U.S. officials unless the United
States wanted to break international maritime law. The sailing of
the *Phyllis Cormack* indicated that protests against nuclear tests
were no longer strictly a case of nationals against nationals. The
tests were seen as threats to other inhabitants of the planet, and the
launching of the *Phyllis Cormack* signaled the translation of that
threat into an international form of protest.

The *Phyllis Cormack* never made it to Amchitka. The crew
ran into bad weather and the U.S. Coast Guard five days short of the
site. Returning to Vancouver, however, the crew realized that the
journey was not in vain as thousands greeted the ship's return. The

trip served as a point of focus for widespread antinuclear feeling. As Robert Hunter put it, "Now the apocalypse had form."[6]

Back home, the DMWC had organized the departure of a second, faster ship, the *Edgewater Fortune* or *Greenpeace Too*. This time, instead of a handful of activists trying to find a ship, captain, and crew, and raise money for the expedition, hundreds of people wanted to be on board and contributions flowed in. Moreover, television camera crews and journalists wanted to accompany the boat. This enthusiasm represented a larger trend of vastly growing opposition to the tests throughout the United States and Canada. For example, U.S. environmentalists were taking their case to the U.S. Supreme Court; Canadians, including former Prime Minister Lester Pearson, took out a full-page advertisement in the *Washington Post* urging cancellation of the test; and the International Longshoremen's and Warehousemen's Union threatened U.S. President Nixon with a boycott of U.S. ships in Canadian ports if the tests were carried out. It seemed that the *Phyllis Cormack* had succeeded in a way that was not originally foreseen. Due to the media attention it received, the *Phyllis Cormack* came to be seen as "a mind bomb sailing across an electronic sea into the minds of the masses."[7] By the time the *Edgewater Fortune* sailed, the mind bomb had already gone off, as it were; thousands of people had joined Greenpeace opposition to the tests.

Notwithstanding growing resistance, the U.S. conducted its test on November 6. The *Edgewater Fortune* was still 700 miles from the test site. While the test did not result in massive tidal waves or cause a devastating earthquake (although it did set off a shock wave that registered 7.2 on the Richter scale), it caused significant damage to the surrounding environment. Aside from ripping a half-mile crater out of the core of the island, it killed countless birds and thousands of sea creatures. According to the U.S. Atomic Energy Commission at the time, the blast killed roughly 1,000 sea otters out of 6,000–8,000 that lived around Amchitka.[8]

The *Edgewater Fortune* sailed back to Vancouver with the spectre of failure. Strangely enough, however, a few days after the test, a U.S. government spokesperson claimed that Amchitka was going to be abandoned as a site for future U.S. nuclear tests. Four months later, it became official. The U.S. Atomic Energy Commission stated that Amchitka would no longer serve as a test site for political and other reasons. This change of mind by the U.S. government, responding in part to a groundswell of opposition from environmental and peace activists, represents one of Greenpeace's first victories. The U.S. originally planned to detonate seven bombs on Amchitka. After exploding only three, it had given up. Amchitka Island was restored to its previous status, a bird and game sanctuary.

For many members of the DMWC, stopping the U.S. tests touched merely the tip of an iceberg. The world was not now safe from atomic explosions nor free from the spectre of nuclear war. Moreover, members saw nuclearism itself as only a part of a larger problem, namely, the unprecedented degradation of the earth's ecosystem by human intervention. Nuclearism was seen simply as another facet of massive threats to the planet posed in part by technological innovation that allows, for instance, strip-mining the oceans and results in driving numerous plant and animal species to extinction, polluting the air, water, and land, and, in the extreme, compromising the life-support system of the earth. To address these larger concerns—especially, at first, threats to marine mammals—the DMWC was formally dissolved in 1972 and reorganized under the name Greenpeace Foundation.

Since 1972, Greenpeace has grown from having a single office in Vancouver to staffing offices in over thirty countries and, until recently, a base in Antarctica. Greenpeace has offices in the developed as well as the developing world, including Russia and Eastern Europe. Its eco-navy consists of eight ships, and it owns a helicopter and a hot-air balloon. It employs over 1,000 full-time staff members, plus hundreds of part-timers and thousands of volunteers. As of July 1994, it had over 6 million members worldwide and an estimated income of over $100 million. All money comes from voluntary donations, 90 percent of which is in the form of small contributions from individual members. Additionally, Greenpeace sends hundreds of canvassers out each night to raise funds and educate the general public about current environmental issues. Finally, it has expanded its area of concern. While originally focused on nuclear weapons testing, it is now concerned with all threats to the planetary ecosystem. In short, from 1972 to the present Greenpeace has grown into a full-scale, transnational environmental organization.

Transnational Organizational Structure

Greenpeace sees the bulk of global environmental problems falling into four categories: toxic substances, energy and atmosphere, nuclear issues, and ocean and terrestrial ecology. Greenpeace works for environmental protection by dividing its attention among these four issue areas, also called campaigns. Within each of these, Greenpeace works on numerous subissues. For example, under the rubric of its nuclear campaign, Greenpeace focuses on reprocessing and dumping of nuclear material, sea-based nuclear weapons and nuclear testing. Under the rubric of ocean ecology, Greenpeace concentrates on whales, sea turtles, fisheries, and dolphins.

As a transnational environmental group concerned with threats to the entire planet, Greenpeace undertakes its campaigns and projects worldwide. The problems associated with toxic substances, energy, and atmosphere and so forth are not limited to individual countries. Almost all parts of the world are vulnerable to the environmental consequences involved. Greenpeace is organized to allow it to address these dilemmas on a global scale.

The top tiers of the organization are made up of the Greenpeace Council, an executive board, and regional trustees. The council is made up of representatives from all the countries where Greenpeace has offices and meets once a year to decide on organizational policy. The council is one of the ways Greenpeace coordinates its diverse activities. The council sets guidelines for the general operation of Greenpeace, approves the international budget, and develops long-term goals. Because council members come from around the world, decisions can reflect a sensitivity to differing regional and local aspects of environmental problems. To provide greater efficiency in day-to-day operations, and to emphasize coordination among campaigns and projects, there is an executive board that ratifies all council resolutions and makes significant decisions for Greenpeace throughout the year when the council is not in session. The board consists of both voting and nonvoting members and is elected by the Greenpeace Council.

In addition to the council and the executive board, there are regional trustees that provide the final stamp of approval for Greenpeace's overall operations. Trustees are representatives of the areas of the world where Greenpeace has offices. These include Latin America, the Pacific, North America, and Europe. While the trustees generally approve all decisions put forward by the council and the executive board, it serves as the final arbiter of Greenpeace policies. Because individual trustees represent diverse regions of the world, as a whole the trustees advance a global rather than a national or even regional orientation within Greenpeace.

Aside from the council and executive board, Greenpeace organizes itself worldwide along the lines of its four campaign areas. Heading each campaign is an international coordinator. He or she designs the way specific campaigns play themselves out in different regional and national contexts. For example, the campaign coordinator of toxic substances orchestrates all Greenpeace projects that contribute to achieving the aims of the toxics campaign. She or he provides the global perspective to different projects.

Underneath international campaign coordinators are project directors. Project directors are scattered across the globe and work on subissues of the larger campaigns. For example, there are nine projects currently being undertaken by the toxics campaign. One of these focuses on the pulp and paper industry. The pulp and paper industry is responsible for 50 percent of all organchlorine discharges into the earth's waterways. Organchlorine is dangerous to both humans and the natural environment; it is known to cause sterility and cancer in mammals. The project's aim is to change the production process of the industry away from bleaching procedures that use chlorine. The bulk of the pulp and paper industry is located in a number of countries, and Greenpeace pursues the project in each of them. The project director oversees all these efforts. Project directors, like campaign coordinators, take a global perspective on their respective projects. They make sure that separate Greenpeace activities throughout the world support each other and fit together to advance the cause of their specific project.

Working under the project coordinators are regional and national campaigners. Campaigners devise specific Greenpeace activities. They identify, what they take to be, the most effective ways to communicate with people and change environmentally destructive practices. For purposes of this chapter, one should think of campaigners as organizers of concrete activities that aim to alter people's perceptions of particular environmental threats. To use the pulp and paper example, there are campaigners in a number of countries including the United States, Canada, Sweden, and Germany. Campaigners focus on the pulp and paper industries in their respective countries, taking into account the governmental, cultural, and industrial attributes of each country to address the problem. Regional and national campaigners are key to Greenpeace's global efforts because they understand the particular contexts within which environmental damage is being caused and fashion appropriate responses. They take the general intentions of projects and over-

all campaigns and translate them into concrete actions that are tai-
lored for specific geographical and political contexts.

Working with campaigners are a host of assistants and volunteers who help carry out specific activities. There are literally thousands of these people throughout the world. They paint banners,
circulate petitions, research issues, organize protests, and take part
in direct, nonviolent actions. All levels of activity are designed, at
least in theory, to advance the goals of specific campaigns.

Greenpeace's Politics

Key to all Greenpeace's efforts is the insight that people do not
damage the ecosystem as a matter of course. Rather, they operate in
an ideational context that motivates them to do so. People are not
machines; they do not respond directly to situations. In the words of
Harry Eckstein, people are moved by "predispositions which pattern
behavior."[9] In the language of social science, human behavior is a
matter of "oriented action." People process experience into action
through general conceptions or interpretations of the world. At the
most general level, but also the most important, then, an important
step toward protecting the earth is to change the way vast numbers
of people understand the world. It involves persuading them to
abandon their anti-ecological or non-ecological attitudes and practices, and to be concerned about the environmental well-being of
the planet. In short, it requires disseminating an ecological sensibility.

People respond to situations through interpretive categories
that reflect a particular understanding of everyday circumstances.
Such mediating orientations are cultural in character. They reflect
customary, socially transmitted understandings that are embedded
in the prevailing values, norms, and modes of discourse. Greenpeace
targets and tries to alter these dispositions. It literally attempts to
manipulate values, norms, and modes of discourse; it seeks to alter
people's conceptions of reality. Greenpeace hopes that in so doing,
people will undertake actions that are more respectful of the ecological integrity of the planet.

Central to Greenpeace's efforts is the practice of "bearing witness." This is a type of political action, originating with the Quakers, which links moral sensitivities with political responsibility.
Having observed a morally objectionable act, one cannot turn away
in avoidance. One must either take action to prevent further injustice or stand by and attest to its occurrence. While bearing witness

often works to stop specific instances of environmental destruction, in general, it aims simply to present ecological injustice to the world. This offers as many people as possible an alternative understanding of contemporary affairs and sets them in motion against such practices. One way Greenpeace does this is by engaging in direct, nonviolent action and advertising it through the media worldwide.

Direct, nonviolent action is a form of political practice that shares much with the passive resistance of Mahatma Gandhi and Martin Luther King. It is a vehicle for confrontation and an outreach to other citizens. For Greenpeace, such action includes climbing aboard whaling ships, parachuting from the top of smokestacks, plugging up industrial discharge pipes, and floating a hot-air balloon into a nuclear test site. Such actions create images that can be broadcasted through the media to spark interest and concern of the largest audience.

Greenpeace is able to capture media attention because its actions are visually spectacular. According to political theorist J. Glenn Gray, human beings have what the New Testament calls "the lust of the eye." This is a primitive urge for visual stimulation; it describes the aesthetic impulse. The urge is lustful because it requires the novel, the unusual, the spectacular. The eye cannot satiate itself on the familiar, the everyday, the normal.[10] Greenpeace actions excite the eye. They portray people taking dangerous risks. These grab attention and thus receive media coverage. By offering spectacular images to the media, Greenpeace invites the public to bear witness; it enables people throughout the world to know about environmental dangers and tries to pique their sense of outrage.

A number of years ago it was difficult to use direct, nonviolent action to change political conditions around the globe. While direct action has always been a political tool for those seeking change, the technology did not exist to publicize specific actions to a global audience. Recent innovations in communication technologies have allowed information to whip around the globe within seconds, linking distant corners of the world. Greenpeace plugs into this planetwide communication system to advertise its direct actions.

For example, in the 1970s Greenpeace ships used Morse code to communicate with their offices on land. Information from sailing expeditions would be translated in a central office and then sent out to other offices and onto the media via the telephone. This was cumbersome and expensive and compromised much of the information that could prove persuasive to public audiences. After weeks at sea, ships would return with still photographs, and these would be the most convincing images Greenpeace could use to communicate about environmental destruction taking place on the high seas.

With the advent of affordable innovations in the field of communications, Greenpeace has been able to update its ability to reach diverse and numerous audiences. Instead of Morse code, Greenpeace ships now use telephones, fax machines, and satellite uplinks to communicate with home offices. This allows for instantaneous information to be communicated and verified. Moreover, Greenpeace uses video cameras to capture its actions. Footage can be taken of whaling expeditions, ocean dumping of nuclear wastes, and discharging of toxic substances into streams and waterways. This documents more accurately actual instances of environmental destruction and the risks that Greenpeace members undertake to protect the environment. Once Greenpeace has footage and photographs of such abuse, it sends them into peoples' homes across the world through the planetwide mass communication system. Greenpeace has its own media facilities and uses these to get its information out to the public. Aside from attracting journalists and television crews to their actions, Greenpeace provides its own photographs to picture editors and has facilities to distribute edited, scripted, and narrated video news spots to television stations in eighty-eight countries within hours.

To see how Greenpeace uses direct, nonviolent action to make the world bear witness, consider its whale campaign. For years, Greenpeace has been trying to preserve whale populations and guard them from extinction. This is part of a larger campaign to generate more awareness and concern for the mass depletion of species currently taking place throughout the world. One technique Greenpeace uses to do this is direct action on the high seas. In one of its early expeditions, for instance, Greenpeace sent a ship to pursue a Russian whaling fleet. One of Greenpeace's first actions was to document the fleet's activities. Greenpeace found that the Russians were killing whales that were smaller than the official allowable size, as designated by the International Whaling Commission. To record this, Greenpeace filmed the killing of an undersized whale and took still photographs of a human being perched over it to demonstrate that it was merely a whale calf. Greenpeace noticed, moreover, that the sheer size and capability of the fleet enabled it to take large catches and thus threaten the sperm whale population in the area. To dramatize this, Greenpeace members boarded inflatable dinghies and positioned themselves between harpoon ships and pods of whales. In essence, they tried to discourage harpooners from firing by threatening to die for the cause. This proved effective as numerous times Russian whalers did not shoot their harpoons for fear of killing Greenpeace members. What turned out to be crucial was that Greenpeace captured this on film. Footage was broadcasted on television stations and still photographs were reproduced in newspapers and magazines worldwide. Greenpeace has engaged in numerous similar actions since then and continues to use such strategies.[11]

A second example of direct action is Greenpeace's campaign to stop ozone depletion. In 1989, Greenpeace members infiltrated a DuPont manufacturing plant in Deepwater, New Jersey. Activists climbed the plant's 180-foot water tower and hung a huge, blue-ribbon banner awarding DuPont a prize for being the world's number-one ozone destroyer. (At the time, DuPont produced half of the chlorofluorocarbons (CFCs) used in the U.S. and 25 percent of world annual production.) The following day, Greenpeace bolted a steel box—with two people inside—onto the plant's railroad tracks and blocked the export of CFCs from the plant. Greenpeace draped the box with a banner that read, "Stop Ozone Destruction Now," with a picture of the earth in the background and used it to stage an 8-hour blockade holding up rail cars carrying 44,000 gallons of CFCs.

What is curious is that, according to Greenpeace, within minutes of removing the blockade, business proceeded as usual. The plant continued to function, producing and sending out substances that are proven to erode the stratospheric ozone layer. Nonetheless, something had happened in those brief 8 hours; something had changed. While DuPont workers continued to manufacture CFCs, they now did so knowing that others knew about and were concerned with the environmental effects. Moreover, because Greenpeace captured its actions on film and distributed video news spots to television stations throughout the world, vast numbers of people were now able to understand the connection between the production of CFCs and ozone depletion. In short, the utility of Greenpeace's activity in this case had less to do with the blocking action and more to do with the message that was conveyed. Greenpeace gave the ozone issue form and used the image of disrupting DuPont's operations to send out a message of concern.[12] As Paul

Watson, an early member of Greenpeace put it, "When you do an action it goes through the camera and into the minds of people. The things that were previously out of sight and out of mind now become commonplace. Therefore you use the media as a weapon."[13]

Political Strategies

Greenpeace obviously does more than perform direct actions. It also lobbies government officials, gathers information, organizes protests and boycotts, produces record albums and other educational merchandise, and carries out scientific research. While many of these endeavors, especially lobbying, are directed specifically at states, a large percentage of Greenpeace's work is not meant to change states' policies per se but is aimed at changing the attitudes and behavior of the more general public. It seeks to change prevailing, and at times internationally shared, values, norms, and modes of discourse. It strives to "sting" people with an ecological sensibility regardless of occupation, geographical location, or access to government officials.

Stinging people is no simple task. It involves knowing how to joggle people's understanding of everyday circumstances and inspire them to reflect on their own commitments and practices in a way that will result in substantive, personal change. Greenpeace uses a number of strategies to move people. Two, in particular, stand out. First, it tries simply to bring instances of environmental abuse to the attention of people throughout the world. CFC production takes place in the guarded corridors of the world's laboratories and factories; harpooners kill whales on the high seas; species extinction takes place in the depths of the world's rain forests; and nuclear weapons are tested in the most deserted areas on earth. Through television, radio, newspaper, and magazine stories, Greenpeace brings these hidden spots of the globe into people's everyday lives. It thus enables vast numbers of people to bear witness to environmental abuse.

Antarctica is the most remote continent on earth. It is hundreds of miles from the nearest country and thus far from widespread public attention. It is also one of the last remaining unexploited regions of the world. As such, it is an ecologist's dream; it stands as a rare example of nature in its close to purest form. Within its boundaries it holds 70 percent of the earth's fresh water and supports 800 species of plant life, 8 seal species, 12 types of cetaceans, and about 45 species of birds. It is the cleanest, least polluted of all continents.

In 1959, twelve nations signed the Antarctica Treaty, dedicating themselves to peaceful scientific exploration of the continent. While this has been hailed as a model of international scientific cooperation, it has not prevented significant environmental destruction. In 1983, for example, the French leveled several islands with explosives to construct an airstrip, destroying Adelie penguin colonies and threatening breeding grounds of Emperor penguins. Additionally, overfishing has led to the near commercial extinction of several species of finfish and the human impact on Antarctica's narrow ice-free shoreline (2 percent of the entire continent) threatens numerous animal and plant species in the area.

Ordinarily these actions would take place out of public view. To counter this, Greenpeace established a research base in Antarctica in the 1980s and continues actions today that monitor and publicize such abuse. The Greenpeace research base was the only one not owned and operated by a state. Greenpeace used the base to document environmentally harmful activities and tried to bring these to the world's attention. More generally, Greenpeace writes articles about the environmental well-being of the continent, produces television films about Antarctica and airs them in a number of countries, and engages in direct actions against polluters and destroyers of Antarctica's environment. In doing so, Greenpeace takes what were previously obscure but environmentally hazardous practices and projects them onto human consciousness.[14]

The second strategy Greenpeace uses to change people's understandings is to expose the gap between the rhetoric and the practices of governments, corporations, and ordinary citizens and to demand explanations for it. Its intention is to point out hypocrisy and to use this to goad people's consciences and thus joggle their conceptions of everyday circumstances. Governments, corporations, and individuals make promises, enter agreements, and tout viewpoints that support environmental renewal and protection. These are codified in laws, advertisements, international accords, and so forth. Greenpeace pushes people to live up to these pronouncements. It engages in what R. B. J. Walker calls "the politics of accountability."[15]

In July 1985, Greenpeace sent underwater divers to Green Bay, Wisconsin, to investigate the emission of toxic wastes from the Fort Howard Paper Company. The state of Wisconsin requires all compa-

nies to document the types of procedures used in handling hazardous wastes, and this includes registering the number of discharge
pipes and the final destination of toxic substances. Outside the
plant, Greenpeace activists photographed three underwater discharge pipes used by Fort Howard that were not reported to state
environmental authorities. By not reporting these pipes, Fort
Howard was pretending to be environmentally responsible when in
fact it was polluting nearby waterways at higher levels than it was
willing to admit. Greenpeace used Wisconsin law as a minimum
acceptable standard of environmentally sound practices and simply
applied it to Fort Howard Paper Company. Publicly Fort Howard
claimed to abide by legal standards, but privately it willfully violated them. Greenpeace pointed out the inconsistency and
demanded explanations for it. It is important to note that in doing
so, Greenpeace took its case not to the courts but to the people of
Wisconsin. By publicizing its direct actions, Greenpeace pointed out
the gap between the rhetoric and actual practices of Fort Howard
Paper and let the victims of this discrepancy—the citizens of Wisconsin—know about it.

More recently, three Greenpeace activists scaled half-way up
the forty-seven-story Time-Life tower in New York to protest the
chlorine-bleached paper used in *Time* magazine. They unfurled a
banner which read, "Chlorine Kills" and "Take the poison out of
paper," against a backdrop of a mock *Time* magazine cover. According to Greenpeace, the production of one year's worth of *Time*
releases 179,400 pounds of organochlorine into waterways in North
America.[16] Like Greenpeace's action against Fort Howard Paper, the
protest aimed to point out hypocrisy. In January 1992, Time Inc.
pledged to request chlorine-free paper from its suppliers. Less than a
year later, it rescinded the pledge but maintained that it was still
committed to environmentally sound production practices. Greenpeace's action, which snarled morning rush-hour traffic around
Times Square, aimed to highlight the discrepancy between *Time's*
stated intention and the reality of its actions.[17]

Greenpeace's overall intention in these actions has been to gar-
ner distrust for business-as-usual, to inspire citizens to take a critical view toward otherwise overlooked circumstances. When people
or companies lie, they implicitly admit that they have violated
acceptable standards of behavior. By exposing such lies, Greenpeace
shows people that the world is not addressing environmental
threats as successfully or as truthfully as it appears. Much more

needs to be done, and it is up to ordinary individuals, as well as state officials and corporate managers, to pursue an environmentally sound future.

Bringing the hidden spots of the earth into people's lives and exposing hypocrisy aim to change the way vast numbers of people see the world. They seek to dislodge traditional understandings of environmental abuse and substitute new interpretive frames. This was put particularly well by Robert Hunter, a Greenpeace activist who participated in the group's early antiwhaling expeditions. For Hunter, the purpose of Greenpeace's efforts was about changing fundamental images about whaling. The predominant view was that whaling was a matter of brave men battling vicious and numerous monsters of the deep. Greenpeace documented a different image. As Hunter put it, "Soon, images would be going out into hundreds of millions of minds around the world, a completely new set of basic images about whaling. Instead of small boats and giant whales, giant boats and small whales; instead of courage killing whales, courage saving whales; David had become Goliath, Goliath was now David; if the mythology of Moby Dick and Captain Ahab had dominated human consciousness about Leviathan for over a century, a whole new age was in the making."[18]

PART TWO

Ecological Sensibility and the Environmental Movement

Disseminating an ecological sensibility is not primarily about changing governmental policies. This may of course happen as state officials bear witness or are pressured by constituents to codify into law shifts in public opinion or widespread sentiment. But this is only one dimension of Greenpeace's direct action efforts. The "new age" envisioned by Hunter is more than the passing of environmental legislation or the adoption of environmental policies. Additionally, it involves convincing all actors—from governments to corporations, private organizations, and ordinary citizens—to make decisions and act in deference to environmental awareness. As governments get smitten by such ideas they will, hopefully according to activists, take measures to protect the environment. When the ideas have more resonance outside government, they will shift the standards of good conduct and persuade people to act differently even though governments are not requiring them to do so. In short, Greenpeace works to disseminate an ecological sensibility to shift the governing ideas that animate societies, whether institutionalized within government or not, and count on this to reverberate throughout various institutions and collectivities.

The challenge for students of international relations is how to apprehend the effects of these efforts and understand their political significance. As mentioned, traditionally scholars have focused on state policy and used this as the criterion for endowing NGOs with political significance. Such a focus, however, misses the broader changes taking place underneath or beyond state behavior that NGOs initiate. To get at these dimensions of change one needs a more sociological orientation toward world affairs.[19] One such orientation is a so-called "fluid approach" which has been used to study domestic social movements but which can be adopted to analyze transnational environmental activist groups.[20] A fluid approach gauges the significance of activist groups by attending to cultural expressions that exhibit cognitive, affective, and evaluative shifts in societies. Observers attune themselves to the quickening of actions and changes in meaning, and they develop an understanding that something new is happening in a wide variety of places. When analyzing the peace movement, for instance, a fluid approach recognizes that activists aim not only at convincing governments to cease from going to war, but also try to create more peaceful societies. This entails propagating expressions of nonviolence, processes of conflict resolution and, according to some, practices that are more cooperative than competitive. A fluid approach looks throughout society and depicts shifts in such expression as a measure of the peace movement's success.[21] Likewise, a fluid approach acknowledges that feminist groups aim not simply at enacting legislation to protect women against gender discrimination. Additionally, they work to change patriarchal practices and degrading representation of women throughout society. Thus, as Joseph Gusfield notes, the successes of the feminist movement can be seen "where the housewife finds a new label for discontents, secretaries decide not to serve coffee and husbands are warier about using past habits of dominance."[22] A fluid approach, in other words, interprets activist efforts by noticing and analyzing, in the words of Herbert Blumer, a "cultural drift," "societal mood," or "public orientation" felt and expressed by people in diverse ways.[23] It focuses on changes in lifestyle, art, consumer habits, fashion, and so forth and sees these, as well as shifts in laws and policies, as expressions of activist efforts.

Applied to the international arena, a fluid approach enables one to appreciate, if only imperfectly, changes initiated by transnational activists that take place independent of state policies. With regard to transnational activists, it allows one to notice how an environmental sensibility infiltrates deliberations at the individual, organizational, corporate, governmental and interstate levels, and how they shape world collective life.

When I talk about the changes that result from the dissemination of an ecological sensibility, these are the types of alterations to which I am referring. These are the kinds of modifications groups like Greenpeace help bring about.

Indications of an Ecological Sensibility

Shifts in attitudes and behavior are extremely difficult to measure, especially when they take place throughout and across societies. Nonetheless, while one cannot precisely quantify the magnitude of such change, one can notice more diffuse, qualitative alterations and interpret these in a way that indicates broad shifts in predispositions and actions.

One indication of widespread shifts in attitudes and behavior is changes in discourse. People express political concerns through language. Changes in vocabulary, then, reflect a shift in the way people conceive of political issues. One indication of the success of women's activist groups, for example, can be charted in the increasingly anachronistic character of sexist terminology. The move away from the word *chairman*, for example, to *chairwoman, chairperson,* and *chair* suggests a shift in the way people conceive of women and their status in society.[24] It registers the existence and success of the women's movement. This is the case with other movements as well. The displacement of *colored* with *Negro, black,* and eventually *African-American,* or *Hispanic* with *Latino,* represent efforts to redefine and reconceive societal groups. To the degree that these terms have gained widespread usage one can talk about shifts in attitudes and even behavior toward and by these peoples. Linguistic change with regard to these terms signals social change around the issues of gender and ethnicity.[25]

One can find similar discursive changes taking place within the field of environmental issues. For example, the word *green* now means more than just a color. It implies a political stance, a set of

values, and a type of activity. A politician, for example, can now be
green. This means he or she takes environmental threats seriously
and works within the political system to protect the earth's ecosystem. This is the case not only with formal politicians but also with
unofficial politicos in general. People describe their political orientation as green to express their commitment to an environmentally
sound world. It means that environmental concerns are high on
their list of priorities. It suggests that of all the issues these people
care about, environmental ones are central. Perhaps the most obvious example of the way the word green has changed in meaning is
that there are now numerous political parties throughout the world
calling themselves green parties. These include *die Grunen* (The
Greens) in Germany; *Vihreat* (The Greens) in Finland; *Comhaontas
Glas* (Green Alliance) in Ireland; *Vereinte Grune Osterreich* (United
Greens of Austria) in Austria; *Di Greng Alternativ* (The Green
Alternative) in Luxembourg; and *De Groenen* (The Greens) in the
Netherlands.[26] By calling themselves 'green,' these parties are
demonstrating that the word *green* has become a loaded term. One
cannot use the word in a political context anymore without it con-
noting a commitment to the protection of the earth's ecosystem. It
suggests change in the way people think about and act toward the
environment. It registers the effects of the environmental movement.[27]

Another indication of widespread societal change is the politicization of circumstances that hitherto were not considered genuinely political. Contemporary social conditions are often
considered, unreflectively, facts of life. One notices widespread
change when such ordinary phenomena become political issues.
Throughout much of history eating disorders among women and the
shapes of women's bodies were understood as private and thus non-
political affairs. *Individual* women suffered from compulsive eating
and fatness; such afflictions were not social or political in nature.
Throughout the 1970s and 1980s, this view changed. Feminists
started looking at the political dimensions that led women to
"choose" compulsive eating and fatness. Many claimed, for
instance, that women gained weight as an adaptation to sexist pressures in contemporary society. Being fat was an attempt to break
free of society's sex stereotypes. People holding this view argued,
then, that eating disorders and being overweight were not simply
private and thus nonpolitical issues. They had to do with matters of
power.[28] The same is true with regard to rape and women's self-

understanding of their own beauty. Many have argued persuasively that these are not private affairs but involve matters of power and are thus political in character.[29] As these perspectives make their way deeper into public consciousness such issues become politicized. This politicization indicates the significance of the women's movement on society.[30]

The politicization of issues can also be helpful for recognizing and charting the environmental movement. Throughout much of history, health was considered a private matter. People got sick and physicians treated them. That is, the causes and alleviation of health problems were personal affairs.[31] In the 1960s and 1970s, people became increasingly concerned with the environmental conditions that give rise to illness and disease. This was especially the case with cancer. People started to realize that cancer is "not an inevitable disease of old age nor one caused by a particular virus. Instead, cancer results from exposure to chemical and physical agents present in our environment."[32] This viewpoint signals that cancer, and more generally health, is no longer seen as a personal concern. It involves questions of power: Who pollutes the ecosystem? What should be done to control disease-causing agents in the environment? And, what mechanisms of authority would bring the necessary changes about? Such questions are public matters; they have to do with collective well-being. What is important to notice is that the blurring of the private and public spheres represents a politicization of human health. The shift from locating the causes of disease in the self to the environment raises concern for the environment itself. It makes the link between human and environmental well-being. As Samuel Hays put it, "This marked innovation in ideas about personal health [from private to public] was an important element in the expanding concern for one's environment as a critical element in well-being."[33] Hays goes on to suggest that changing notions of health are an integral part of widespread environmental awareness and concern.[34]

A third indication of societal change is the widespread acceptance of previously controversial values, attitudes, and practices. Social movements begin with a critique of particular contemporary circumstances. Specifically, they arise when a handful of people start to see societal problems less as misfortunes and more as injustices and demand changes to rectify them.[35] Because they are critical, these voices of dissent are, at first, marginal and out of sync with mainstream thought and practice. One can chart the success of a movement by looking at the degree to which such critical ideas find their way into conventional social life. According to Richard Falk, one indication of the success of antinuclear weapons groups is a normative repudiation of nuclearism by physicians, lawyers, clergy, artists, and a number of prominent military personnel. This signifies, what he calls, a "shift in the balance of legitimacy." "It is a clear indication," writes Falk, " of the existence of cultural reinforcement for restrictive attitudes on the acceptability (and legality) of nuclear weaponry."[36] It signifies the extent of influence of the antinuclear weapons movement.

One sees a similar shift in the "balance of legitimacy" in environmental issues. Early environmental concern was predominantly a youth-based movement.[37] Age was more important than class, geographical residence, political orientation, or gender when it came to identifying the social bases of environmental concern and activism.[38] More significantly, as a youth-based movement, environmentalism was considered marginal and thought to be fragile and short-lived. Indeed, for years environmental issues remained a low priority among voters and there was only a narrow base of support for the movement itself. Throughout the 1980s and early 1990s, this has changed significantly. Many more people now express concern about environmental quality; in fact, people from various age groups claim they are willing to make personal economic sacrifices to enjoy better environmental conditions.[39] Environmental concern now enjoys a broad base of support. Like the antinuclear weapons movement, environmentalism has been shifting the balance of legitimacy. Now, environmental concern is found not only in the alternative press but also in places like *Time* Magazine and *National Geographic.*[40] Additionally, physicians, lawyers, and clergy are expressing concern for the environment. In 1989, for example, Pope John Paul II argued for the need for all peoples to confront global environmental problems and, before leaving office, Prime Minister Margaret Thatcher and Mikhail Gorbachev called themselves environmentalists as did George Bush.[41] (One should note here that even if these stated concerns by politicians are rhetorical, seeking merely to cater to widespread public support, it still suggests a broadening of concern or the widespread acceptance of previously controversial or ignored values, attitudes, and practices.)

A last indication of a social change beyond state action is the expansion of areas of concern. That is, one notices the effects of a social movement when related issues become matters of attention.

In the late 1960s, the hospice movement was getting under way in both England and the United States. People began to set up shelters, or more accurately homes, where terminally ill patients could be cared for in a supportive, warm, and open environment. This early wave branched out into other arenas. Soon the medical community started to question the appropriateness of its intensive-care and life-support technologies. Furthermore, people started to criticize traditional notions of prolonging life through contemporary medical practice, supported various forms of euthanasia, and began seeing the dying process as an important learning experience. In short, concern for more appropriate care of the terminally ill has grown into other areas having to do with contemporary approaches to death, dying and the prolonging of life. It has spawned what many call the new "death awareness movement."[42]

One sees a similar trend in the environmental movement. In the early 1960s, many people who considered themselves environmentalists understood environmental issues in terms of litter cleanup and scenic planning. For them environmentalism meant enhancing the aesthetic quality of one's community. Thus, there were campaigns to clean up nearby parks and rivers. From the late 1960s onward, people have been broadening their concerns. Looking back on the evolution of environmentalism over the past twenty-five years or so, one notices how more and more issues have fallen into the fold of environmentalism. According to Samuel Hays, community litter clean-ups gave way to concerns about trash in general and eventually to the notion of recycling. An understanding of reprocessing materials spilled over into larger ideas of natural cycles. In time, people started to see the importance of ecological processes themselves.[43] More generally, the concept of environmental protection itself constantly expands. As UNCED demonstrated, environmental protection now fundamentally includes improving the lot of the world's poor. Indeed, one can no longer ignore the underdevelopment of much of the South when thinking about and taking action to improve the quality of the environment.[44] Furthermore, as debates over the North American Free Trade Agreement (NAFTA) and the General Agreement on Tariffs and Trade (GATT) demonstrate, trade issues have now become a matter of environmental concern. According to many, one can no longer discuss international trade without considering its environmental ramifications.[45] Finally, social justice issues have become part of environmentalism. For years, the environmental movement stayed clear of

problems such as racism and class relations. With a growing awareness that toxic waste dumps, and garbage incinerators are disproportionately situated in low-income or minority neighborhoods or that
lands owned by minorities have traditionally been the most
exploited, there is now a sense that environmentalism must focus
on social justice issues. In fact, for some, social justice has come to
define genuine environmental protection.[46] The expansion of environmental concern represents a broadening of issues. It indicates
the presence of the contemporary environmental movement.[47]

Noticing changes in discourse, the politicization of issues,
mass acceptance of previously controversial perspectives, and the
broadening of concern is a way to apprehend the kinds of changes
environmental activist groups try to bring about. Granted such
alterations are diffuse and it is hard to appreciate the effect they
have on the environmental conditions throughout the world.
Nonetheless, they represent widespread changes in people's attitudes and values concerning the well-being of the environment.
They signify increased ecological awareness or environmental concern. They indicate the spread of an ecological sensibility.

Transnational environmental organizations are, obviously, not
responsible for all facets of this sensibility. As mentioned, they are
as much a result of the dissemination of an ecological sensibility as
a further source of amplification and diffusion of it. In this latter
capacity they play a central, although undetermined, role, and it is
this activity to which I wish to draw attention. As I have shown,
Greenpeace deliberately works to increase worldwide awareness of
environmental issues and persuade people to take actions to protect
the ecosystem. It tries to change people's understanding of environmental abuse and thus inspire them to work in the service of the
environment. This contributes to a *greening* of the world's publics.
It heightens human concern for the environment, and one can see
the widespread expression of that concern in changes in discourse,
politicization of ordinary circumstances, and so on.

An Ecological Sensibility and World Politics

An ecological sensibility is rippling through societies all over
the world. It is percolating throughout social, cultural, and economic practices in addition to governmental ones. It manifests
itself, for example, when corporations voluntarily cease producing
chlorofluorocarbons (CFCs) that deplete the ozone layer and con-

tribute to global warming, and when they plant thousands of trees to offset the carbon emissions from coal plants.[48] It surfaces when households and communities voluntarily cease using toxic substances to clean their homes and offices and stop eating and drinking out of styrofoam containers (which until recently, contained CFCs). It also emerges when farmers reject pesticides and pursue organic agriculture in an effort to preserve topsoil. When corporations, households, communities, and farmers take these measures it is not because governments are breathing down their necks. They are pursuing environmentally sound practices because they are aware of the severity of environmental problems and want to contribute toward alleviating such dangers. They are being "stung," as it were, by an ecological sensibility. This sting is a type of governance. It represents a mechanism of authority that is able to shape human behavior.

In 1970, one in ten Canadians said the environment was worthy of being on the national agenda; twenty years later, one in three felt not only that it should be on the agenda but that it was the most pressing issue facing Canada.[49] In 1981, in the United States, 45 percent of those polled said that protecting the environment was so important that "requirements and standards cannot be too high and continuing environmental improvements must be made regardless of cost"; in 1990, 74 percent supported the statement.[50] This general trend is supported around the world. In a 1992 Gallup poll, majorities in twenty countries gave priority to safeguarding the environment even if it entailed slowing economic growth; additionally, 71 percent of the people in sixteen countries, including India, Mexico, South Korea, and Brazil, said they were willing to pay higher prices for products if it helps protect the environment.[51]

These figures suggest that over the past two decades there has been a significant shift in awareness and concern about the environment. It is worth noting additionally that people have also translated this sentiment into changes in behavior. In the 1960s, the U.S. Navy and Air Force used whales for target practice. Twenty-five years later an international effort, costing $5 million, was mounted to save three whales trapped in ice in Alaska.[52] Two decades ago corporations produced products with little regard for their environmental impact. Today, many corporations are working hard to reduce environmental repercussions at the production, packaging, and distribution phases of industry.[53] When multilateral development banks and other aid institutions were formed after the Second World

War, environmental impact assessments were non-existant. Today, they are commonplace.[54] Until recently consumers cared little about the environmental consequences of their buying habits. Today, in contrast, vast numbers of people living in diverse settings are boycotting environmentally unsound products and industries are working hard to claim that their products do not damage the environment.[55] Furthermore, twenty years ago most people did not think twice about throwing recyclables into the garbage with the rest of their refuse. Today, recycling is mandatory in many municipalities around the world, and voluntary recycling in some areas has generated a profit-making industry. (Between 1960 and 1990, the amount of municipal solid waste recovered by recycling in the United States nearly quintupled.)[56] In each of these instances, people are voluntarily shifting their behavior in part because of the messages being publicized by activists. If one looked solely at state behavior to account for this change, one would miss a tremendous amount of significant world political action.

A final, if not controversial, example of the dissemination of an ecological sensibility is the now greatly reduced practice of killing harp seal pups in northern Canada. Throughout the 1960s, the annual Canadian seal hunt took place without much public awareness or concern. In the late 1960s and throughout the 1970s and 1980s, Greenpeace, along with the International Fund for Animal Welfare, the Sea Shepherds Conservation Society, and a host of smaller preservation groups, saw this—in hindsight, according to many, inaccurately—as a threat to the continued existence of harp seals in Canada and brought the practice to the world's attention using, among other means, direct actions. As a result, people around the globe, especially in Europe, changed their buying habits. They refused to purchase products made out of the pelts and, as a consequence, the market for such merchandise all but dried up.[57] After this happened, the European Economic Community (EEC) actually banned the importation of seal pelts. Significant is that the EEC did so clearly after a dramatic drop in consumer demand.[58] The incident suggests that governmental policy may have simply been an afterthought and ultimately unnecessary. People acted in response to the messages propagated by activist groups or, put differently, increased awareness.[59]

In each of these instances, genuine changes took place or are taking place with respect to the way people treat the earth and use its resources. At work are forces that involve power and thus are matters of world politics. Put differently, an ecological sensibility is a form of governance that operates partly worldwide. Unfortunately, many students of international relations have difficulty appreciating the political dimension of such a sensibility. There are three reasons for this. First, there is a tendency to dismiss ideational factors because they are difficult to get an analytical handle on; it is much easier to ascribe patterns of thought or behavior to more structural or institutional elements of society. As Elkins and Simeon claim, "structural or institutional variables are simpler, more easily measured, more widely applicable and more universally understood [than cultural variables]."[60] Thus, many seek to understand phenomena in these terms. Social scientists, in other words, are wary of cultural variables; they always want to explain them away as derivative of deeper, more material animating factors. There are many sound reasons to support this point of view. In fact, I would be the first to admit that the existence of an ecological sensibility is difficult to define, too unwieldy to characterize elegantly, and almost impossible to measure with any degree of accuracy. Moreover, there is a strong incentive to explain it away by claiming it is merely a superstructural reflection of deeper processes. This, however, would be a mistake. It would involve privileging methodological, and even epistemological, rigor over an appreciation for important, yet clearly intangible, factors in political analysis.

The second reason many scholars of international relations ignore sensibilities is that even those who focus on the role of norms, values, and shared ideas understand them in terms of interstate behavior. They acknowledge and study them only to the degree that these ideas are involved in the formulation of state interests and, by extension, international cooperation and discord. This is what the vast majority of the regime literature is about. Indeed, even Peter Haas's work on epistemic communities, which departs from the regime literature in its attempt to explain the diffusion of knowledge among elites in general and not simply the origins and longevity of particular state norms, takes ideas seriously only to the degree that they shape state interests with the ultimate goal of international cooperation. Or, put more accurately, he is mainly interested in epistemic communities when they involve state policy makers.[61] Such focus on ideas only to the degree that they are picked up by states is partial because it ignores the fluid dimension of social movements and thus remains blind to the impact of societal phenomena in public affairs.

The third and final reason students of international relations avoid discussing sensibilities is that many of them are skeptical about cultural factors existing in the global arena. Many students of international relations are communitarian. Communitarians see the social group as the source of identity and the ground for shared customs, understandings, and so forth.[62] According to communitarians, predispositions develop only within particular societies where people enjoy a common history and culture, and such commonality is currently lacking on a worldwide scale. As mentioned, social predispositions, to the degree that students of international relations even talk about them, are merely *state* attitudes. They are not common attitudes held by peoples of the world and expressed throughout societies at large.

This third objection to acknowledging the governing potential of an ecological sensibility may have been relevant fifty years ago but it is harder to maintain at this point in time. Advancements in communication technologies are bringing societies into intimate contact, making people dramatically more aware of each other and thus more vulnerable to each other's beliefs, values, and concerns.[63] Perhaps the greatest indication of this is the proliferation of television throughout the world. From 1965 to 1986, the number of televisions per 1,000 people nearly tripled in the United States, France, and Australia. In Mexico, Hungary, and the former Soviet Union it quadrupled. In El Salvador, Singapore, and Jamaica it rose by 1500%.[64] From 1970 to 1989 the number of television sets worldwide increased about threefold.[65] Such an increase suggests that the percentage of people plugged into mass communication is greater than at any other time in history.[66] When people tune into their televisions they are accessing channels of communication that are almost instantaneous and global in scope. While television programming is neither neutral nor beyond state control, it promotes cultural diffusion in an unprecedented manner.[67] Interpretations of life, or simply cultural expressions, fly around the globe at greater speed and scope than at any previous time in history. They are creating what Ivo Duchacek calls "perforated sovereignties."[68] According to Walter Truett Anderson, a result of this is that "more people have modified their values and beliefs over the past few decades than over any other comparably brief period of time."[69]

In my view, this certainly does not mean that the world enjoys a robust culture. It does suggest, however, that ideas and predispositions are not the sole purview of nation-states. They develop, migrate, and fertilize transnationally.[70] And, to the degree that people's actions reflect their values, attitudes, and concerns, it is important to consider widely held sensibilities, such as the ecological one, as significant forms of governance.

Globalism Versus Supra-statism

In chapter 2, I claimed that there are three traditional approaches to global environmental governance: statism, supra-statism and sub-statism. I also suggested that one can move beyond these schemes by looking at transnational environmental activist groups. Such organizations take a process-oriented, as opposed to an institutional-based, approach to global environmental problems and pursue a type of politics that is not oriented merely toward the institution of the modern state. In this chapter I have been outlining one dimension of this type of politics. This is the dissemination of an ecological sensibility throughout the world. If one thinks about statism, supra-statism and sub-statism as the primary avenues for approaching environmental governance, disseminating an ecological sensibility represents an alternative to the supra-statist option. It is a practice that, while not attempting to construct a world government, is directed at the global level of political life. The idea behind disseminating an ecological sensibility is not to design a set of agencies on the scale of a world state or to devise blueprints for a global governing body. Rather, it is to budge the social and cultural dimensions of global collective life toward an appreciation for the critical condition of the planet's ecosystem and inspire vast numbers of people to undertake action to defend the earth.

World government is a "design" approach to environmental problems. It seeks a blueprint for relations of power and suggests that once the correct configuration is arrived at, human behavior will be successfully controlled so as to solve global environmental dilemmas. It represents an architectural orientation that sees world politics strictly as a matter of governmental structures and thus believes that only a change in structural arrangements will provide answers to global environmental problems. It suggests that global environmental dilemmas can simply be legislated away, if only human beings enjoyed an institution that could legislate on a worldwide scale.

The idea that global problems could be solved if only the world were run by a supra-statist institution is grossly misguided. It assumes that law backed by force is the only way to alter human behavior. It thus takes a conflated view of environmental dilemmas—seeing their continued existence as a result of the absence of a world authority that can develop and enforce laws to regulate behavior. The dynamics of environmental problems are more intricate and cross-sectoral than this view assumes. Environmental dilemmas are embedded in social practices that permeate most levels of human experience. They are the result of the entire complex of social, economic, and governmental elements that support environmentally unsound practices. Hence, a world governmental solution will not provide the answer to global environmental problems. Responses to such difficulties must come from changes within the entire range of social arenas. Transnational environmental groups recognize this. They engage the social and cultural dimensions of human experience—aspects of global life that are not simply amenable to governmental action—instead of focusing exclusively on institutional arrangements.

To emphasize the difference between statism and the efforts of transnational environmental groups, one could say that the politics of disseminating an ecological sensibility is a matter of *globalism*. Globalism is traditionally used to describe a heightened sensitivity to the fragility of the life-support system of the planet and a sense of human solidarity in a world of increasing interdependence.[71] One should also think of it, however, as a type of politics, as an activity committed to bringing about conditions that will alter the behavior of others in matters of public concern and involvement. While supra-statism proposes solving global environmental problems by creating some form of world government—specifically recreating the institution of the modern state on a world scale—globalism is not oriented to the notion of the state in any form. It thus represents a type of political action that deprivileges or ignores nation-states as sovereign entities and pushes for an environmentally sound world without being enamored with the state itself. Globalism as world politics is not foremost about building institutions but changing people's attitudes and behavior. It is about raising concern for environmental issues among the largest audience possible and therewith pushing the cultural element of human enterprise toward a respect for the environment. It seeks to inspire people to express concern for the environment and work toward its well-being not only at the ballot box (where it exists) but in the marketplace, at work, and in the home. Globalism is, in short, the attempt to infuse all people's practices with a conscience about environmental well-being. It seeks to instill an ecological sensibility so deeply into the human psyche that it will act like a norm or predisposition. That is, it will be "so well-entrenched through habit and ceremony, so broadly, even intuitively, honored that it exercises its sway with minimal reflection."[72]

Greenpeace and other transnational environmental groups work to disseminate an ecological sensibility throughout the world. They seek to persuade people to care about and take actions to protect the earth. In their most ambitious moments they aspire to reacculturate all of humanity and thus create an environmentally sustainable way of life for generations to come. While this may never happen on such a scale, it is taking place already among critical numbers of people throughout the world. Today millions of people know and care about environmental threats and have undertaken significant practices to protect the earth. Such a change is obviously not *the* answer to global environmental problems. It is, however, a necessary component of any set of approaches to such dilemmas.

As will become clear in the next few chapters, disseminating an ecological sensibility is only one dimension of the politics of transnational environmental activist groups. In this chapter I have tried to show that it is an important one. Such dissemination, which I choose to characterize as globalism, is akin to what Andre Brink calls a "revolution in conscience."[73] It is politics not of rifles or tanks but of words and images. It is a politics not over territory or votes but over ideas and feelings. It is, in short, the attempt to permeate the values, attitudes, and eventually the behavior of others. Granted, this kind of enterprise is a slow process. Indeed, compared to world population, only a handful of people at this time possess an ecological sensibility. Nonetheless, social dynamics work in mysterious ways. As poet Paul Eluard writes:

> They were but a handful—
> Suddenly they were a crowd.[74]

4   World Wildlife Fund and Political Localism

The poor are not the problem; they are the solution.
—Robert Chambers

There are parts of the world that are unresponsive to an ecological sensibility. Even though access to televisions, magazines, newspapers, and so forth has increased dramatically over the past few decades, many people live in ways that muffle the message of environmental concern when it is expressed in globalist terms. This is especially the case among the world's poor. Over one billion people live in dire poverty, with 400 million close to starvation.[1] While many of these people actually know and care about environmental issues,[2] they are subject to external, largely economic, constraints which make it difficult for them to act to protect the global environment. Many of them cut trees, cultivate crops, or graze cattle for a livelihood in ways that often undermine the ecological integrity of the earth. To be sure, as individuals, the poor destroy the environment at a fraction of the rate of the affluent; moreover, their practices are often in response to the consumption patterns of the rich. Nonetheless, the sheer number of the world's poor and the biologically rich character of their immediate environment magnifies the environmental ramifications of their actions.

Working among the poor for environmental protection requires a special kind of activism. It calls for focusing on economic development and using local economic improvement as a route to safeguarding the environment. As long as basic human needs remain unmet, the poor will (rightfully) exploit the natural world. Activists concerned with preserving habitats and species among the poor, then, must find ways of linking the struggle to stay alive or simply improve one's economic well-being with environmental protection. Many transnational activists are, indeed, finding such linkages and their work stands as an important example of enlisting the poor in halting or at least slowing environmental degradation.

In this chapter, I study the eco-development efforts of transnational environmental groups and evaluate their world political significance. I examine how activists work in the field to foster sustainable development projects and trace the effect this has on the behavior of collectivities throughout the region and the world. The central argument of the chapter is that eco-development efforts work to empower local communities and, as those communities interact with wider economic, social and governmental institutions and processes, they effectively shape widespread practices. For this reason, when activists focus on the local level and empower communities they are engaging in a significant form of world politics.

This argument fits into the overall theme of the book insofar as it examines an additional form of governance that transnational environmental groups use to create a more environmentally sound world. Working with local residents, mostly in the Third World, is a form of political activity that takes place outside the immediate grip of state power. The local realm, in all its social, economic, and political complexity, is not completely captured by the state. To be sure, there are important overlaps and these often become relevant for activists' work. Nonetheless, the overlaps are not what make activist efforts political nor necessarily significant. Environmental groups manipulate the incentive structures of local residents, reorient the productive mechanisms of certain societies and forge links between communities and the outside world which support sustainable development. Moreover, by simply enabling communities to succeed in securing both economic and environmental aims, activists embolden local people and thereby magnify the influence of local communities. *These* activities and their effects make the efforts of transnational groups political and significant. And, because these take place underneath or around the state, depicting them illustrates another facet of world civic politics.

This chapter is similar to the last one in that I use one transnational environmental organization to illustrate my point. In the following, I concentrate on World Wildlife Fund (WWF) to articulate the dynamics of a transnational politics of empowerment. While WWF disseminates an ecological sensibility and engages in other types of political action (including lobbying governments), it spends the bulk of its time in the field; the majority of its energy is devoted to specific environmental projects that target particular areas of the world. For this reason it serves well to illustrate the hands-on type of politics of many transnational environmental groups. Another similarity between this chapter and the previous one is that I use the categories of sub-statist, supra-statist, and statist orientations to conceptualize the overall meaning of WWF's politics. In the following I show that WWF's empowerment efforts take place at the sub-statist level of political life, but are not intent upon creating institutional structures of the state variety. Rather, in the same way Greenpeace works at the global level without trying to build a world government (thus engaging in *globalism*), WWF undertakes a type of politics called *localism*. This is the attempt to empower local communities so they can better control their environmental and development destinies and, in so doing, have an impact on wider spheres of collective life.

Before focusing on WWF and its localist politics, it is important to make a general point about transnational environmental groups working in the Third World. There is a widespread assumption that the poor—either because they are short-term maximizers or because they lack resources to undertake sustainable practices—categorically destroy the environment. Furthermore, many believe that it is only because rich, First World environmental groups get involved in Third World environmental issues that the poor are able to develop any semblance of environmentally sound practices and, at times, become environmental activists in their own right. Much of the following may sound like it subscribes to these assumptions but this would be a misreading. Research shows that the poor are not categorically foes of the environment and, under certain circumstances, are, in fact, at the forefront of environmental activism. Moreover, such activism is not usually the consequence of a relationship with First World environmental groups but is indigenous to specific countries, given specific conditions.[3] By focusing on the strategies that transnational environmental groups use to promote environmental protection in the Third World, then, I am not claiming that the efforts of transnational groups are the only or best form of environmental protection among the world's poor. Rather, I am simply trying to understand how transnational environmental activist groups devise relevant strategies for environmental protection in areas that are often unresponsive to messages of global environmental degradation. The localist politics of WWF and others represent a type of political practice undertaken by transnational groups that aims to change widespread behavior in the developing world. It is not the only or best route to environmental well-being among the world's poor nor more promising than activities initiated by the poor themselves. It is, however, one key way transnational groups practice their politics in poorer parts of the world.

PART ONE

Origins of World Wildlife Fund

After the Second World War, with the decolonization of much of the Third World, many people hoped that the countries of Africa, Asia, and Latin America would follow the path of development pursued by the First World. Such development, according to these people, would eradicate poverty, malnutrition, and rampant disease; cut down on population growth; and bring Third World societies up to the living standards of those in the "civilized" West. Over the past four decades, First World countries have undertaken significant actions and have loaned or given vast sums of money to promote Third World development. From an economic standpoint, these efforts receive mixed evaluation. Some observers see them as success stories that have lifted at least some people from dire poverty and created a better life for many people throughout the Third World. For others, development strategies—often based on theories of modernization—have failed to improve the lot of the world's poor and, in some ways, have actually worsened it. Many argue, for example, that they have led to dependent economies, corrupt regimes, enfeebling social stratification, and increased poverty due to ill-conceived projects motivated more by a commitment to make money than alleviate poverty. From an environmental standpoint, the record is less confused. There is widespread agreement that development projects—even those that some people feel have improved the lot of many—involve high costs to the natural world. Increased deforestation, desertification, pollution, salinization, and so forth are all partly associated with efforts to develop the Third World along a First World development model. Most projects along these lines use resources in an unsustainable fashion and encroach upon wildlands that possess their own ecological integrity.

The beginnings of WWF can be found in the discontent among many conservationists with the environmental costs of development. As far back as the 1950s, observers noted that many development projects threatened African, Asian, and Latin American wildlife. For WWF, this discontent was given particular expression in 1960 when the biologist and zoologist Sir Julian Huxley wrote three articles for the London weekly *The Observer* on growing threats to African wildlife. The articles chronicled a recent trip he had taken to East Africa. As luck would have it, the articles were read by Victor Stolan, a German who had become a naturalized Briton and was living in London. Stolan wrote Huxley a letter suggesting that to save African wildlife researchers must go beyond surveying the degree of loss and actually work to protect remaining but endangered areas and species. According to Stolan, the main obstacle to doing this was a lack of funds for the already existent but weak worldwide conservation movement. There were plenty of people dedicated to protecting wildlife; the only problem was that they did not have the resources to carry out necessary projects. Stolan suggested that he had ideas about how to raise money and would like to discuss some of them with Huxley or others who shared his concern. The gist of Stolan's letter was the need for a professional organization to raise funds necessary to put the worldwide conservation movement on a strong financial footing.

Huxley passed on Stolan's letter to a friend, E. M. Nicholson, who was Director-General of the British Nature Conservancy (now the Nature Conservancy Council). Nicholson had been thinking along the same lines as Stolan for quite some time, and the letter served as a catalyst to put the idea into actual material form. Nicholson discussed the scheme at various speaking engagements in the United States and Britain and found much support for it. Particularly enthusiastic were Guy Mountfort and Sir Peter Scott. Mountfort was a successful businessman and prominent member of the British Ornithologists' Union. Sir Peter Scott was the Vice-President of the International Union for the Conservation of Nature and Natural Resources (IUCN).[4] Since its inception in 1948, the IUCN had been greatly hampered by a lack of resources to carry out its work. Stolan's idea, passed on through Nicholson, was a perfect opportunity to improve IUCN's effectiveness. Nicholson, Mountfort, and Scott drafted a paper that was discussed and approved by the executive board of the IUCN. This set the ball rolling. A month later a preparatory group was formed, which included Victor Stolan, to examine the requirements and prepare plans for the establishment of a worldwide fund-raising organization. This would work in collaboration with existing associations to bring enormous financial support to the conservation movement.

In its preparatory work, the group chose the name World Wildlife Fund with the subsidiary title, "An International Foundation for Saving the World's Wildlife and Wild Places." This captured most accurately the groups initial mission. Also during this time, H.R.H. Prince Philip, Duke of Edinburgh, expressed interest and agreed to become president of the British national association. He enlisted the support of Prince Bernhard of the Netherlands who became the first patron and later president of the WWF international office. What put the organization on its feet during this time were contributions from two anonymous donors totaling 3,000 pounds (equivalent to 20,000 pounds in 1986) and a donation of 10,000 pounds from Jack Cotton, a well-known British businessman. This enabled the organization to set up an international headquarters in Switzerland and apply for tax-exempt status. In September 1961, WWF was formally constituted under Swiss law.

The main reason to set up WWF was to raise money. The organization was given an important initial boost by a special issue of the London newspaper the *Daily Mirror*. On October 9, 1961, in collaboration with WWF, the *Daily Mirror* ran a "shock issue," which highlighted threats to endangered wildlife. Seven full pages alerted readers to the wildlife emergency. On the back page was a coupon that allowed readers to send in donations. The response was dramatic. Readers sent in sums ranging from a few pence to hundreds of pounds. It took people days to sort out the mail bags of letters. In total, donors contributed 45,000 pounds (equivalent to 300,000 in 1986) and this was deposited into a central WWF International account.[5]

Since its establishment in 1961 and its opening of an international headquarters in 1962, WWF has grown into a genuinely transnational environmental activist group.[6] With a central international office in Gland, Switzerland, and a second central hub in the United States, the WWF family is made up of offices in twenty-seven countries, spanning five continents. While the bulk of these are in the First World, there is a substantial number of WWF offices in the Third World. For example, there is a WWF–Pakistan, WWF–Malaysia, WWF–India, and WWF–Hong Kong. World Wildlife Fund enjoys a membership of over 6 million supporters and an annual budget of roughly $200 million. Over the past thirty-plus years, WWF has funded or engaged in over 4,000 projects in 140 countries. These range from building fences around a forest preserve and providing trucks, rifles, and other antipoaching equipment to local authorities to setting up environmental research stations. Funding comes from a variety of sources. WWF relies on contributions from individuals, as well as grants from foundations and corporations. The bulk of it comes from private, individual contributors. WWF has been, and continues to be, concerned with preserving wildlife. Protecting wild animals and lands, and thus working in the service of biological diversity, is its chief goal. Nonetheless, as it became clear that safeguarding wildlife involves issues of economic development, pollution, climate change, and other more general environmental concerns, it has expanded its focus. It now has programs on pollution, the greenhouse effect, and ozone depletion in addition to traditional conservation projects. The former, however, are not as yet as well-funded as the latter. Finally, WWF has changed from an organization that simply contributes money to ongoing projects to an initiator and active participant in field-oriented conservation. It actually undertakes conservation work itself. This, as I will show, represents its most important contribution to addressing global environmental problems.

Transnational Organizational Structure

World Wildlife Fund conceptualizes conservation issues in terms of geographical areas. It sees Latin America, Europe, Africa, North America, Asia, and the Pacific as unique regions each demanding special attention. Its programs are designed to develop projects that address the particular needs of wildlife within each area. WWF coordinates its offices in a way that targets these specific regions.

While all areas on the globe deserve attention, the Third World is particularly in need of special effort. A host of economic, political, and demographic factors work together in the Third World to heighten the severity of threats to wildlife. For this reason, while WWF engages in many projects throughout the First World, it directs most of its energy to countries in Africa, Asia, and Latin America. WWF does so by establishing two lead offices that coordinate all WWF activity in these regions. WWF–U.S. acts as the lead office for Latin America, and WWF–International in Switzerland acts as the lead office for Asia and Africa. All projects in the Third World are administered through these offices. Local WWF chapters which wish to support conservation efforts in the Third World contribute part of their funds to these offices. WWF-U.S. and WWF-International pool this money and this allows them to carry out extensive projects. Additionally local offices often wish to see specific projects undertaken in the Third World, that is, projects that they themselves conceive. In such instances, they must still work through one of the lead offices. This will ensure that any actions are well integrated into other WWF efforts in the region.

While projects in the Third World are administered through one of the two lead offices, the overall programs undertaken in Latin America, Africa, and Asia are supervised by WWF–wide committees. These committees are made up of representatives from a number of WWF offices. They meet a few times a year and, while not responsible for setting strict policies, formulate the general orientation of WWF programs. The transnational character of these committees complicates the process of formulating programs. Often people from different countries hold varying conceptions of goals and strategies of how to pursue wildlife conservation. Nonetheless, this diversity can, many times, provide a more informed sensitivity and understanding of the difficulties involved. Indeed, because committee members come from separate countries, this ensures a more cosmopolitan or at least nonnational perspective on the development of wildlife programs.

In addition to designing programs for particular regions, WWF also has a set of cross-cutting programs that inform all regional projects. These can be thought of as conservation methods to be employed within diverse geographical areas. These include programs on Creating and Preserving Protected Areas, Linking Conservation and Human Needs, Protecting Species, Building Effective Institutions, and Addressing Global Threats. Each of these is meant to develop particular strategies for conservation, which WWF employs in different regions. For example, the Linking Conservation and Human Needs Program focuses specifically on sustainable development. It recognizes that human beings must be economically secure if they are to use natural resources in an ecologically sensitive manner. It thus seeks to link management of natural resources with grassroots economic development. The program has mastered a number of techniques for doing this. Such techniques have become an integral part of projects in Thailand, Zambia, Cameroon, Mexico, and Costa Rica. Likewise, the Protecting Species program involves campaigns to save flagship species, halt global trade in endangered plants and animals, and train and equip antipoaching teams. The program is active in almost all areas where WWF works. Like the Linking Conservation and Human Needs Program, it should be thought of as complementary to larger, regional WWF projects.

The transnational character of WWF manifests itself in cross-cutting programs in the same way that it does in regional ones. Committees, comprised of representatives from a number of countries, formulate the overall orientation of these cross-cutting initiatives. This, again, brings about differences of opinion and thus makes the process of formulation difficult. It also, however, lends a broader perspective to the work of WWF. It serves as a check against nationalist biases. The transnational program committees, like their geographical counterparts, are not responsible for devising specific policies concerning the way programs are pragmatically implemented. Rather, they simply set general guidelines.

While this describes the overall organization of WWF, it is important to note that there is a fair amount of leeway for individual offices to pursue projects within their home countries. Indeed, every office undertakes at least some conservation action within its own region. For example, WWF–Pakistan is working to protect the blackbuck antelope from extinction. It is doing so by breeding and reintroducing the antelope within Pakistan's Kalabagh Natural Park. WWF–Japan is helping to create a protective sanctuary near the city of Nakamura for the more than sixty-four species of dragonflies that are indigenous to the island of Shikoku. WWF–UK has provided fences and notice boards for several county naturalist trust areas to protect them from destruction and has purchased lands around a number of national nature reserves in North Berkshire to provide ecological buffer zones. When individual offices undertake these kinds of actions, they pay for them from money that they have raised but did not send out to the two lead offices.[7] It is important to note that while individual offices undertake local conservation work, their activities are conceptually and practically integrated into larger regional programs. As part of the WWF network, offices are aware of other projects taking place in their particular regions and design their unilateral projects to fit into the larger framework of conservation in the area.

The institutional make-up of WWF consists of coordinating its offices around the world and the workings of an executive committee to oversee the entire network. Most offices, except those in Switzerland and the United States, are called national appeals. They raise money and, after paying their own operating expenses, send a significant amount of their funds to WWF–International and WWF–U.S. Most of the time they relinquish control when they send this money, although, as mentioned, they can retain some say over how their contributions are used if they have specific projects in mind. Each year, representatives from the national appeals meet and share information. This includes devising ways of improving communication between offices and discussing broad issues and strategies for wildlife conservation.

The executive board of the WWF is known as the Program Committee (formerly the Conservation Committee). This is a body made up of representatives from those WWF offices that raise the most money and meets every few months to work out problems with the overall coordination between offices and to provide general direction to the organization as a whole. The executive board is not as active as, say, the international board of Greenpeace. In fact, for many years, there was not much international coordination between the two hubs, WWF–U.S. and WWF–International. They each enjoyed their respective areas of administration and the most coordination that took place was in terms of transferring funds from individual offices to one or the other of these two lead countries. This is changing, although not at lightning speed. The WWF executive board is becoming more prominent and serves an important organizational role by providing cohesion and direction for the international WWF network. It is not powerful enough, however, to run the organization in a strict supervisory fashion.

World Wildlife Fund's Politics

The basic notion behind WWF's politics starts with a critique of traditional conservation practices. Most conservation efforts are launched and carried out from a distance. They are undertaken by nonnationals or at least nonlocals. This tradition was set in place in the early days of the international conservation movement. At the time, those concerned about wildlife lived mostly in northern, First World countries and believed that Third World people could not appreciate the value of wildlife, or were simply too strapped by economic pressures to be able to conserve nature. Conservation programs, then, had to be developed and financed by the North. Local inhabitants could never be expected to participate extensively in them. Initially, WWF took this approach. All its research and activities undertaken in the Third World were performed by staff people of the First World. Over the past few decades, however, it has been developing a more comprehensive understanding of conservation and this is giving way to a less paternal type of politics.

Originally, WWF saw conservation as a matter of saving specific species. It was concerned, for example, with protecting the great panda bear or the Bengal tiger. These animals were threatened with extinction and WWF saw its mission to keep them alive. The bulk of WWF's work in these early days consisted of researching the characteristics of particular species. The idea was that if one could understand the biological needs of animals one could take steps to protect them. Most of this research entailed sending First World scientists into the field and working through international agencies to disseminate findings.

While WWF made some progress in saving certain animals from extinction during this time, it also recognized that it was, overall, fighting a losing battle. The amount of resources it was devoting to wildlife research was not stemming the tide of massive species depletion and extinction. It was this realization that first altered WWF's notion of conservation. WWF recognized that conservation was not merely a matter of preserving individual species. Animals are situated in given ecosystems that perform particular functions. The existence of certain plants, access to water, a predictable climate, and the presence of other animals to provide a robust food chain are all significant for preserving species. Animals cannot be saved if their habitats are being destroyed. The needs of animals extend beyond their individual mating practices, ability to ward off disease, and migration patterns. They also include the preservation of healthy habitats. During this period of WWF's experience, WWF sought mainly to establish wildlife preserves. This locked-up pieces of territory so human beings could not disrupt significant ecological processes and thus throw off the balances that sustained wildlife habitats. The main way WWF established parks was to work through national governments. WWF would provide funding to governments to designate preserves, hire rangers, buy patrol and maintenance vehicles, and so forth.

While wildlife parks have gone a long way toward protecting vast numbers of species, they have not proven to be sufficiently effective. Over the past few decades, vast numbers of species have been decimated both within and around national parks. Moreover, parks could never prove to be complete solutions to threats to biological diversity because there are vast regions that are rich in wildlife but that cannot be protected under the rubric of a national park. WWF recognized this as it witnessed the numbers of species dramatically decreasing despite its efforts to establish wildlife preserves.

Eventually WWF started to notice that the central problem with a preserve system of wildlife conservation is that while it attends to the needs of animals, it ignores the needs of human beings. Much of the earth's remaining biological wealth is in parts of the world where the poorest peoples draw their livelihood from the land. As demographic and economic constraints grow more severe, these people will exploit otherwise renewable resources in an attempt merely to survive. Indeed, it does not matter if such areas are officially designated as parks or not, the poor and hungry will (rightfully) seek resources to keep themselves alive. Recognizing this aspect of environmental conservation, WWF has expanded its conception of conservation to include human needs. It now tries to improve the quality of life of the rural poor through projects that integrate the management of natural resources with grassroots economic development. For, if human beings living in areas of rich biological diversity cannot live economically viable lives, they will inevitably destroy the resource base that keeps wildlife alive as well as kill the animals themselves. In other words, people are an important element to wildlife protection.[8]

This evolution in conservation thinking has given way to a unique form of WWF politics. WWF no longer pursues conservation simply from a distance—either through international agencies or national governments—nor is it as paternalistic as it used to be. It now works closely with local inhabitants and tries to develop indigenous forms of economic development and conservation. This involves demonstrating how local communities can become more economically successful if they use their resources in a sustainable way, as well as setting up infrastructures that can ensure local participation and thus long-term viability. Another way to say this is that WWF seeks to empower local people to protect their own environments. It works so closely with local residents that it can be receptive to their needs, give expression to their visions, and set into motion mechanisms that will enhance the ability of local people both to live economically productive lives and protect wildlife.

Zambian Conservation Project. Sub-Saharan Africa holds some of the most magnificent wildlife in the world. Elephants, buffalo, lions, leopards, impalas, hippopotami, crocodiles, and numerous exotic species of birds bless this region of the world. For over thirty years, WWF has been initiating and supporting projects to protect these animals. One of its most impressive efforts is in Zambia.

Zambia protects its wildlife in the same way as many other sub-Saharan African countries. It has established a number of national parks and forbids people to live or hunt within park borders. Parks act as the main preserver of wildlife. At present there are nineteen national parks in Zambia. Surrounding these parks are lands known as Game Management Areas (GMAs). These are semiprotected regions designated for game utilization. Safari hunting, for example, is legal within these zones, and most of them support traditional communities. There are thirty-two GMAs throughout Zambia, accounting for 31 percent of Zambia's land area. GMAs are much larger than the national parks and thus serve as buffers. They are meant to relieve the pressure of hunting in national parks. By allowing hunting within these regions, the theory goes, national parks will be spared invasion.

Unfortunately, this system of conservation has been unsuccessful. While designating boundaries for national parks and trying to protect animals within these regions is a worthwhile endeavor, the patterns of wildlife do not always respect zoning laws. Animals have a hard time reading boundary notices. Because their habitats extend across national park boundaries, they migrate into GMAs and beyond. In itself, this is not a major problem. The level of official hunting in GMAs from professional safari groups is inside sustainable limits. Problems arise due to illegal poaching. Poaching for elephant ivory, black rhino horns, leopard skins, crocodile hides, and so on has depleted wildlife stocks considerably and forced a number of species to the brink of extinction. For example, poaching reduced the elephant population in one Zambian park by 70 percent throughout the 1980s, and diminished the number of black rhinos in the area to only a small handful. In nearby Kenya, the black rhino population has dwindled from 20,000 in 1970 to only 450 in 1990. In addition, 85 percent of Kenya's elephant population has been killed since 1973 (although the rate of killing has decreased due to the ban on elephant ivory trading). Similar stories can be told about wildlife in Uganda, the Sudan, and Tanzania.[9]

Poaching is a lucrative business. For local people it represents one of the easiest ways out of extreme poverty. Selling horns from a single black rhino on the black market can yield the equivalent of several months of income in the fields. For middlemen who sell such products to foreign consumers, the price of tusks and rhino horns yield so much money that there is little incentive to stop the butchery. A single rhino horn can fetch as much as $24,000 in Asia or Yemen where it is considered, respectively, an aphrodisiac and the traditional material for making dagger handles.

For over a decade, WWF has been working to halt the slaughter of wildlife by poachers in Zambia. It supports and helps manage an antipoaching project which builds on the traditional park/GMA program but addresses many of its insufficiencies. The main problem with the traditional Zambian scheme of conserving wildlife was that it left the needs of local people out of the picture. In fact, it operated in ways that made local inhabitants almost victims of conservation efforts. One can see this, for example, in the law enforcement schemes within GMAs. Until a few years ago, park and GMA enforcement officers were civil servants appointed by the Zambian government and brought in from outside. Given the duty of arresting poachers, these officials found it easiest to pursue local, small-time hunters and poachers. Such residents were not nearly as well armed or organized as professional poachers and thus represented easy targets. This caused much hostility to develop between game officials and local communities. "The department would track a suspect to his house and inspect his fire, even if he was only cooking a rat," claims Willard Ntalasha, a governor of an area that falls within the Mumbwa GMA in western Zambia.[10] Such hostility allowed professional poachers to cooperate with local inhabitants. Professional poachers could easily bribe residents not to inform on them. Thus, a tacit alliance was set in place between local people and professional poachers. In this situation, it was clear that conservation efforts worked against the interest of local inhabitants.

An additional source of ineffectiveness came from the discord between local inhabitants and professional safari hunters. Hunters secured permits to kill game that was off-limits to residents. Local people saw hunters, then, as legalized poachers. This was particularly troublesome because safari staff and hunters also came from outside the area and enjoyed the local fruits without giving back benefits to the GMA communities. In contrast, poachers many times hired community residents as porters and assistants. This gave local people a source of income and livelihood in an area poor in employment opportunities. The result of these pressures formed a major stumbling block to conservation efforts. Even with sophisticated equipment such as helicopters and fleets of airplanes, state law enforcement failed to stop increasing levels of poaching.

It was in such a climate that WWF started to fund and direct a new approach to antipoaching. The program is called the Administrative Design for Game Management Areas (ADMADE). It breaks the link between poachers and local residents by enlisting GMA communities in the struggle to protect wildlife. The key source of allegiance between poachers and residents stems from the lack of economic opportunity in the region. Essentially, local people must eke out livelihoods on the land, and this provides only minuscule income. Under such conditions, poaching, or being bribed by poachers, becomes almost an economic necessity. ADMADE works against these conditions by making it more profitable for local residents to protect wildlife than to support poaching.

ADMADE rests on two central features. First, it includes local residents in antipoaching and conservation operations. Under the program, young men from the area become village scouts who are trained in antipoaching techniques, data collection, and resource monitoring, and operate in units which patrol designated areas within GMAs. Village scouts also accompany safari hunters and record which animals are killed and thus monitor legal wildlife utilization. They are paid a steady salary and receive clothes, food, and a small number of amenities. The village scout program provides employment to people who would otherwise look to poaching for income.

The second major feature of ADMADE is that revenues from tourists and safari hunting, the most significant form of income in the region, are reinvested into local communities. This creates an incentive for GMA inhabitants to conserve wildlife. For many years the money received from park admissions, hunting fees, and concession charges paid by safari companies went to the national Zambian finance ministry. It was used to pay for the upkeep of the national parks and to promote tourism within Zambia as a whole. Under the ADMADE project, a significant portion of this money is returned to local communities. Fees, concessions, and so forth now go into the Wildlife Conservation Revolving Fund. This is divided between national and local entities. Under this scheme, over 40 percent of revenues is channeled back into community development—which includes building schools, health clinics, and wells for local residents—and into upkeep of the GMAs. This latter money generates much employment through the scout program. The key to both features of ADMADE is that through increased employment and participation at the local level, and due to revenues received from wildlife utilization, villagers can earn a better living caring for and protecting their game than by supporting poachers. In fact, some people who used to be poachers are now employees of the program; and present-day local poachers are excommunicated from their villages. Professional poachers are kept out of GMAs or arrested by village scouts.

Although ADMADE has only been in operation a number of years, it can already claim a number of significant accomplishments. From 1987 to 1990, 545 poachers were arrested throughout the GMA system. In the Lupande valley, adjacent to the South Luangwa National Park, such efforts have reduced poaching by 90 percent and doubled wildlife population across the board. In the Mumbwa GMA, which borders the Kafue National Park, elephants, which had all but disappeared, have returned to the sparse forests and open grasslands, and populations of buffalo, zebra, and hartebeest are beginning to recover. Another measure of success is that local employment in wildlife-related activities has risen tenfold since 1986. This is due mainly to the scout program, although support for the infrastructure of the entire ADMADE program has enlisted the work of nonscout residents as well. Additionally, the program is working so well that WWF has won support from the U.S. Agency for International Development (AID). Since 1990 U.S. AID has contributed significantly to the financial stability of the project. U.S. AID money is being administered by WWF in cooperation with the Zambian government and the Zambian National Parks and Wildlife Service (NPWS), which oversees the ADMADE program. The success of ADMADE can also be measured by the number of other communities throughout Zambia that have requested that their areas be reclassified as GMAs. Popular sentiment shows that the idea of sustainable wildlife utilization, as a way to provide people living near parks and protected areas with direct, tangible benefits from wildlife conservation, is growing significantly. The NPWS is having difficulty mapping and surveying all areas under consideration for reclassification. Perhaps the most impressive success story of the program is the amounts of money being channeled back into local communities. In 1989, former President Kenneth Kaunda presented the first cash disbursements from revenues raised from the sustainable uses of wildlife in ten ADMADE units. Kaunda gave checks totaling 2.3 million kwacha

(US $230,000) to nine local chiefs to finance community development projects. This money has been used to build schools, wells, maize grinders, and health clinics in the region. Similar amounts have been presented back to the community since then.

The ADMADE program represents one of WWF's more successful projects for saving wildlife through local participation and economic development. WWF knows that the future of wildlife conservation in the Third World does not lie in the hands of those in the "civilized" North. If local people cannot live economically viable lives, species will continue to be threatened if for no other reason than to secure short-term economic benefits. Before the ADMADE project was established, poaching represented an attractive source of cash income for villagers. The project has changed this. Local residents now see how their own livelihoods are better protected by saving wildlife. Wildlife conservation gives them more control over their lives. The ADMADE program represents, then, a way for local people to participate in environmental protection and not be victims of it. WWF is experimenting with transporting this approach to wildlife management to other areas of the Third World.[11]

Cameroon Kilum Mountain Project. The ADMADE project works on the assumption that wildlife will attract tourists and hunters to national parks and GMAs and that the revenues from these activities will fuel the local economy. In this manner, residents can build a sustainable economy through wildlife conservation. The backbone behind the project is that much of Zambia is blessed with large mammals and exotic birds. Consequently, villagers need only protect these species in order to develop a type of economic stability that works in the service of wildlife conservation.

Much of Africa and the Third World does not enjoy the attraction of large mammals and exotic birds. Tourism and safari hunting are almost unheard of throughout the vast majority of these regions. These areas do, however, house numerous plant and animal species that exist nowhere else in the world and whose existence is crucial to the maintenance of local ecosystems. WWF is committed to protecting these regions of the world's wildlife treasures as well as the flashier areas that capture attention of tourists and hunters from the North. One of its more impressive efforts is in the area surrounding Kilum mountain in northwest Cameroon.

Kilum mountain, standing 10,000 feet high, is the second-highest mountain in West Africa. Along its slopes are 17,000 acres of forests that support a high concentration of indigenous plants and animals. These include the Pygaeum tree, the black-and-white Preuss monkey, and over twenty species of birds. While not as well known or dramatic as African wildlife in the lowland forests, these species exist only in the Kilum mountain region and their extinction would be a permanent loss to the store of biological diversity on earth. Their survival hinges on the healthy maintenance of the Kilum mountain forests. Unfortunately, these forests are under heavy assault from a growing and more agriculturally active human population.

The Kilum forests are inhabited by three different ethnic groups; the largest is the Oku people. For decades if not centuries, these peoples have depended upon the forest to supply resources for their livelihoods and to provide conditions to raise sustainable agriculture. They have harvested bark from the Pygaeum tree, which is used internationally as an effective medicine for prostate problems, extracted honey from beehives throughout the forests, and cultivated different varieties of trees for wood products. Furthermore, the forest cover guarantees a reliable flow of freshwater even during the November to February dry season. This enables local people to grow maize, potatoes, yams, beans, and coffee throughout the year.

Over time, demographic, economic, and political pressures have changed the interaction between inhabitants and the environment. A number of years ago, goats were introduced into the area and large portions of the forest understory were eaten as a result. This reduced the ability of the forest, as a whole, to reproduce. Additionally, farmers moved deeper into the forest and used slash-and-burn methods of agriculture. This cleared the land quickly but, among other things, compromised the fertility of the soil, as the forest cover could no longer protect against the elements. Moves to go deeper into the forest also included the attempt to cultivate land on steeper, more precipitous slopes. This resulted in erosion as deep-rooted trees were removed and replaced with shallow rooted crops. Furthermore, local residents harvested and simply destroyed trees faster than the trees could reproduce. This ruined many of the areas where bees could build hives and where numerous species could live. Finally, the reduction in forest cover lessened the amount of freshwater flow during the dry season and thus decreased agricultural productivity. The end result of all these occurrences is that, for many years, the forest area shrunk in size. Throughout the 1970s and 1980s, over half of it was destroyed. A third of the remaining forest is severely degraded.

From 1988 through the early 1990s, WWF worked to halt the decimation of the forest. Its involvement included financing, advising and providing other resources for a conservation team that put into place a sustainable conservation program in the region. The team was initially led by two WWF staffers, the only two non-Cameroon people involved in the field. They worked with local residents to devise methods of increasing agricultural productivity and protecting natural habitats and ecosystems.

Starting in 1988, one of the first things WWF did was establish the remaining areas of the mountain as a forest reserve. This sought to protect the most fragile and richest areas in the region. While this entailed submitting a proposal to the Cameroon government and working with state officials, the most important aspect of it required enlisting the help of local residents, for these were the people who would be immediately affected and who posed the most direct threat to the montane ecosystem. WWF staffers gathered together village leaders from the area and explained the importance of preserving the forest. This included reassuring people that all existing claims to land on the mountain would be respected but that boundaries had to be established to prevent further destruction of the forest. Over a number of months, WWF staffers, along with village leaders and officials from the Cameroon forestry department, hiked through the area and negotiated where the forest boundary should be set. They hung signs and whitewashed trees to designate the protected area. Because local residents were intimately involved in the process, the preserve enjoys a high level of legitimacy. As of 1993, there has been only negligible infringement on the forest and this has been addressed effectively by traditional authorities in the area. This is especially noteworthy in that, although the area has been considered for legal preserve status, as of this writing it has no official protection. Local residents have been respecting the preserve's boundaries due to their own involvement in its establishment and in the importance its ecological well-being has for their farms and living areas.

Another aspect of the project was setting up horticultural nurseries. Diverting water from a nearby stream, the WWF conservation team was able to irrigate a number of vacant plots of land. They set these up as breeding grounds for raising trees and crops to be transported to other parts of the region. They produced, for example, seedlings for a wide range of indigenous trees and introduced new, but seemingly appropriate, types of crops. These included cabbage, kale, onions, cauliflower, and a "java" variety of coffee. Up until the introduction of these foodstuffs, people in the area lived mainly on maize, yams, and potatoes. The introduction of these crops greatly expands their diet and diversifies their agricultural production. Moreover, with the destruction of so many trees in the area due to faulty farming and harvesting methods, the production of tree seedlings has played a major role in the reforestation of the area. Within two years of the project's beginning, 8,000 seedlings were transplanted and, over the following years, WWF staffers helped others set up satellite nurseries throughout the montane region. The idea was to create a network of nurseries to reforest the area and increase agricultural production.

World Wildlife Fund also worked to preserve topsoil on the mountain. Topsoil depletion is a problem wherever farmers overwork the land. Soil depletion on Kilum mountain is a significant threat to sustainable agriculture as it renders more and more areas unsuitable for cultivation and hence forces farmers to move deeper into the forest in search of arable land. Among their many efforts, WWF staffers raised legumes in the nurseries (which fix nitrogen in the soil), removed eucalyptus trees (which hog nutrients and water), set up composting practices (which increase the fertility of the soil), and introduced the use of goat manure as an organic fertilizer. What is significant is that, in all these efforts, WWF enlisted the participation of local residents and arranged for local people to carry out the work themselves. This aimed both to ensure long-term, sustainable agriculture and increase productivity.

Another aspect of the Kilum mountain project is environmental education. In many ways, the efforts described were part of an educational campaign to teach people how to conserve the wildlands and to live agriculturally sustainable lives. In addition, however, WWF also carried out direct, explicitly educational projects. For example, WWF produced a slide show, called "Trees for Life," which emphasizes the importance of saving the forest and specifies the dangers of not doing so. It is narrated in the Oku language and consists of photographs taken from the area and from comparative regions throughout Africa. A portable generator and slide-tape equipment is used to present showings at many community gatherings throughout the region. Additionally, WWF, in collaboration with local leaders, started publication of a ten-page newsletter, which, among other things, argues for forest conservation, specifies forest reserve boundaries, and defines rules governing behavior within the reserve. Because the newsletter invites local responses and editorials, it serves as important source of communication between Kilum mountain residents.

The final aspect of the Kilum project worth mentioning is the revitalization of a local honey cooperative which traditionally served as an important source of income for local residents. For years Kilum mountain residents had been collecting honey by destroying hives in the forests and bringing them to a central building within which the honey was extracted. In the process, wax and bees got mixed in with the solidified honey. Often this mixture remained at the cooperative for months before it was boiled, strained, and packaged for sale within Cameroon. The result was that beekeepers did not get paid for at least six months after they brought in their honey. Moreover, the mixture was boiled over an open fire and this created a smokey taste that made it less competitive on the Cameroon market. WWF worked hard to change the style of the cooperative. It introduced ways of retrieving honey without destroying the hives, a pressing process that replaced burning over open fires, and a revolving fund—created on the basis of a direct grant from WWF and later Birds Life International—that enabled prompter payments to beekeepers and processors. Improving the bee collective was an attempt to link further the economic fate of the Kilum peoples with the well-being of the forest. For, if the bee industry remains successful, there will be an incentive to preserve the forest that contains the nectar and pollen upon which the bees depend.

The success of the Kilum mountain project is difficult to measure. Because it does not take place on the level or enjoy the scope of the Zambian ADMADE project, one cannot gauge it at this time by the increase of wildlife in the area or by the degree of cash flow through national or international channels. Nonetheless, there are a few indicators that suggest that significant achievements have been made. First, incomes in the area have improved. Increased agricultural productivity has placed the local economy on a quasi-steady footing, and this has enabled residents to integrate their economy more efficiently within the broader national market. Second, the forest preserve, while still not enjoying official sanction, is being respected by the inhabitants. As of 1993, no new lands were carved out of the forest reserve for agriculture or grazing. While trend is not destiny, this appears to be extremely significant given the pattern of moving deeper into the forest before the WWF program. Finally, the program stands as a testament that agroforestry systems can be introduced and work in the less flashy areas of Africa. (Agroforestry is a method of conservation that entails integrating reforestation with improved crop yields.) In fact, it has worked so well—establishing a set of principles for such conservation schemes—that it is now being used in other areas of Cameroon. In particular, a similar program is being instituted in the area between Kilum mountain and Mount Cameroon along the Atlantic coast.[12]

Debt-for-Nature Swaps. The Zambian and Kilum mountain projects illustrate how WWF works with local inhabitants and enhances indigenous methods of combining wildlife conservation with economic development. WWF does the same thing, only at a more abstract level, in its debt-for-nature programs. Here the idea is to rechannel financial resources, specifically targeted for wildlife conservation, back into Third World countries. It is similar to the Zambian and Cameroon projects insofar as it enables local people to carry out environmental protection on their own.

At present, Third World nations owe over $1 trillion to lending institutions. Throughout the 1970s these nations borrowed heavily to finance balance of payment deficits; cover domestic policy errors, such as overvalued exchange rates; and invest in capital intensive projects, such as new roads, large-scale modern agricultural programs, and hydroelectric plants. During this time, due to the overall strength of the world economy, First World countries were able to loan vast sums of money and actually competed for Third World clients. Unfortunately, when the global recession occurred in the early 1980s and commodity prices plummeted and interest rates soared, the costs of outstanding debts became prohibitive. Banks quickly cut back on lending to most developing countries. This drove many debtor nations to the brink of default because they depended upon these new funds in part to pay back previous loans. Moreover, the recession itself was driving debtor nations into default because of increased oil prices, lower prices for export commodities, and variable interest rates. The situation was highlighted in 1982 when Mexico announced it could not service its debts. Since then, over forty countries have experienced similar difficulties in meeting their obligations.

The debt crisis is spelling economic and environmental disaster for much of the Third World. The continued heavy debt burden, in part, prevents many developing countries from resuming the growth rates they experienced in earlier years. In Latin America, for example, the average annual growth of GNP per capita went from 4.6 percent during 1965–1973 to .5 percent during 1980–1990. Similarly, in sub-Saharan Africa the average annual growth rate went from 1.6 percent to -1.1 percent over the same periods.[13] Additionally, reduced growth itself is creating further disincentives for banks to loan more money. Thus, developing countries are stuck in a vicious cycle: they cannot demonstrate growth to attract further credit and yet, only additional credit will enable their economies to grow.

On the environmental side, the attempt to increase production and boost exports is forcing many Third World countries to exploit their natural resource base. This includes clearing forests for farmland, pastures, mining, and timber without taking measures to ensure long-term sustainability. Furthermore, the debt burden is tying up funds that could otherwise be allocated to protecting the environment. Since the 1970s, Third World countries have been devoting an increasing proportion of GNP to interest payments. This takes away from productive investment and funding for environmental protection as well as from other social programs. This economic crunch is particularly troubling to conservationists because Third World countries are the richest storehouses of biological diversity and hold some of the most important natural treasures. For example, Brazil is the leading debtor among developing countries and holds nearly 30 percent of the world's rain forests.[14] (Rain forests are the most mature and diverse ecosystems on the planet.) To save vast numbers of species from extinction and to protect wildlife in general in these regions, people must, among other things, devise ways to relax the Third World debt's stranglehold on development and reverse the unsustainable use of natural resources.

In October 1984, Thomas Lovejoy, then vice president for science of World Wildlife Fund, suggested a method of converting Third World debt into support for conservation activity. In an op-ed piece in the *New York Times*, he suggested a way in which conservation organizations could acquire Third World debt at a discount and, by redeeming it for local currency, use it for conservation purposes.[15] Since 1984, a number of conservation groups have undertaken debt-for-nature swaps. World Wildlife Fund has taken the lead. Since 1984 WWF has entered into debt-for-nature deals with a total face value of close to $70 million.

Debt-for-nature swaps work on a principle similar to that used in debt-for-equity schemes. Developing countries may not be able to provide U.S. dollars needed to repay their debts. They can, however, offer creditors something else instead. In many cases, they offer creditors some form of ownership in domestic businesses. In particular, debtor countries redeem portions of their external debt in local currency for use in commercial or industrial projects. What makes debt-for-equity schemes viable is that since the early 1980s banks have written down or sold high-risk debts at substantial discounts. This means that buyers can obtain control over debts at a fraction of their original cost. This has created a secondary debt market.[16] Because debts can be bought at significant discounts yet redeemed at face value within debtor countries, there is a strong incentive to buy up debt on the secondary market and turn it into equity.[17]

Debt-for-nature swaps rest on the notion that debts can be bought on the secondary market and redeemed not only for equity investments in the industrial sector but also for investments in conservation. The scheme works in the following way. First, conservation organizations in the First World, such as WWF, identify a local, Third World conservation group that is willing and able to make effective use of funds. While First World groups maintain some oversight, the idea is to enable local groups to use their own discretion in using the funds.

Second, WWF actually purchases debt on the secondary market. Banks seek to sell high-risk, outstanding loans for a number of reasons. They may see it as one of the only ways to recoup at least some of their investment; they may feel "overexposed" in a single country and want to reduce their capital at risk; or they may simply want to clean up their books by reducing the amount of doubtful debt. As a result, the banks will offer the loans at rates well below the hard currency face value. For example, they may sell debt notes at rates as low as 15 percent of the original value. Thus, a bank might sell a debt note with a face amount of $100,000 for only $15,000. When these notes are converted into local currency at face value, this multiplies the impact of conservation dollars. Discounted rates yield a better return on investment than directly spending money in developing countries; one dollar of acquired debt can yield the equivalent of several dollars worth of local currency. In this way, debt-for-nature swaps can be seen merely as a better form of investment by First World conservation groups.

The third step is converting the debt into local currency. This must be worked out with debtor governments.[18] This stage is important because unless it is done with sensitivity to local conditions it can cause dislocations in the economy. The most feared consequence is a rise in inflation. This can happen when debtor governments agree to convert debt into cash and must print more money to pay off loans. To avoid this, depending on the situation, governments issue bonds. In these cases, local conservation groups receive interest on the bonds each year to use for operating costs and projects. Eventually, at the time of maturation, they receive the principle as an endowment.

The final step involves working out and executing a conservation program. This is the most important and trickiest stage. While First World conservation organizations want to avoid eco-imperialism and hence do not dictate the exact use of funds, they also have a strong interest in making sure monies are spent in an effective way. Indeed, they have a responsibility to their members (donors) to ensure that the money raised for debt-for-nature swaps actually contributes to protecting the environment. First World groups try to work through this problem by collaborating with their Third World counterparts. In many instances this is not difficult because, as transnational organizations, they may have developed strong ties over the years. In some cases, the Third World group may actually be an affiliate of the First World organization.

World Wildlife Fund has participated in a number of debt-for-nature swaps. In 1989, for example, WWF concluded a debt-for-nature swap with Ecuador. Ecuador is blessed with a wide variety of natural treasures. It has Amazonian rain forests; Andean highlands, coastal savannah and mangrove forests; and the famous Galapagos Islands, which have plants and animals found nowhere else on earth. One of the leading nongovernmental conservation groups in Ecuador is the Fundacion Natura (FN). WWF arranged to channel money to the FN by acquiring up to $10 million worth of debt. In December 1987, WWF purchased its first installment of $1 million. At the time, the Ecuadorian dollar debt was selling for about 35 cents on the dollar in secondary markets, and thus WWF paid roughly $354,000 for $1 million worth of Ecuadorian sucre. Between 1987 and 1989, WWF bought an additional $5.4 million and persuaded the Nature Conservancy, another environmental NGO, to buy $3.6 million. The money has been put into nine-year bonds. The interest rate on these bonds was 31 percent the first year and has been tied to the interest paid by Ecuador's five largest banks since then. This interest funds ongoing projects, with the principal eventually being used for a permanent endowment with FN as beneficiary. WWF has collaborated with FN to design a number of conservation projects. These include management of existing national parks, identification and acquisition of small nature reserves, training forestry personnel, and environmental education activities throughout the country. Moreover, providing FN with such a large amount of money puts the organization on financially secure footing and thus ensures a long-standing, nongovernmental conservationist presence in Ecuador.

Aside from Ecuador, WWF has arranged debt-for-nature swaps with Costa Rica, the Philippines, Madagascar, Zambia, Bolivia, and Poland. While each case is unique, they all follow the general characteristics previously outlined. Debt-for-nature swaps are not an answer to the world's debt problems nor will they, in themselves, protect wildlife throughout developing countries. They do represent, however, an innovative way of linking development issues with environmental conservation. They attempt to alleviate economic hardship while taking measures to protect the environment. Moreover, they represent a way to empower local people to take economic development and wildlife protection into their own hands. The fundamental principle of debt-for-nature swaps is to shift financial resources away from First World nations and into the hands of Third World ones.[19] Putting money in the hands of these entities—and out of those of the First World—is a significant form of local empowerment.[20]

Strategies of Empowerment

These three projects represent only a fraction of the work in which WWF engages. Worldwide it is involved in literally hundreds of similar efforts. Behind all of WWF's endeavors, however, one can discern a set of strategies that contribute to local empowerment. Three stand out as particularly significant. First, there is an emphasis on antipoverty. Many of the world's biologically richest regions are located in rural areas where people eke out meager existences on the land. This is unfortunate, from some perspectives, because faced with economic hardship such people will rightfully exploit otherwise renewable resources. Indeed, the most direct threat to wildlife throughout the Third World is the poor's need to use resources in an unsustainable manner. This is why WWF sees economic development to be a part of wildlife conservation. In fact, they are two sides of the same coin. As Michael Wright put it, WWF focuses "on both conservation and development simultaneously, in the belief that neither can truly be attained independently of the other. Sustainable development is not merely a conservation tactic but an interrelated and coequal goal."[21] In the Zambian project, it was the lack of economic opportunity and the harsh conditions that led local inhabitants to side with poachers as opposed to conservation officials. Only when WWF helped develop a program wherein residents could benefit economically from wildlife conservation (through scout training and so forth) was an effective system of environmental protection able to work. In the Kilum mountain project, it was the inability of the mountain people to farm in a sustainable manner that drove villagers further into the forest. In this case, conservation became viable only when WWF devised ways of boosting agricultural production (through nurseries, honey making, and so forth). In the debt-for-nature swaps the same dynamic is at work. WWF buys up Third World debt in order to relieve the economic pressure on Third World countries. This releases money to be used for conservation and productive in-country investments. In short, environmental protection can only work in the Third World if it addresses development issues. WWF cultivates methods for local people to lead economically viable lives through their ability to sustain environmental well-being.

A second strategy of empowerment is local involvement. Wildlife conservation, like many aspects of environmental protection, is not a one-shot deal. One will never devise a system that will ensure the continued existence of various plants and animals forever. It is a constant challenge that requires both a long-standing commitment by those carrying it out and a system that is flexible enough to respond to changes and robust enough to remain intact over the long run. Local participation is a prerequisite to such an approach. Only if local residents are involved in the processes of conservation will it work successfully. In each of the projects mentioned, WWF sought local participation. In fact, it was a central factor. In the Zambian project, WWF hired local residents to staff the scout program and relied on village leadership to oversee and disperse funds received from tourism and hunting. In the Kilum mountain project, while WWF introduced the nurseries, a new method of making honey, and innovative procedures of soil conservation, it utilized local materials and, almost immediately, enlisted local participation. This has been essential to ensuring that the boundaries of the forest preserve are respected and to the continued viability of the nurseries, honey collective, and fertility of the soil. Finally, local participation is almost the raison d'être of the debt-for-nature swaps. The whole idea is to shift financial resources from First World banks to Third World peoples. Indeed, in most cases local NGOs administer the money and this greatly bolsters local participation.

Closely related to the strategy of local involvement is ensuring sustainability. Any form of external intervention in development and conservation projects risks the problem of paternalism. Paternalism is a form of disempowerment. It entails either giving things to or doing things for other people. This is disempowering because it engenders dependence on outside aid as opposed to encouraging self-reliance. Moreover, both giveaways and doing work for people are expenses that no project can sustain over the long term. In each of the projects I mentioned previously, WWF works toward sustainable programs. In the Zambian project, WWF created a revolving wildlife fund that would finance the system of conservation over the long run. In the Kilum mountain project, WWF introduced only appropriate technology. The pressing method of making honey and soil conservation techniques rely on tools that can be integrated into existing practices, can meet actual needs, and can be fixed on the premises. This is extremely important for ensuring sustainability. Finally, the debt-for-nature swaps were negotiated in a way that would guarantee a level of significant sustainability. When local governments convert foreign debt into local bonds, the principal of the bonds is created as an endowment for local NGOs and thus in-country conservation projects. As such, it can yield interest every year to pay for ongoing projects.

These strategies are at the core of WWF work. They aim to empower the people who are most vulnerable to and greatly responsible for environmental degradation. After years of experience, WWF has determined that this is the most promising way to guarantee effective conservation programs.

PART TWO

Empowerment and State-Society Relations

A strategy of empowerment may seem important from a micro-perspective although marginal from a world political one. After all, creating sustainable development in one village or shifting even millions of dollars from First World banks to a mere handful of

Third World NGOs do not, at first, appear to have much impact on the larger dimensions of global environmental problems. They represent pockets of successful environmental work in a world of massive environmental degradation; they are "antlike" attempts to wrestle with world political phenomena.

One should not underestimate the world political significance of antlike efforts. On paper they may look merely like cells of empowerment and environmental protection; in practice, however, their success ripples through interlocking networks of social, economic, and political life and actually affect world environmental affairs. In the following I describe these wider implications.

Before doing so, it is important to point out that even the most micro-efforts of activist groups in the field can have world significance, even if not in a strictly political sense. Activists target key areas for environmental protection. They focus upon the richest, most fragile, or most immediately threatened biological regions. Many times these areas house unique species whose extinction would be a permanent loss to the world. By protecting them, activists perform a world significant role. Think about, for example, what it means to save the elephant or the Bengal tiger from extinction. Such acts, although small in scale, are immense contributions to the well-being and richness of the world. When people actually save a plant or animal from extinction they are doing so for all times. To be sure, protecting species is a never-ending challenge; there will always be threats against numerous species. Additionally, saving selective species does not solve the ultimate problem of extensive biological depletion nor restructure political relations on a global scale. Nonetheless, to take a stand against imminent extinction is an act of world significance. It preserves the biological fabric of life on earth and that, in itself, is of considerable importance.

There are, actually, world political implications to grassroots environmental protection. To appreciate these, it is helpful to look first at the political ramifications of empowerment within the domestic arena of Third World countries. To do so, it is necessary to review briefly theoretical work on the relationship between the state and society.

Over the past decade and a half, students of comparative politics have focused significant attention on the state as the primary unit of study. This effort to "bring the state back in" argues that scholars should consider the state an independent variable when trying to explain social and political phenomena.[22] This emphasis on the state was a welcome response to a previous overemphasis on society. Society-centered studies—of the pluralist, structural functionalist, and neo-Marxist variety—put too much weight on social forces. They saw the state simply as an arena within which different social groups compete for resources, a mechanism that translates societal *inputs* into governmentally sanctioned *outputs*, or a set of institutions controlled by the ruling class. Government itself was never taken seriously. State-centered research serves as an important corrective to this earlier work.

The most important contribution of the state-centered approach, in my mind, is not so much that it calls attention to the state as such, but that it highlights the interface between the state and civil society. By circumscribing the state as a unit of study and endowing it with causal significance, it has opened up an entire research agenda that focuses on state-society relations. Scholars now see the state and civil society as tangible entities whose interaction itself plays a key role in structuring collective life.[23] This has caused some scholars to conceptualize the state *within* society. The state, from this perspective, is one of a number of organizations that coexist and interact with each other. This has given rise to a number of significant studies that try to understand the resources and instruments states use to control competing actors.[24]

A heightened sensitivity to state-society relations provides a conceptual framework for understanding the significance of a transnational politics of empowerment. If one focuses on the interface between the state and society, one notices the relations between them are dynamic and that the realms themselves are hard to distinguish. Indeed, the relations between the state and civil society ebb and flow over time and in different settings and intersect.[25] When activist groups undertake environmental work to empower local peoples they are augmenting social agency within civil society and thus shifting the balance between state and social forces. They are nurturing and increasing the amount of lateral social interaction, and this is adding political weight to the efficacy of local communities.

As mentioned, much of the earth's remaining biological wealth is in parts of the world where the poorest peoples draw their livelihood from the land. Without being overly simplistic, it is fair to say that throughout most of these regions people have traditionally eked out lives in a relatively high degree of autonomy from official institutions. With the emergence of a world capitalist market throughout the mid-1800s this changed dramatically. It opened up even the remotest regions to vertical relations. As a result village chiefs, landlords, and strongmen provided the outlines of social structure and authority. Through these actors, interlocking networks emerged linking local, national, and international peoples. What is curious, however, is that during most of this period those networks were not controlled by states. In fact, the state was very much out of the picture. The state in most parts of the Third World remained superfluous to the lives of vast numbers of rural people until the mid-twentieth century.[26] Local, rural people represented, in the words of Goran Hyden, the "uncaptured peasantry."[27] During this time, one can talk about a disengaged relationship between rural poor communities and the state. Both existed relatively independent of each other. The rural poor operated according to their own, indigenous social conventions—for example, devising an "economy of affections,"—and the state carried on its duties without much regard for these regions.[28]

With decolonization and the rise of the modernizing state throughout the Third World from the late 1940s onward, this changed. As new states were born and weak ones became more active, the state as a political and social force in the Third World came of age. In all shapes and sizes state institutions from health clinics to marketing boards penetrated even the most remote villages of Asia and Africa. The result was that the interlocking networks between local, regional, national, and international spheres were now objects of conflict between state and society. The state tried to forge the contours of these interconnections along statist lines or at least lace them with statist objectives. This, of course, was no surprise. As the main coordinator of development activity and industrialization, the state often had the resources and the will to do so. Many societies in these regions, however, did not stand by idly and invite state penetration. The state met resistance. This was a function of either unassimilating rural people who clung for security to traditional folkways and institutions or the machinations of the state itself. (In this later regard, Migdal shows how state actions themselves sow the seeds of resistance.)[29] Either way, since mid-century the state has lived a mixed existence throughout the Third World. In some countries it has established itself as the sole political authority and enjoys enhanced capabilities of social control; in others it has had to struggle consistently with other organizations for political governance. In all instances, however, the battle has been about controlling the interlocking networks that structure social life. The state is in a constant struggle to control local societies.

When transnational environmental activist groups undertake eco-development projects in these areas of the world, they intervene in the web of associational life. When they introduce alternative production processes, utilize villagers in conservation activities, or enhance the capability of local NGOs, they reorient the material, social, symbolic, and political dimensions of rural life. At a minimum, this consolidates people into new forms of social interaction. On the one hand, it strengthens existing patterns of social intercourse—for example, when activists enlist traditional community leaders in conservation efforts. On the other hand, it changes or reorients them by providing additional, meaningful frameworks for collective life. One sees this impact most clearly in the emergence of new networks of distribution, avenues of communication, and forms of accumulation. From a transnational activist perspective, such reorientation can provide a sense of political efficacy among communities with respect to environmental and development issues. Eco-development projects inject a sense of mission into communities, which, to be sure, may not be to everyone's interest, but, nonetheless, articulates a particular perspective on a community's economic and environmental destiny.[30]

One result of a thickened web of associational life informed by a particular orientation toward environmental and development issues is that it restructures the way communities interact with wider domains of social relations. For instance, local communities are no longer easily penetrable by outside forces when economic or environmental affairs are involved. In fact, many times they act as agitators toward outside institutions and processes when it comes to these domains of collective life. To put it in formal terms, when environmental activist groups empower local communities they add weight to civil society. They stimulate and release popular energies in support for community goals.[31] The result is that the state cannot railroad its development strategies or other policies over local preferences. Indeed, it must now compete more explicitly with civil society for control over broad economic, political, and social networks. The balance between the state and civil society in these regions has shifted. To put it crudely, although not inaccurately, eco-development projects turn peasants into citizens or, more accurately, civilians.[32]

Strengthening Civil Society and World Politics

Altering and at times strengthening civil society has important consequences for world politics. To appreciate these it is first necessary to recognize that the accelerated extraction of resources is not merely a domestic phenomenon. While national governments oversee development projects throughout the Third World and play a key role in the production of raw materials for industry, they do not act on their own. They are enmeshed in larger, international economic and governmental networks that determine, to a significant degree, the character of resource utilization.

One of the most pervasive myths is that environmental abuse is driven solely by overpopulation in the Third World. Using the logic of Malthus, people argue that threats to the environment stem simply from too many mouths to feed and too many bodies to house and keep warm. By many counts, there *are* too many people living on an earth with a limited amount of resources. Overpopulation as such *is* an important factor in environmental degradation, especially in the Third World and, while I do not address it at length, I am very much aware of the debilitating effect it has on Third World environmental well-being. Nonetheless, the deeper issue is not merely *how many* people inhabit the earth but their consumptive practices. According to Shridath Ramphal, the average citizen from the developed world consumes twenty times more resources than the average citizen of the developing world. This means, for instance, that the average person from the First World uses 120 kilos of paper compared to 8 kilos in the Third World and roughly 450 kilos of steel compared to 43 kilos. In terms of energy consumption, 25 percent of the world's population accounts for 80 percent of energy usage. This means that while the average U.S. citizen uses 280 gigajoules annually, the average person from Tanzania, Ethiopia, or Mali uses one.[33] In short, throughout the First World in general the average person uses over ten times more nonrenewable energy than the average Third Worlder.[34] To secure resources, the First World reaches into the depths of Third World lands. Japan pulls timber from tropical rain forests; Germany imports fruit from Latin America; the United States buys up minerals from southern Africa. If one could stand above the earth and note the transfer of natural resources, one would see lines running from the periphery to the center of economic power, that is, from the South to the North. Seen in this way, environmental degradation is not merely a domestic issue. It is international in scope. Poor people do not wreck the environment on their own. The resource guzzling North often creates pressure through the international economic system for them to do so.[35]

To blame the North, however, is too easy. The pattern of consumption—from the periphery to the center—is replicated at the domestic level as well. The richest Third World people, living mostly in urban areas, consume many more resources than their poorer rural counterparts. Rio de Janeiro, Calcutta, and Mexico City are magnets that draw resources from even the remotest parts of their countries.[36] Standing above the earth, then, one would notice transfer lines running from the countryside to the cities in the South, as well as from the cities of the South to those in the North. If one further understood these lines in terms of economic constraints—pressures on rural poor to exploit their environments—one would see that environmental degradation results from multiple outside pressures on the local people. Absorbed in the global market yet based mainly on agricultural production, local people find that one of the only ways to survive economically is continuously to extract raw materials from the environment. Thus, regional, national, and international processes simultaneously impinge on their utilization of resources. A helpful way to imagine this situation is in terms of the skin of an onion: there are multiple layers of economic constraints forcing people to extract resources without much sensitivity to longer-term sustainability.

One can begin to appreciate the world political significance of local empowerment and strengthened civil societies when one sees them as part of a strategy for resisting and transforming outside constraints. Speaking in the most general terms, there are two broad strategies for casting off outside pressures. The first recommends starting from the outermost layer and working inward. It entails ripping-off or fundamentally changing the global processes, which, in this case, continuously support environmental degradation. It suggests altering the worldwide structures—for example, the international economic system—that pattern human behavior. The second strategy proposes starting from the center, at the innermost dynamics of collective life, and working outward. The idea is to "burn-off" conditioning structures. It calls on small groups to nurture local resistance and creativity, as well as to build sufficient political intensity to gain geographical spread. Both approaches are, obviously, ideal types. Nonetheless, if we conceive of them as two ends of a spectrum, one can locate the activity of transnational empowerment closer to the latter strategy than the former.[37] When transnational groups empower local communities—helping to shape them into politically efficacious units—local inhabitants can better resist wider national and international extractive pressures. They can take control of their own lives and environments and no longer fall easy prey to national or international pressures. Furthermore, the effects of their efforts can fan out to the larger dynamics of international politics.

One way grassroots empowerment spreads to international circles—or, burns off external conditionings—is when local communities resist international development programs administered or sanctioned by their home governments. Throughout much of the world, local NGOs and community leaders have traditionally served as conduits for government policy. They have been unofficial arms of the government that can more efficiently institute development projects in the countryside. The empowerment politics of transnational groups have helped change this. Many more NGOs and village heads are now acting as obstacles to the grand designs of international agencies and development banks rather than as facilitators.[38] They are no longer at the service of their own governments; in fact, many times they explicitly struggle against official development projects. One sees this, for example, in the protests against hydroelectric projects throughout the Third World. In India, for instance, activists stopped construction of the Silent Valley and Bedhi dams and, have been demonstrating against the Sardar Sarovar dam, which is part of the Narmada River Project.[39] The protest against Sardar Sarovar is the largest against a development project in India's history. While these latter protests have not halted construction, the outpouring of political expression itself has, at a minimum, redefined debates over the environmental efficacy of large dam projects as well as those having to do with displacement and rehabitation. They have also introduced a profound hesitation on the part of the Indian government, World Bank, and other aid agencies concerning future dam projects—indeed, in 1993, the Indian government withdrew its request for World Bank funding to support the Sardar Sarovar project.[40] Finally, they have served notice, through local peoples insistence to drown rather than be displaced, that local communities are now better organized to resist large-scale, external environmental and development designs in general.[41] Resistance to the Sardar Sarovar dam represents only one of the flashier instances of resistance. Similar struggles are taking place throughout the Third World.[42] These resistances are reacting to international and national pressures at the capillaries of power. They are attempts to oppose the reach of multinational corporations, development agencies, and national governments. To mix metaphors, they aim to stop intrusive and ill-advised enterprises by biting the fingertips of outside sponsors. Local communities hope, however, to make the pain felt throughout the entire system. To be sure, transnational environmental groups are not responsible for all or even most instances of local resistance. Yet, to the degree that their efforts strengthen civil society and enhance the capabilities of local NGOs, they contribute to such resistance.

Resisting outside interference is only the beginning of the wider impact of grassroots empowerment and strengthened civil societies. As mentioned, the worldwide accelerated extraction of resources has enveloped local communities in broader economic, social, and political networks. It has initiated them into larger economic markets, governmental jurisdictions, and social interactions. Also as mentioned, as new states emerged and others became more active, states tried to capture, with mixed success, these networks. Many observers look at this incorporation strictly in terms of further state penetration. They argue that the state has, on the whole, co-opted vertical networks and that the entire process is simply an advanced phase of state formation. That is, emerging interlocking structures serve as additional forms through which the state can control, repress, and exploit civil society.[43] To be sure, states have been the main beneficiaries of vertical networks. Nonetheless, the broader frameworks have also had to react to grassroots empowerment. That is, the direction of control does not travel simply in one direction. Interlocking networks serve as channels for local expression and demand adjustment from governmental, economic, and social institutions and processes. As Migdal and others point out, the center does not always directly affect the periphery. Many times the periphery conditions the center.[44] Broad networks twist and reorient themselves as local communities make themselves felt within a wider context.[45] Thus, strengthened civil societies bend and restructure national and even international agendas and activities.[46]

This becomes especially true when local NGOs and communities enjoy sustained contact with transnational environmental groups. When transnational environmental activists build up civil society they both create politically efficacious nonstate actors and inaugurate an alliance with them. This connection takes place through numerous mediating factors. When it involves the transfer of funds, it almost always involves sanctioning by the home state and entanglement with tax structures, import-export conditions and market arrangements. In 1989, Northern NGOs distributed $6.4 billion to developing countries, which is roughly 12 percent of all public and private development aid.[47] Much of this aid went to local NGOs and contributed to the empowerment of local communities.[48] Additionally, when it entails collaborating on actual projects, it can involve issues of park management, agricultural pricing, or broad health, education, and environmental policy.[49] None of these arenas belong exclusively to the state. Each represents a mechanism that can potentially be influenced by a host of different actors. To be more accurate, each is the result of changing patterns of social and political relationships that take place within and across state borders. Local communities can have more of an influence on these mechanisms the more politically efficacious they become and the more they interact with larger institutions and processes.

One sees this most explicitly in debt-for-nature swaps. Formal debt-for-nature negotiations involve governments in both First and Third World states, banks in more than one country, transnational environmental groups, and local NGOs. The issues at hand entail tax revenues, purchasing bonds, currency conversion, payments to local NGOs, and debt-readjustment.[50] When debt-for-nature agreements are implemented, the configuration of these factors change. Governments, banks, transnational groups, and local NGOs work out new arrangements and thereby create new pressures on existing financial institutions and processes. The connection between local groups and transnational environmental organizations, then, acts like a thread reverberating through diverse and complex vertical networks. This thread, though thin, is an important avenue through which strengthened civil societies affect world political phenomena.[51]

In addition to affecting broad interlocking layers between local and international collective life, the transnational connection between activist groups and their Third World counterparts creates world political changes of a different sort. As links between transnational and local NGOs solidify and as local groups become inte-

grated into the international arena, questions arise over the legitimate exercise of power. In many instances, states take a backstage
seat to the transnational activities of activist groups. Consequently,
one begins to ask: Who has the right to assert local leadership? Who
should operate the development enterprise? Through whom should
assistance be channeled? Who has the ability to organize people and
allocate resources? Increasingly, it is getting harder to answer these
questions by referring simply to the state. NGOs—in both the First
and Third World—are progressively undertaking development/envi-
ronmental work. This is threatening the state especially in the
South, although First World governments also have reason to be
wary about extensive transnational NGO operations.[52]

Third World governments have a schizophrenic attitude
toward transnational relations. On the one hand, they welcome
transboundary private initiatives. These attract additional resources
to the country and thus boost development and environmental
work. On the other hand, transnational alliances threaten state governments. In terms of funding, local groups do not always attract
additional money, but many times appropriate funds that were previously slated for official use. Indeed, while foreign assistance has
declined over the past decade, NGOs have received an increasing
share of it. In 1975, donor governments channeled $100 million
through local NGOs; in 1985, they channeled $1.1 billion through
them.[53] This represents a shift on the part of Official Development
Assistance (ODA) countries from donating only 0.7 percent of their
funding through Third World NGOs in 1975, to 3.6 percent in
1985.[54] By 1988, this figure rose again bringing the total to $2.1 bil-
lion of the amount governments were funneling through NGOs.[55]
(At the UN Conference on Population and Development in September 1994, the United States pledged $595 million for population
relief work in 1995. Slightly less than half of this was slated for
NGOs.)[56] Moreover, the issue of rechanneling funds is only a part of
a larger problem, viz., the shift in legitimacy from governments to
NGOs. NGOs have proven to be more effective at times in providing development assistance and devising environmental projects
than governments. Furthermore, due to changes in development
theory, which now partly stresses small-scale rural projects instead
of large-scale urban ones, and the desire of First World governments
to bypass what they often think are corrupt regimes in less developed countries, more development assistance is channeled through
local NGOs[57] One consequence is that as local groups gain interna-

tional visibility through transnational relationships, Third World governments can lose international prestige. International recognition for local NGOs, then, eclipses the prominence of state governments.[58] A final threat is simply the international penetration of Third World states. Governments see themselves as the sole legitimate source of political power within a given territory. While they coexist with other organizations—families, corporations, and religious groups—they ultimately seek predominance over them. Transnational links scramble this effort. They puncture the veil of state sovereignty. Governments no longer completely control development and environmental projects. Thus, they do not enjoy supreme authority over their territories.

From an international relations perspective, it is worth noting that transnational NGO relations affect First as well as Third World governments. For reasons stated earlier, First World governments have been often turning to transnational environmental and development NGOs for guidance when it involves development and environmental assistance. In fact, many First World governments fund projects initiated by transnational groups instead of undertaking assistance themselves. According to a 1989 OECD report, by the early 1980s virtually all First World countries adopted a system of cofinancing projects implemented by their national NGOs. "Official contributions to NGOs' activities over the decades have been on an upward trend, amounting to $2.2 billion in 1987 and representing 5 percent of total ODA," according to the report.[59] While much of this was funneled through voluntary relief organizations, such as Catholic Relief Services, overall there has been a shift in expertise. Governments have become students of transnational groups. These latter organizations enjoy the knowledge and have the experience to carry out development/environmental projects more effectively.

Taking these points together, it could be said that we are witnessing an upgrading in the status of NGOs concerned with development and environmental issues. Development and environmental work is no longer the sole responsibility of the state. Nonstate actors are proving many times to be more efficient and knowledgeable than states and thus undertaking significant amounts of development/environmental activity. In some ways we are seeing the beginnings of what the international functionalists predicted: nonstate organizations undertaking functional activities on an international scale.[60] To be sure, this has not spilled over dramatically into the international politics of war and peace or international political economy. Nonetheless, the beginnings of a nonofficial layer of political activity is being set into place in the development/environmental field and, as such global issues grow worse, we can expect this dimension of world political life to become more prominent.

The last way grassroots empowerment is affecting world politics is by weighing in on the continuing debate about Third World economic development. Specifically, it has been largely responsible for linking the economic and environmental dimensions of the debate.[61] Until recently, a guiding theme of traditional development strategies was that economic progress entailed environmental destruction. Environmental resources represented the major forms of Third World assets, and the best way for developing countries to advance was to extract them in profitable ways. Both the efforts to expand export markets and to institute import-substitution models operated under this assumption. Exploitation of the environment, the argument went, was the sad but necessary consequence of economic progress. It represented the path the First World took and thus provided guidance for Third World development.[62]

Grassroots development/environmental projects, including those initiated by transnational environmental groups, did much to turn this thinking around. To be sure, there was much "theory" during this time that questioned the equation of economic development and environmental destruction. Many scholars thought economic progress need not entail environmental degradation. Nonetheless, there were no actual instances in which both the environment and the economy were mutually prospering. The types of pilot projects I mentioned previously provided the first set of such models.[63] They demonstrated that the most sustainable forms of economic progress rest on using resources in a renewable fashion. The natural environment provides the resource base upon which people build their livelihoods. Environmental destruction does more harm than good when it comes to economic development. It literally takes the floor out from under people's feet. It denies them access to clean water and air and fertile soil and long-term economic productivity. Model grassroots projects initiated by transnational groups act as actual instances that link theory and practice. They attest to the fact that eco-development is a genuine alternative to earlier, resource guzzling approaches.[64]

Each of these activities—resisting official development schemes, altering the mediating factors between transnational and local NGOs, creating nonstate mechanisms for global environmental protection, and shifting the debate about development—represent, in part, the effects of direct environmental protection by transnational groups. They reflect the result of augmenting Third World civil society along environmental lines and the impact of this on world affairs. What is crucial to recognize in all of this is that the lines of impact and the local communities themselves were not necessarily fated to become mechanisms of environmental well-being to the degree that they have. They represent potential political tools that lay dormant—neither, necessarily, anti- or pro-environmental protection. Transnational environmental groups turn these seemingly uncommitted entities and processes into forms of governance in the service of the environment. They enlist them as mechanisms of influence. (To be sure, many local communities do this on their own.) Their approach is to empower local residents to take control of their lives and environment, and to count on and provide ways for this to affect larger world environmental affairs. Put differently, the idea is to turn Third World villages and peoples into politically efficacious units endowed with a commitment to environmental protection and enable them to "shoot" their concerns up through the ranks of international environmental politics.

Localism Versus Sub-statism

In chapter 2, I claimed that there are three traditional political approaches to world problems and that these represent the main conceptual responses to global environmental threats. These are statism, supra-statism, and sub-statism. In chapter 3, I examined how Greenpeace works at odds with supra-statism. This chapter follows this line of interpretation. It discusses the way transnational environmental groups undertake direct environmental action and the world political significance of this. This type of political action is parallel to, but different from, sub-statism.

Sub-statism is the notion that the most effective solution to global environmental problems involves breaking up the contemporary state system into political units that are smaller than present-day states. The fundamental cause of environmental dangers, according to sub-statists, is the scale of economic, social, and political processes. Sub-statists claim, for example, that large-scale activity and organization call for the use of advanced and high technologies that significantly disrupt fundamental environmental processes. They also argue that greater degrees of scale and power overwhelm the capacity of ordinary human beings to understand and control their environments. From a political perspective, sub-statists claim that political institutions mimic the large-scale dimensions of these processes and thus further accentuate the big-ness of contemporary life. The contemporary state system creates allegiances, understandings, sources of authority, and commitments that draw people emotionally, intellectually, and practically out of their local environments. The result is a profound nonappreciation for the needs and dynamics of local ecosystems. On a world scale, this means living in a way that will necessarily abuse the earth.

When transnational environmental groups undertake direct environmental work they operate at the local level of political life, although they do not intend necessarily to break up contemporary states or de-link from larger processes and institutions. The idea is almost the opposite. They aim to generate political intensity and ecological expertise on a small scale and cultivate ways for this to affect successive, expanding layers of collective life. For transnational groups, the layers of integration among local, regional, national, and international collective life are lines of power that can be used in the service of global environmental protection. That is, while they are not anti- or pro-ecological in their own right, they can be co-opted or enlisted in the service of environmental well-being.

A guiding theme in sub-statism is that global environmental problems would be eradicated if each community was sensitive to the ecological needs of its immediate environment. The idea is kind of an "I'll take care of my plot, and you take care of yours." Transnational environmental activists take a different stance in their politics of empowerment. The notion is more like, "you take care of your plot, and then apply that experience in wider interactions; that is, express it through the mechanisms which connect your plot with that of others." Activists politicize communities. They initiate them into the fold of larger environmental concerns and catalyze them so they will have an impact on the wider dimensions of environmental problems.

The same point can be made in a different way. Sub-statists propose utilizing resources close to home. They suggest that particular communities can generate a type of local wisdom that will both appreciate the dynamics of immediate environment processes and develop practices that will be appropriate for sustaining resource use over the long term. Ideally this will entail small, self-sufficient communities. While transnational activists are equally concerned with local people taking control of their own environments and being responsible for resource use, they do not call strictly for local resource utilization. Rather, they encourage integration into larger economic markets but demand that local communities maintain control over the *way* resources are extracted or cultivated. They emphasize control of utilization rather than the geographical scope of distribution. In short, the notion is that local communities should regain control of resource use and this reappropriation should be in the service of local economic and environmental well-being as well as wider transformation.

The way transnational environmental groups do this, as I have been outlining throughout this chapter, is through fostering environmental and development projects. Eco-development projects at the grassroots level can speak to local inhabitants and help turn their efforts into local success stories and embryonic strivings for a more ecologically balanced world. This, by the way, relates to the overall theme of the book. Undertaking actual environmental protection through development work is itself a form of governance. It seeks to create conditions that will make people act in ecologically mindful ways. It can be thought of as a further mechanism for changing people's behavior—in addition to disseminating an ecological sensibility.

Notwithstanding their importance, ideational factors associated with disseminating an ecological sensibility can go only so far. A sensibility, essentially, targets widely held notions about the environment. It works to induce large-scale cognitive shifts in people's consciousness. In many ways, however, it is too blunt. It aims at too broad an audience and thus can fail to mobilize significant parts of the world.

There are regions of the world within which the message of global environmentalism sounds irrelevant. Concern about global warming, ozone depletion, and even threats to biological diversity can fall on deaf ears unless it is translated into the everyday needs of local people. Undertaking actual eco-development work is a way for transnational groups to "flip the environmental switch" in particular places in the world. Specifically, transnational activists try to set in motion certain elements of environmental protection that will create long-term benefits in areas where people are resistant to governmental directives or out of touch with norm creation at the global level. Activism itself, then, is a form of governance. It is a way to create conditions that will direct and order the activities of others.

There is a word that captures this political strategy· *localism*. Localism suggests a type of political activity that takes place across state boundaries yet remains sensitive to local situations. It focuses on the actual conditions of everyday life and uses these as jumping-off points to launch broader political enterprises. Fundamental to localism is that political strategies are forged by actual people in the context of their concrete struggles for economic and environmental well-being. Transnational activists listen to local inhabitants and try to articulate their visions. This entails, as mentioned, local participation. Localism, then, is a matter of enabling inhabitants to make their own communities. It involves helping them devise forms of political activity that will improve the quality of their individual lives and the surrounding environment. Central to localism is that it is out of this that people devise appropriate forms of political intensity that can affect broader institutions and processes. That is, a world politics emerges through a local one. Only by coming to terms with actual conditions of a particular community or people can transnational groups generate a solid, effective type of world political activity.

Localism is based on empowerment. For people to act in a politically efficacious manner, they need to feel that there is something they can influence and control and in which they can trust. Localism cultivates faith in one's own community. It nurtures capabilities that enable people to get a handle on the processes that affect their immediate lives and thus develop trust in their own abilities. Its intent is to lend cohesiveness and strengthen social agency at the local level. This provides the foundation for a wider politics.

Localism finds its conceptual origins in the grassroots traditions that emphasize local organization as a form of larger transformation. It has affinities with, for instance, the community organizing of Saul Alinsky, the village rule (*gramraj*) of Mahatma Gandhi, the issue-specific constituency organizing of Cesar Chavez, the local economic initiatives of the German Greens, and the populist citizen movement ideas of Harry Boyte. Each of these invites greater involvement of ordinary people in the processes that affect their lives and sees this as a necessary building block for changing conditions throughout their respective countries and the world. It is this impulse that informs the transnational politics of empowerment.

The wider political implications of this kind of activity are always difficult to gauge. Indeed, many times it is hard to assess even small-scale political ramifications. "How do you measure," Ariel Dorfman asks, for example, "the amount of dignity that a people accumulate? How do you quantify the disappearance of apathy?"[65] Couple this with the difficulty of untangling and measuring the intricate causal relations between different layers of local, regional, international, and global collective life, and one faces an almost impossible task. In this chapter I tried to negotiate my way through this challenge by presenting a sort of "sociology of action." I tried to give voice to the political dynamics that take place at the interface of strengthened civil societies and broader economic, social, and political networks. It is at this juncture, this conjunction of force relations, that one can identify the shimmerings of wider political implications. It is here one notices the world political significance of a transnational activist politics of empowerment.

5   Friends of the Earth and
Political Internationalism

*When we try to pick out anything by itself, we find it
hitched to everything else in the universe.*
—John Muir

In the last two chapters I outlined ways in which transnational environmental activist groups operate outside the arena of the state system but, nevertheless, engage in world politics. In both cases, although I did not emphasize it, there are obvious ways in which their nonstate activities actually intersect with and affect the behavior of states. As mentioned in the Introduction, while global civil society is distinct from the state system, it is not wholly autonomous. The two realms overlap and cross-pollinate each other so that activities in one have consequences for the other. For example, when Greenpeace disseminates an ecological sensibility, it is true that it is not targeting the state per se, nor mobilizing citizens to pressure state officials. Nonetheless, state executives and administrators are obviously susceptible to such dissemination and may, in fact, act in the service of environmental protection as a result. Additionally, citizens may translate their newfound concern for the environment into governmental pressure, even though Greenpeace does not necessarily instruct them to do so. This is also the case with World Wildlife Fund. While WWF targets local areas and seeks to empower communities, WWF would be naive to think that its actions do not involve states. Local communities are nested within national governmental systems, and in some countries efforts to empower local civil society may appear to blunt the ability of the state to rule. In these instances, the state certainly gets involved. Furthermore, insofar as empowered communities operate in successive circles of collective interaction, they are always rubbing up against the state and ultimately the state system. In short, while transnational environmental groups focus directly on civil society when they operate in ways specified in the previous chapters, they are also getting themselves into the thick of state politics.

In this chapter I focus directly on the interface between world civic politics and state actions. My intention is to highlight the relationship between the society-oriented activities of activists and the workings of the state system as they relate to environmental affairs. In particular, I show the way transnational groups work in global civil society to corner states into environmentally sound behavior. No matter how much transnational environmental groups appreciate the efficacy of world civil society, they are not blind to the importance of state action. They recognize that national governments exist and represent effective institutions for altering human behavior. They know that through laws, policies, and programs states can greatly manipulate the way people interact with the earth. States, however, are not easily moved. Environmental groups are not, themselves, states and thus can not use the traditional mechanisms of statecraft—war, trade, diplomacy—to change state behavior. Furthermore, while they engage in lobbying activity to influence states, they recognize its limits. In various settings, confronting the state head-on through lobbying is difficult if not impossible. This is especially the case in authoritarian regimes but can also be true in settings where environmentalists are effectively shut out of influence because other groups enjoy greater government access. In such circumstances, transnational environmental activists frequently search outside formal state processes for mechanisms that can, nevertheless, affect state action. The central argument of this chapter is that when activists do so they find these mechanisms in global civil society in the form of global interdependencies. Specifically, they "colonize" significant strands of complex interdependence and use these as levers of power to make states more sensitive to global environmental dilemmas. Their political work, then, even when it involves states, is of such a society-oriented character that it often takes place in the sphere of world civic life as opposed to the more official interstate arena. For this reason it must also be considered a form of world civic politics.

Ever since Marshall McLuhan said that the world was becoming a global village, it has become somewhat of a cliché to say the world is shrinking and that all persons are becoming increasingly linked socially, economically, culturally, and politically. In international affairs, scholars pay tribute to increasing links between people and collectivities through the concept of interdependence. Interdependence describes the reciprocal effects between countries or actors as a result of transnational activity taking place within a world context.[1] Economically, it refers to the interpenetration of markets, culturally it alludes to the intermeshing of symbolic meaning systems, and socially it refers to transnational collective endeavors. In each instance, transactions are taking place that involve flows of goods, money, information, or people across state boundaries with the result that states and their societies are being mutually (although not symmetrically) affected.

Interdependence is more than a description of the contemporary international system. Additionally, it has been used as a prescription for state policy. *Linkage politics*, whereby states seek leverage in negotiations by tying issues together and *regime politics*, by which states assume a leadership role in international regimes to maintain arrangements that are in their long-term interests, represent perhaps the two most well-known types.[2] More recently, a number of scholars have argued for the importance of what could be called *leverage politics*. This is a result of the end of the cold war and the prominence of environmental issues. It suggests that the poor states of the world can use global environmental concerns to their advantage when bargaining with rich nations over economic issues.[3]

In this chapter, I show that interdependence is not simply a strategy open to states but is available to other actors, including transnational environmental groups. In fact, ironically, it is being used by environmental activists to pressure states into particular types of behavior. Transnational groups target and manipulate the interdependencies of world collective life to corner states into environmentally sound action. They recognize that global interdependencies can operate as levers of power with which to entangle states and thus govern, in imperfect but significant ways, state behavior. Such activity represents another example of how transnational environmental groups engage in societal forms of political action to shape widespread behavior.

The principal conclusion of this chapter is that by engaging in interdependency politics, transnational environmental groups are creating a thin but nevertheless significant form of global accountability in the world. They are turning the nettings of world affairs into strictures that partially hold states responsible to global environmental well-being. Throughout most of the history of international relations, states have been accountable only to themselves. They have pursued their national interests unanswerable to anyone except the dominant members of their societies. Over the past century or so, a number of institutions have emerged that attempt to create a sense of global responsibility. The League of Nations, United Nations, International Court of Justice, and numerous international agencies such as the International Whaling Commission have presented themselves as (or evolved into) organizations that ostensibly look out for the well-being of the entire world and thus demand at least partial respect from nation-states. If nothing else, these institutions represent forms for the expression and registration of world opinion; they thus establish a weak, but nevertheless existent, institutional presence for worldwide conscience. In many instances, states (and at times individuals and nonstate collective entities) must justify their actions to these international bodies or rethink their behavior before acting in deference to them. The kinds of accountability mechanisms transnational environmental groups create are similar to but different from those institutionalized in the UN and so forth. These latter organizations are, essentially, manifestations of the state system and thus reflect, in many ways, not so much the global interest as the interests of the most powerful states. As I will show, the watchdog role of activist groups is different because it is generally unhinged from statist arrangements. Transnational environmental activist groups are "sovereignty-free" actors, and this allows them to approach environmental issues from a nonterritorial perspective.[4] Although there are questions of accountability to be leveled at transnational groups themselves— something I address at the conclusion of this chapter—by manipulating global interdependencies, they provide an additional and, as I will show, unique dimension to the institutionalization of global accountability.

This chapter is similar in format to the previous ones. I focus on one transnational group, Friends of the Earth, to exemplify interdependency politics. While FOE shares much with Greenpeace and World Wildlife Fund, it spends a tremendous amount of energy targeting the interdependencies of global collective life to ensnare states and induce them to work for environmental protection. Further, while the studies of Greenpeace and WWF reveal and lend specificity to alternative renditions of supra-statism and sub-statism respectively, a focus on FOE illustrates an alternative to statism. In the following I show how FOE works at the level of state interaction but does so by intangling states in interdependencies that partly exist in global civil society—a strategy I call *internationalism* in contrast to statism. In the following, then, I study FOE to familiarize the reader with another transnational environmental group and to highlight the actual dynamics involved when transnational organizations work outside the strictly statist arena to protect the earth's ecosystem.

PART ONE

Origins of Friends of the Earth

Friends of the Earth began, ironically, as the consequence of a feud between members of the Sierra Club, one of the oldest environmental groups in the United States. In 1969, after serving seventeen years as the club's executive director, David Brower found himself embroiled in a number of heated disputes over issues, commitments, managerial style, and budgeting.[5] These included arguments about the club's stance toward nuclear power, the decision to publish environmental books, and how to spend (or overspend) club funds. Brower was at odds with members of the executive board over each of these and eventually faced dismissal as a result. Undaunted, Brower chose to resign from the Sierra Club and start a rival organization. At his resignation speech he made clear that the new group would be many of the things the Sierra Club was not. Instead of merely national, it would be international; instead of delegating publications as secondary to the organization, they would be central; instead of being highly bureaucratized, establishing multiple oversights on individuals' activities, it would be decentralized and more anarchic; finally, it would take an unabashed stance against nuclear power and nuclearism more generally. Within months after his resignation, Brower established this new organization. It took its name from a quotation from Muir: "The earth can do all right without friends, but men, if they are to survive, must learn to be friends of the earth."[6]

Brower eventually left FOE for reasons not unlike those that spurred his departure from the Sierra Club.[7] With or without him, however, the organization has grown tremendously since 1969.[8] It now has offices and multiple local chapters in over fifty countries. Many of these are in the Third World and Eastern Europe; it has affiliates, for example, in Malaysia, Sierra Leone, Indonesia, Estonia, and Poland. Each of these offices publishes a magazine for its members and the general public, and the international office, which is located in London, puts out a semiannual newsletter reporting on the club's worldwide activities. Membership varies from office to office. Worldwide there are between 700,000 and 1 million members. Funding comes from a variety of sources. The bulk of it, however, comes from charitable foundations. In 1993, FOE offices worldwide had a combined annual budget of approximately $15 million. FOE potentially focuses on all environmental issues. It limits itself geographically and substantively only according to which issues appear most pressing and where FOE can be most effective. In this sense, it has spearheaded a number of campaigns that were hitherto not being addressed successfully by the NGO community. For example, FOE has been on the forefront of alternative energy policy (pushing a soft-energy path relying on nonnuclear renewable sources), was the first group to work against acid rain, and one of the first to define nuclear war as an environmental issue. Perhaps the organization's most important strength as a transnational environmental group comes from its global reach. By staffing offices in over fifty countries, it keeps abreast of developments worldwide and thus maintains a concrete understanding and political presence concerning environmental dilemmas plaguing the earth. It has often been pointed out that, like the British Empire of old, the sun never sets on Friends of the Earth.

Transnational Organizational Structure

Most transnational environmental activist groups are organized like republics. Individual offices are subordinate to an official council, president, or board of directors that oversees international policy and coordinates transnational activity. While affiliates can make suggestions and push for particular policies, all major decisions must be authorized by the executive of the organization. Friends of the Earth is different in this respect. Instead of a republic, it appears more like a confederation. Individual offices are, for all intents and purposes, on their own to decide policy, spend money, take partisan stands, and so forth. It is genuinely grassroots in this sense. Chapters of FOE throughout the world are bound to the organization formally only in name and orientation. All groups must be committed simply to the "conservation, restoration and rational use of our planet's resources," as an early FOE pamphlet put it. The way they pursue this end is up to them. In practice, however, there is a tremendous amount of voluntary coordination between regional offices.

Part of the reason for the confederate structure is that it allows FOE groups to work on genuinely local environmental issues. For example, *Les Amis de la Terre* (FOE–France) has worked to block the construction of dams on the Loire River in northwest France, *Amigos da Terra* (FOE–Portugal) has protested the dumping of 3,000 Japanese cars off the coast of Portugal threatening coastal wildlife, NOAH (FOE–Denmark) has pushed for an alternative transportation system in Copenhagen to reduce smog and noise, and FOE–New Zealand has worked successfully to stop a planned food irradiation plant in Auckland.

Perhaps the best way to describe this confederate structure is to compare the way FOE brings new chapters into its network with the way other organizations do so. When Greenpeace, for example, wants to open an office in a particular country it locates interest in environmental issues among local people and then sends Greenpeace representatives to help organize this interest into a functioning Greenpeace group. This entails socializing local people into the Greenpeace system. Many times, Greenpeace members from established offices will live in foreign countries for a number of years, trying to establish well-functioning offices. In contrast, FOE does not send out missionaries to set up offices but simply awaits interest by organized environmental groups throughout the world. People contact FOE and ask to be part of the network. This does not entail sending representatives from established offices but simply informing interested parties about how FOE works and the obligations that come along with affiliate status (discussed below). Groups that apply for membership must be approved by FOE, and then they are on probation for one year. After that time, established FOE offices evaluate the activities and contribution of the group and either welcome it into the FOE network or reject it. Part of that decision is based on how well these new groups voluntarily work within the larger FOE network. There is no need to forge the new group in the image of already established FOE offices.[9]

The most important element of the international administration is the Coordinating Council. This body is made up of representatives from all member offices and meets once a year. The council reviews and votes in new members, reports on individual campaigns, shares information, coordinates the broad outlines of international campaigns, and elects an executive committee and a chair for the committee. At these annual meetings, FOE solidifies its international presence and develops a partially cohesive orientation toward global environmental problems. This is the only time all groups meet in one place.

The executive committee is made up of seven individuals and represents the council when it is not in session. The committee is the international arm of the organization throughout the year. It tracks international campaigns, officially speaks for the FOE–International network, and sends people to international conferences and major environmental fora. This ensures a FOE presence at all significant environmental events. While the executive committee is important for coordinating international activity, it is not nearly as powerful as similar international boards in other organizations. It does not oversee the budgets of all member offices nor allocate funds to particular projects. The autonomous structure of FOE throughout the world leaves this to individual chapters. The only resources it controls are the dues member offices pay to FOE–International, which roughly is 1 percent of gross annual income.

The executive committee appoints an international secretariat. This person acts as a liaison between groups. The secretariat responds to requests from member offices working on particular campaigns, writes and distributes a quarterly internal newsletter that informs members of the activities of fellow FOE groups, and publishes an external international newspaper twice a year about FOE organizations worldwide.

This thin international structure, which allows for autonomous action among member groups, reflects a goal of David Brower's when he first organized FOE. This is its quasi-anarchic character. One of Brower's main contentions with the Sierra Club was that bureaucratic oversight, wherein staff members had to secure authority for individual initiatives from the board of directors, hampered individual enterprise and censored creativity. Friends of the Earth is set up to foster autonomy and creativity insofar as it is not a "top-heavy" organization. There is plenty of room for individual offices to pursue the projects they feel are important.

While the loose confederate structure is characteristic of FOE, it should not be overemphasized. This is especially the case in recent years. Because all offices are concerned about the environment, there is actually a great deal of coordination and sharing among them. As the organization has increasingly focused on global environmental problems, transnational coordination has become progressively more significant.

The final aspect of FOE's organizational structure worth mentioning is its practice of working closely in coalition with other environmental groups. In the early days of the modern environmental movement, environmental groups claimed various areas of expertise and concern, and pursued their goals almost independent of each other. Greenpeace, for example, was originally concerned with nuclear weapons testing; the Wilderness Society was concerned with protecting wilderness areas from development; the Jacques Cousteau Society focused on marine ecology. These organizations considered these issue areas their "turf" and, since they competed for membership and media attention, resented invasions into their claimed area of expertise. This caused problems insofar as activist groups carried out their own research, disseminated information through different channels, produced diverse opinions about particular issues, and supported distinct pieces of legislation. The result was that environmentalists could easily be ignored because, when they voiced their position, they sounded more like a cacophony than a chorus. Throughout the 1980s, links started to form between activist groups. Organizations started sharing information, political strategies, publications, and even personnel. In the United States this was reflected in the formation of the Group of Ten.[10] Internationally, groups started to coordinate formally through the Environmental Liaison Centre in Nairobi. Friends of the Earth has played a central role in building these coalitions. Such coalition building allows activists to pool resources and expertise, and to speak often with one powerful voice.

Friends of the Earth's Politics

Key to FOE's work is the understanding that states play the central role in protecting the earth's ecosystem. States represent the most advanced institutions able to influence human activity throughout the world. Thus, their commitment is crucial to earnest environmental protection. As an early member of FOE put it, "The government is probably going to play a major role in the next few years, and perhaps decades, in environmental issues. Everyone wants clean air and clean water and open space and good transportation, but no one (including us [FOE]) really knows how to get them. Government is in a position to encourage the research and the implementation of the techniques and programs necessary. It seems to me that government is the only institution in society capable of handling (or likely to handle) the really monstrous problem confronting us."[11] To win the support of states, FOE many times acts like an interest group intent upon lobbying state officials. It nurtures direct contact with state representatives, helps formulate and advance its own versions of specific policies, musters public pressure on particular individuals and even, in some countries, tries to affect elections. Lobbying is one of the most efficient ways to affect state action.

While lobbying is important to FOE's political work, in its traditional form—putting direct pressure on government officials—it is often ineffective or, depending on the context, impossible to carry out. In those places where it is permitted, such as Western democracies, stronger interest groups frequently overshadow environmental organizations. In nondemocratic regimes, environmental activists usually do not have access to state officials. As a consequence, FOE also tries to influence states indirectly by manipulating those things that condition state action. In this way, FOE aims to corner states into environmentally sound behavior rather than directly lobbying them.

States are entangled in a host of processes that splice, penetrate and enmesh their activities. In the language of international relations theory, they are snarled in numerous interdependencies that impinge upon their maneuverability and behavior. These include economic, cultural, social, and governmental activities that are interstate, transgovernmental, or transnational in character.[12] FOE identifies particular strands of these nettings that it can influence and turns them into mechanisms which will position states to be more actively responsive to the ecological needs of the earth.

Local-National-International Interconnections. There is a movement throughout the world known as municipal foreign policy. It entails city or community involvement in international trade, cultural exchange, and global politics. The idea is that municipalities themselves can carry out international political work independent of their national governments. Cities have, for example, established offices of international affairs, engaged in selective investment of city council revenues, declared their territories nuclear free zones, and undertaken sister-city projects that involve formally adopting and sharing resources with a counterpart in a different country. One intention of this movement is to democratize foreign policy, that is, to disperse foreign policy decision-making power throughout domestic polities. Additionally, the movement aims to exploit the interdependencies that exist between municipalities and the larger configuration of economic, cultural, social, and governmental forces throughout the world and use these to shape collective behavior.[13]

Municipalities are essentially pockets of jurisdiction; city governments formulate and implement local policies. Because of the transmunicipal character of economic, social, and cultural life, when cities enact policies, many times they influence activities outside their specific borders. In these instances, local restrictions can act as barriers or regulatory conduits for the flow of goods and services across city lines and thus serve to shape large-scale activities. This can work in the service of environmental protection, insofar as many practices that affect the environment operate across municipal jurisdiction and thus must tailor themselves to local regulations. The most obvious example of this is corporate behavior, which, because of economies of scale, seeks to standardize products and services. When municipalities pass laws or set regulations that are more stringent than other areas, corporations must adapt their products accordingly and this, many times, is expensive. For instance, when Berkeley, California, declared itself a styrofoam-free city—in an attempt to cut down on the release of chlorofluorocarbons (CFCs) into the atmosphere—corporations such as McDonald's had to alter their production processes or forfeit the Berkeley market.[14] Likewise, moves to restrict the use of polyvinyl-choloride grocery bags in places such as Suffolk County, Long Island, and Portland, Oregon, have put pressure on supermarket chains and their suppliers.[15] Friends of the Earth has been working in coalition with local groups on these types of issues. It represents an important FOE strategy.

One area of municipal foreign policy where FOE has been particularly influential is in its ozone-layer protection campaign. Prior to the Montreal Protocol in 1987 and shortly thereafter, FOE worked locally to get cities to enact strict laws on the production and use of CFCs. FOE's actions aimed to create pockets of CFC-free areas with the idea that this would persuade companies like Johnson Wax and DuPont to stop CFC production, and ultimately, generate momentum for national and international legislation. By late 1989, FOE, in coordination with other organizations, persuaded over twenty-four U.S. cities to pass laws to reduce ozone-depleting gases more quickly than regulations outlined in the Montreal Protocol and to recover and recycle CFCs from all products that contain them.[16] (Significantly, although the initial agreement at Montreal was later upgraded in London and then in Copenhagen, no national or international attempt has been made to recover and recycle existing CFCs or halons. FOE has been working to persuade states and municipalities to enact such policies.)[17] The theory behind this type of activity is that once a critical mass of cities enacts such measures, pressure will be exerted on the national governments to take a stronger stand and work for stricter international regulation.

This strategy is based on a broader type of political action that focuses not only on municipalities, but on provinces, principalities, and states within a particular country. The idea is to use those pockets of jurisdiction to advance initiatives with national and global impact. California, for example, has been on the forefront of passing environmental legislation that is stricter than federal standards. Its automobile emission standards, for instance, require antipollution equipment on all new cars and light trucks, the reformulation of gasoline ingredients, and the introduction of thousands of electric cars. These measures affect industries associated with automobiles and have forced corporations to alter their products or practices or both to remain competitive. Additionally, they have worked to motivate some companies to push for national standards in line with California's regulations because they have adapted quickly and can take early advantage of national legislation. Finally, as more states follow California's lead, the federal government feels increased pressure to enact stricter standards.[18] (In 1994, twelve states in the Northeast asked the U.S. Environmental Protection Agency to impose California tail-pipe standards on the Northwest region of the country.)[19]

FOE has often tried to work at this broader level. For example, throughout the 1970s, FOE worked in the United States with other organizations and in tandem with scientific associations to restrict CFC propellants in aerosol sprays at the state level. By 1975, eleven states had legislative proposals regarding CFC regulations. Oregon became the first state to ban completely the sale of CFCs in aerosols. It stipulated that shopkeepers selling CFC products could be fined or put in prison or both. New York soon followed suit requiring labels on aerosols stating that they were harmful to the environment. Moreover, similar efforts helped persuade Johnson Wax, the fifth-largest manufacturer of aerosols to end all uses of CFCs in its products.[20] To be sure, FOE was far from being single-handedly responsible for these actions. Its efforts were part of a whole host of initiations coming from diverse directions pushing for state action on CFCs. Nonetheless, FOE's role and subsequent attempts at marshalling support for environmental action at the municipal, provincial, and state levels was and continues to be significant. One sees this, for example, in FOE's efforts in other countries.

Due in large part to the efforts of *Vereniging Milieudefensie* (FOE–the Netherlands), close to two thirds of all Dutch municipalities have passed laws banning use of tropical timber in municipal projects and have encouraged private architects to stop using tropical timber in their work. This is part of FOE's transnational campaign to protect tropical rain forests. In the late 1980s, Dutch tropical timber consumption per capita was among the world's highest, second only to Japan. Every year, 43,000 hectares of tropical rain forest were being destroyed to satisfy Dutch timber demand. Less than 1 percent of the imports were produced in a sustainable way. Throughout the late 1980s and early 1990s, *Vereniging Milieudefensie* worked to persuade Dutch cities to adopt restrictions on tropical timber consumption.[21] By 1994, the Netherlands cut consumption between 6 and 40 percent.[22] And, due to the fact that the timber companies that import to the Netherlands are multinational and that the Dutch are active participants in international, intergovernmental fora, it is hoped that such measures will have an effect on the processes that facilitate the destruction of tropical rain forests.[23]

National-International Interconnections. A strategy of municipal foreign policy works at the local level and uses overlapping jurisdictions to influence national and, by extension, international activity. FOE targets interconnections between national and international domains more specifically and uses these to shape state action.

In 1989, a coalition of environmental, investor, and church interests, known as the Coalition for Environmentally Responsible Economies (CERES), met in New York City to introduce a ten-point environmental code of conduct for corporations. One month later, CERES along with the Green Alliance launched a similar effort in the United Kingdom. The aim was to provide criteria for auditing the environmental performance of large domestic and multinational industries. The code called on companies to, among other things, minimize the release of pollutants, conserve nonrenewable resources through efficient use and planning, utilize environmentally safe and sustainable energy sources, and consider demonstrated environmental commitment as a factor in appointing members to the board of directors. FOE, along with thirteen other environmental organizations, publicize the CERES Principles (formerly known as the Valdez Principles, inspired by the Exxon *Valdez* oil spill) and enlist corporations to pledge compliance.[24]

The CERES Principles are valuable for a number of reasons. For pension funds, the code can be used to foster shareholder pressure on companies to improve their environmental performance. For investors, it serves as a guide to help them decide which companies are acceptable for socially responsible investment. Environmentalists can use the code as a measuring device to praise or criticize corporate behavior. Finally, the principles are being used to alert job-seeking college graduates about corporate compliance with the code and thus insert environmental considerations into the career paths of the young. Taken together, these measures signal an element of corporate accountability driven by consumer action.[25] Corporations are in the business, ultimately, of selling products (including selling themselves as investment opportunities). To do this successfully is a function of maintaining a consumer-friendly corporate image. In an age when environmentalism is partly guiding the choices people make, the CERES Principles can alter this image and thus sway consumer preferences.

What is promising about the CERES Principles, from an international relations perspective, is that signatories include at least one Fortune 500 company and a number of multinational corporations. Sun Company, General Motors, Polaroid, and a host of other MNCs have pledged compliance or are at least seriously considering doing so. These companies operate in numerous countries and thus their actions have transnational effects, and, to the degree that they subscribe to the Principles, their actions will introduce a green perspective into many areas of transnational economic relations. Given the transnational character of MNCs, then, sponsoring the CERES Principles is a means of exploiting the interdependencies between national and international domains.

The CERES Principles also reveal a strategy of interdependency politics insofar as those companies abiding by them will, themselves, become lobbyists for national and international environmental legislation. When companies voluntarily meet environmental standards they often push for such standards to be codified into law so that their commitments will not leave them at a comparative disadvantage vis-a-vis their competitors. If company 'A,' for instance, has cut back on, say, CO_2 emmissions, then it would like companies 'B,' 'C,' and 'D' to do so as well so they will not undersell 'A' due to cheaper, less environmentally sound production processes. Moreover, as such standards get written into domestic law, the same dynamics encourage companies to push for international standards. For, in a global marketplace, comparative disadvantage works across state boundaries. While FOE's work associated with the CERES Principles is no guarantee that this will happen, its efforts represent a step in this direction.

One area where such dynamics have already been at work is the pressure Friends of the Earth and others have put on corporations that produce CFCs. I said a bit about this in the last section, but the analysis can be extended beyond the aerosol ban and municipal and state action. In the late 1970s and early 1980s, the domestic pressure FOE and others placed on U.S. corporations, municipalities, state legislatures, and the federal government made it clear that, while domestic regulation may not come immediately, it was definitely going to come sometime in the near future. This was presaged by the 1980 EPA proposal for a no-growth formula that would restrict CFC production to current levels. While U.S. industries successfully fought the measure, it sent a message to them that sooner or later the United States would impose some form of CFC regulation.[26] The threat of domestic regulation scared U.S. industries. For, if the United States was the only country to impose restrictions, then U.S. industries would be at a competitive disadvantage to foreign CFC producers. To put it in more theoretical terms, the interdependencies of the global marketplace threatened to hurt U.S. firms disproportionately. In the face of such circumstances, industrial lobbying groups, such as the Chemical Manufactures Association and the Alliance for Responsible CFC Policy, began to call for international standards. Arguing that the U.S. economy would suffer disproportionately, these industrial lobbying groups claimed that the United States could only call for cutbacks in production if it did so internationally.[27] According to Alan Miller and Irving Mintzer, the pressure from U.S. industries to internationalize restrictions provided much of the momentum for the United States to enter into international negotiations and agreements.[28] This is confirmed by Richard Benedick, chief negotiator of the Montreal Protocol, who points out that industry support in the United States hinged on measures that protected U.S. corporations against unfair competition from countries not party to the treaty.[29] Thus, paradoxically, U.S. industry was a driving force behind international accords. It pushed the U.S. government to the negotiating table, and since the United States is the largest producer of CFCs, this was instrumental in getting international agreement. FOE was obviously not single-handedly responsible for pressuring corporations or successive levels of government to support international legislation. Its efforts, along with other NGOs, were one of several parallel forces involved, including advancements in scientific work and shifts of view within significant segments of the CFC industry.[30] Nonetheless, its targeting the interdependence of global economic processes played a significant role in advancing international regulation on CFC products and highlights its overall political strategy. Referring to the 1992 ozone agreement in London and the work of FOE in particular and NGOs in general, Bramble and Porter state that, "It is impossible to assess how much the achievement of the London agreement can be attributed to NGOs, but there is certainly enough evidence to suggest that it happened sooner because of the NGO campaign."[31]

In both these instances—the formulation of the CERES Principles and the push for domestic controls on CFC producers—FOE pinpoints the intersection between national and international processes. In these cases, FOE focuses on transnational economic practices and uses the international market to create incentives for international accords. Friends of the Earth recognizes that economic practices are becoming global in scope and that constraining them in one domestic setting can have international implications.

International-National Interconnections. While FOE pursues much of its work by expanding outward, that is, from local to national to international settings, it also pinpoints the interdependencies that function in the other direction. It manipulates processes that are, at first, international, and uses them to impose environmental constraints at the national and local levels of interaction. This is one of FOE's most significant endeavors. Foremost in its strategies, FOE focuses on international regimes. International regimes, to cite one of the most widely accepted definitions, are "principles, norms, rules, and decision-making procedures around which actor expectations converge in a given issue-area."[32] They reflect the institutionalization of acceptable modes of behavior in international relations. In the absence of a worldwide sovereign entity, states experience collective action problems. To use the language of rational choice theory, they fail to realize feasible joint gains resulting in suboptimal outcomes. States establish international regimes partly to counter this situation. Regimes facilitate cooperative efforts by providing a quasi-permanent and consistent structure for interstate relations. In other words, regimes institutionalize international behavior by developing rules, norms, and conventions.

What is important to FOE is that, in the process of facilitating international cooperation, international regimes act as constraints on state behavior. One can see this most clearly when regimes are codified in international governmental organizations (IGOs). IGOs are associations, created by governments, that address particular collective action problems. The main participants in such organizations are states, and the predominant topic of discussion is intergovernmental relations. As IGOs mature, however, they gain a sense of autonomy, legitimacy, and power in themselves. That is, while IGOs are established and staffed by governments, they take on a life of their own. In theory, a delegate is meant to represent his or her government at international proceedings. In practice, however, this is not always the case. The extent to which a delegate is governmentally bound is a function of personality, the issue in question, home country, and character of the IGO.[33] Moreover, the secretariats who service IGOs act, many times, more like international bureaucrats than state representatives. Thus, when it comes to delegates and secretariats, there is leeway for IGO officials to act in nonnational ways. Indeed, over time, as officials identify career-wise with their duties, they begin to defend the principles of the organization. This is also the case with less formal aspects of international regimes. As norms and conventions become entrenched they win their own legitimacy and power. They establish modes of behavior around which expectations converge. Violating these modes, then, carries costs. Ostracism, diplomatic isolation and public rebuke raise the stakes of noncompliance. They act as forms of constraint on state behavior.[34] To FOE, the more autonomy international regimes muster, the better for international environmental politics. For, to the degree that international regulations, policies, and norms restrict state behavior, they work against the narrow nationalism that generally animates interstate relations and hinders global environmental protection. In short, international regimes act as entanglements within which states function, and FOE uses these to advance environmental well-being.

Since the signing of the Antarctica Treaty in 1959, Antarctica has remained a nonmilitarized, denuclearized area where scientists from around the world carry out research in a cooperative and peaceful setting. Part of the reason for this is that governments have established the Antarctic Treaty System (ATS) within which all major political issues are addressed. Throughout most of its history, Antarctica has been spared intensive ecological disturbance. In fact, it represents the last close-to-pristine ecosystem on earth. Developments over the past few decades, however, have raised concerns about Antarctica's environmental well-being. Scientific programs and the number of stations are growing, and greater numbers of tourists are visiting the continent. This is increasing the human impact on Antarctica's fragile environment. Additionally, the Southern Ocean is being regarded as an important source of food for human societies. Throughout history it teemed with abundant quantities of seals, whales, fin fish, and squid and today sustains the world's largest population of krill. Overfishing is becoming a serious threat to these marine animals. Finally, there has been sustained speculation that Antarctica holds vast amounts of minerals and, until recently, there was tremendous pressure to open up the continent to mineral exploration. Friends of the Earth is committed to protecting the ecological integrity of the continent and takes these threats seriously.

Friends of the Earth works for the environmental protection of Antarctica in coalition with other environmental organizations. It is most active through the Antarctic and Southern Ocean Coalition (ASOC). Established in 1978, ASOC represents a worldwide association of over 200 nongovernmental organizations situated in forty countries. Prior to 1978, activists concerned about Antarctica worked independently of each other. The most effective organizations were the Center for Law and Social Policy (CLASP), the International Office of the Sierra Club, and the International Union for the Conservation of Nature (IUCN).[35] As large-scale exploitation of marine resources and the possibility of mineral development increased—and thus the fate of Antarctica's ecosystem came into greater focus—it became clear that a stronger NGO presence was necessary. This paved the way for ASOC. Friends of the Earth has been a key member of the coalition. In fact, James Barnes, a member of the FOE–International executive committee, founded ASOC and for years the organization has operated out of FOE's U.S. office.

ASOC's main strategy is to target the ATS and use it to make states more responsible to the environmental well-being of the continent. It has done so by infiltrating ATS negotiations and meetings. For example, since 1983 a representative from ASOC has been on the delegations of Australia, New Zealand, France, the United States, and Denmark at ATS meetings.[36] As such, ASOC members have advocated their position at all national preparatory meetings and, while not completely capturing each of these delegations, have gotten a number of them to support ASOC policy stands. Such influence was crucial in defeating a proposal to open up Antarctica to mineral exploration (More on this later).

In addition, ASOC influences the ATS as an independent observer at all international meetings. ASOC sends representatives to all relevant conferences, informal gatherings, and treaty negotiations. In each of these settings, ASOC provides information, advances its own positions, and facilitates the exchange of ideas. Moreover, ASOC's formal observer status entitles it to participate at many levels of international deliberation. While ASOC members cannot vote on final decisions, they can be present and contribute extensively to debate. They can address ATS fora, submit material to the secretariat for distribution to delegations, and have access to all documentation presented at formal negotiations. This allows ASOC to keep up to date with all proceedings and to exert its presence at all stages in the international policy process.

One of the most effective ways ASOC influences the ATS is by publishing the newspaper *ECO*.[37] *ECO* was originally produced by FOE and the magazine *The Ecologist* in 1972 during the UN Conference on the Human Environment in Stockholm. It served as a daily news sheet that distilled and analyzed the major events going on at the conference. With thousands of pages of separate proposals, *ECO* allowed delegates to stay abreast of all significant developments.[38] Since 1972, *ECO* has been published at all major international environmental negotiations (at times, under a different name). Often it is the only document that is produced on a daily basis, and thus delegates rely on it for information about the previous day's events, relevant proposals, and latest information. What is of central importance is that *ECO* does not advocate the position of any specific country but rather the NGO community. Its analysis and recommendations represent ASOC's views. And, to the degree that

ECO is considered almost mandatory reading at ATS meetings, it serves as an important source of ASOC influence.

While it is difficult to assess the effectiveness of ASOC, it is clear that it has been instrumental in the formulation and implementation of certain policies and political positions. One of the most significant results of its efforts is the resilience of the idea of making Antarctica a world park. In 1972, members to the Second World Conference on National Parks called on states that were party to the Antarctic Treaty to establish the continent and the surrounding seas as the first world park under the auspices of the United Nations. In 1975, New Zealand formally proposed the idea but, finding stiff opposition, soon dropped it. Throughout the 1980s, speculation grew concerning mineral resources on the continent and, in 1988, the twenty countries operating research bases in Antarctica signed a minerals development agreement, the Convention on the Regulation of Antarctic Mineral Resources Activity (CRAMRA).

This agreement established regulations for future mineral exploration and extraction. Environmentalists, including ASOC, opposed the convention because, while it aimed to regulate future mining activities, it nonetheless still allowed mineral extraction and thus could be used actively to facilitate minerals exploitation with little regard for environmental damage.[39] Instead of CRAMRA, ASOC and others supported the moribund World Park proposal and worked during the ratification stage of CRAMRA for its adoption. They found their first glimmer of success in 1989, when Australia refused to ratify CRAMRA largely because of environmental reasons; three months later, France followed suit. This basically defeated the overall ratification of CRAMRA because, as countries holding territorial claims, their support was mandatory for the convention's adoption.

Within a year a number of other countries joined the French and the Australians, and by October 1991, all ATS members refused ratification and supported instead the 1991 Environmental Protocol, which prohibits mineral and oil exploration on the continent for at least fifty years and establishes a normative and institutional framework for preserving the continent as a world park.[40] The protocol states that, "The Parties commit themselves to the comprehensive protection of the Antarctic environment . . . and hereby designate Antarctica as a natural reserve, devoted to peace and science."[41] What is crucial to notice is that since 1975, the idea of a world park and a complete mineral ban was kept alive only because of NGO support, with ASOC playing a particularly active role.[42] Commenting on the Australian and French moves to reject CRAMRA, Jim Barnes said, "the Australian and French initiative reflects the thinking of the environmental community."[43] While it would be inaccurate to say that ASOC, or even the NGO community, single-handedly defeated CRAMRA, it played a critical role. It inserted itself, along with other NGOs, into every fora in which CRAMRA was discussed and attempted to influence the ATS toward the world park idea. In fact, one of the original reasons for founding ASOC was to promote the concept.[44]

ASOC has also had a strong influence on the ATS by helping to implement ATS agreements. Agreements negotiated within the ATS are difficult to enforce; in fact, as mentioned, this is the case with all international agreements. There is no worldwide police and thus no strong incentives for compliance. ASOC serves an important role within ATS by trying to assume part of the task of implementation. For instance, in the 1980s, the French built an airstrip near the d'Urville base at Pointe Geologie in Terre Adelie. Construction damaged the fragile environment, and many aspects of it were in violation of the Antarctica Treaty System's rules and codes. Although it was unable to block construction, ASOC acted as a watchdog to ensure that construction would be, at least partially, respectful of environmental standards. For example, it published a chronology of events associated with the airfield, documented violations, and presented a legal analysis of these violations. These were originally circulated to all consultative parties and to diplomats at the UN in 1986 and have been presented at all international meetings of the consultative parties since then.[45] Additionally, ASOC and others have worked as watchdogs at McMurdo Base, the home of U.S. researchers and at Argentina's Marambio Station. In this capacity they have monitored and criticized garbage dumping in landfills, fuel storage in leaky containers, and toxic chemical contamination in both areas.[46] While ASOC has not become an effective police force in Antarctica, its role in this instance and others has won it credibility within the regime and has bolstered its ability to influence ATS affairs.[47]

The ATS works as a constraint on states. As parties to the ATS, states agree to abide by its policies even when their own actions are curtailed as a result. To be sure, there are infractions; sometimes states pursue actions that they deem to be in their best interests but that are at odds with ATS agreements. Nonetheless, as a regime, the ATS constrains, to a degree, state autonomy. Through a complex set of inducements and punishments, states find it, on the whole, easier to comply with ATS policies than not. ASOC recognizes this and infiltrates and manipulates the ATS to the best of its ability to adopt stricter measures against environmental destruction. Friends of the Earth works for the environmental well-being of the continent through its participation in ASOC. This represents another instance in which it targets the entanglements of world politics as a way to affect state behavior.

Transnational Interconnections. The interdependencies of global collective life do not operate merely in a vertical direction. That is, economic, social, and political processes do not proceed simply along a local-national-international trajectory (or vice versa). There is also a strong horizontal component to worldwide practices. One sees this explicitly with multilateral development banks. The World Bank, the International Monetary Fund (IMF), and a host of other institutions, including the Inter-American, Asian, and African Development Banks, are directly responsible for large flows of international capital. For example, in 1989 and 1990, the World Bank alone lent close to $40 billion.[48] As these flows make their way through successive layers of international and eventually national and local interaction, they greatly shape the way governments and societies treat the natural world.

Throughout most of their histories, multilateral development banks (MDBs) have been all but ignorant of the environmental effects of their loan programs. For example, their stipulations, which generally call for increasing exports and decreasing government expenditures, work against environmental conditions. In the first instance, one of the easiest ways to increase exports is to extract resources at an accelerated pace. In agricultural production, this involves using soils and groundwater at rates higher than natural systems can replace them; in mineral development, it means using greater quantities of energy to extract from poorer and poorer ores; in timber production, it entails harvesting without replanting. Each of these practices makes it extremely difficult for countries to pursue sustainable development. In the second instance, one of the easiest targets for cutting government expenditures is conservation. Development banks generally do not instruct governments to cut expenditures in particular areas; they leave such decisions to recipient nations. Unfortunately, in many Third World countries, conservation projects are seen as expendable. They do not contribute directly to immediate economic growth (although they may in fact do so in the longterm), and hence can be cut without much public outcry. In other words, the demands of economic austerity generally take precedence over all other considerations. For this reason, governments often forego long-term resource management for short-term economic production.[49]

In addition to the conditionality of loans, MDBs also support environmental abuse because the projects they fund, many times, adversely affect local environments. For example, the introduction of inappropriate technologies has often destroyed the productive potential of ecosystems. The most striking instances are hydroelectric projects whose environmental costs—the inundation of productive land, drying of downstream lakes, and reduced downstream productivity due to salinization and erosion of deltas—have in most instances, exceeded the benefits of irrigation and hydroelectric power.[50] In addition, the conversion of tropical forests to agricultural and livestock use ends up stripping land of its productivity (in a matter of a few years). Furthermore, multilateral development banks encourage "packages" of high-yield crops that require heavy use of pesticides, and increased reliance on pesticides causes serious long-term environmental (as well as economic) problems. Each of these projects greatly damage the ecological well-being of Third World environments as well as cause severe social dislocations.[51]

For these and other reasons, FOE has been organizing NGO lobbying of multilateral banks. Its main focus has been on the World Bank and the IMF. In the early 1980s, FOE started a campaign to change the structure, staff, and basic policies of these institutions. Because governments are donors and shareholders of multilateral development banks, much of FOE's effort aims at pressuring officials of specific governments to withhold country contributions to the World Bank and IMF. Additionally, however, FOE has also tried to influence directly multilateral banks themselves. It has, for example, presented bank officials with assessments of the environmental impact of past loans, met with bank members and executive directors, drafted and disseminated proposals for international legislation that set conditions on loan approval, and organized media and public opinion campaigns to voice opposition to particular projects.[52] The results of these actions have been uneven. With the first wave of criticism, the World Bank promised to integrate environmental assessments into project cycles and to fund environmentally sustainable projects. It partially made good on these promises by suspending loans to build roads in Amazonia, Brazil, and to transport populations within Indonesia from Java and Bali to outlying, tropical regions, such as Kalimantan and Irian Jaya. As criticism continued, it went further and took measures for making environmental concerns more central to all bank operations. This included raising the number of environmental specialists from three in 1977 and five in the mid-1980s to over 200 by the mid-1990s, establishing a department of environmental affairs (which publishes *Environmental Bulletin* and numerous working papers), increasing loans specifically for population and forestry programs, and setting environmental assessment guidelines as a criterion for loans.[53] Moreover, as it assumed responsibility for the Global Environmental Facility (GEF) in 1990 and, as this institution was given greater significance at the Earth Summit, its decision-making operations have become more transparent, thus inviting more pressure from environmentalists. To be sure, these measures have not made the World Bank a model environmental institution. It still funds projects that, by most accounts, degrade the environment and are not sustainable over the long term and has yet to allow its newfound concern for the environment to be fully integrated into its operations.[54] Nonetheless, the World Bank has budged a bit in its commitment to environmental issues, and this is largely attributable to pressure from NGOs such as FOE.[55] NGOs have been less successful with regard to the IMF. The IMF has yet to fully staff an environmental affairs office, hire experts in environmental issues or target special funds for environmental programs. Moreover, while it has stated an intention to integrate environmental concerns more seriously into its work, there is no overarching commitment even rhetorically to do so as of yet. In fact, it claims that its structural adjustment programs inherently preserve the environment by reducing economic distortions.[56] Nonetheless, the IMF is experiencing significant NGO pressure, led mainly by FOE. It has been served notice that it can no longer continue loan practices that are dismissive of envirnmental concerns without incurring outside criticism.

What is key to notice in FOE's actions as they relate to MDBs is the interconnection between the banks and the state system. States are constitutive members and administrators of MDBs. They both experience and must approve changes in loan policies. When FOE pressures MDBs and fosters change, it is fixating its efforts at the interface of states and MDBs and working to alter the character and processes of both entities. It is in this way that FOE corners states into actions that they could not ordinarily take and refashions institutions that are themselves greatly responsible for the earth's ecological well-being. FOE's efforts in this regard, then, represent another instance of their world civic politics.

PART TWO

Political Interdependence

The strategies of pressuring MDBs, engaging intergovernmental organizations, working at the municipal level on global issues and forcing multinational corporations to change their behavior are all predicated on the view that these actors and domains of activity intersect with wider spheres of practices and thus changes undertaken by or within them will affect broader patterns of activity. When FOE works to convince the World Bank to fold environmental concerns into its lending practices, for example, it does so not because it cares about the character of the World Bank per se, (although this is part of it), but also because the World Bank interacts with and sets conditions on governments, corporations, and societies at large.[57] Likewise, when FOE infiltrates the ATS it is not simply trying to change the sensibility of the treaty system for the sake of the system's self-character but because it interacts with and affects other organizations, most importantly state governments. The same is true when FOE targets municipalities and multinational corporations. These are world politically significant because they are embedded within broader nets of jurisdiction and activity, and their actions will influence collective practices. In almost every instance, what is crucial is that, at some point in the interaction, the governments of states become entangled in the processes of global civil society, and thus FOEs overall strategy entails targeting the interdependencies of world affairs to corner states into greater environmental activity.

States can be cornered, as it were, because the world has become much more interdependent. Transactions between countries have been increasing, and the costs involved have become so high as to engender dependence between actors.[58] For students of international relations, interdependence has become genuinely significant because transnational flows very often interface with state action or at least involve domains of activity for which states are responsible for regulating or controlling. In the study of international relations, recognition of this spawned the view of complex interdependence, which argues, among other things, that states are not autonomous, or even unitary, actors, but rather they are partially conditioned by the nettings of world affairs. In more recent years, as more international regimes have emerged codifying much transnational activity, scholars have developed the so-called neo-institutional view that emphasizes the amount of influence international regimes have on state action.[59] Neo-institutionalists argue that institutions can lessen the inhibitory effects of international anarchy on states' willingness to cooperate with each other, especially when they share common interests. Institutions increase interactions among states and provide rules, norms, and principles to facilitate interstate relations. In this latter regard, they work by lowering transaction costs and creating a host of inducements that help states move toward Pareto-optimal conditions.[60] Both complex interdependence and neo-institutionalism, while different in crucial regards, share the view that states are not on their own but are rather embedded in multiple, intersecting structures that pattern behavior.

Transnational activist groups are practitioners of complex interdependence and neo-institutionalism. They deliberately target the constraints on states and use them to move states toward more ecologically sound actions. They do so specifically by influencing the way states calculate and pursue their national interests.

No one questions that states act in their own interests. What is less clear, however, is how they perceive those interests. A traditional international relationist line is that states formulate their national interests autonomously. They have a set of national goals that are a function of domestic politics and regime type, and pursue these to varying degrees depending upon the constraints of the international system (i.e., balances of power, geographical positioning, and threats to security).[61] As a host of writers point out, including and especially regime and neo-institutionalist theorists, this is a narrow understanding of national interest and state behavior. The world political system has its own conditioning factors that play into the formulation of national interest. The entanglements that I have been discussing represent one such factor. They represent "social facts," which make up the context within which states formulate interests.[62] As Keohane and others suggest, interdependencies alter the incentives facing states. As constraints, they affect the costs of certain actions and many times induce states to reconceptualize their interests. Additionally, interdependencies serve an educative role in world affairs. They restrict states' maneuverability and, as states rub up against conflicting processes, "teach" them about significant issues that are occupying world political life. This moves states to reevaluate their national interests. Finally, entanglements alter states' understandings of their own roles in the international system and change their assumptions about others' motivations. Interdependencies, in this capacity, determine how one's position and the actions of others are interpreted.[63] In each of these ways, international entanglements form and act as international social structures. They condition the formulation of national interest. (This, by the way, is simply part of a larger phenomenon wherein states not only help constitute the world political system but are also shaped by the transnational processes that evolve within it.)[64] Transnational environmental activist groups target international networks of entanglement and use them to influence state behavior.

When one talks about constraining states through entanglements, one implicitly speaks about a form of governance. To the traditional observer of international relations, entangling states may not seem like an important form of governance. Because it does not wield power directly over the fundamental actors of world politics, viz., nation-states. Rather, it is a type of governance that works through the complex of economic, social, cultural, and governmental dimensions of world affairs all at once. Transnational groups do not streamline their efforts and thus do not target states in a direct way. On the contrary, they engage simultaneously in a host of different arenas to surround states. For this reason, many observers may not even see the activities of transnational groups as genuinely political. After all, if activists are busy only tinkering with the nettings of world affairs—and not directly taking on nation-states— then their actions can be analyzed simply as collective fluff: interesting forms of collective action, although having no effect on larger, more significant events. This view, in my judgment, represents a narrow and naive understanding of politics in general and world politics in particular. As people such as Antonio Gramsci,[65] Alain Touraine,[66] Adam Michnik,[67] and others[68] make clear, "tinkering" with the wider configurations within which states are enmeshed (especially in the realm of civil society) can be an effective form of politics. This is the case, even when the ultimate objective is not seizing state power. As I have been emphasizing throughout, politics is not simply about governmental action per se, and world politics is more than interstate relations. Politics, in its broadest sense, is a practice undertaken by actors who wish to direct and order collective life. World politics, likewise, involves all activities devoted to creating conditions that will shape collective behavior within a world context.

When transnational activists manipulate the entanglements of states they are attempting to create conditions that will constrain the activities of all significant actors, especially states. To be sure, they pursue this type of politics circuitously, and they do not simply lobby government officials. But this does not make it any less political. They want to direct states to certain types of behavior.

Interdependencies and Global Accountability

To direct someone is to control them. It is to impose conditions on them. When environmental groups manipulate transnational interdependencies, they are constricting the area of maneuver for states. Raised to a higher level of abstraction, one can think of this as creating a form of global accountability. Accountability means being answerable or responsible to someone else. For most of their histories, states have been accountable only to the dominant members of their societies. States heeded the voices of a particular class, an ethnic group, the military, or even, at rare moments, the entire citizenry of given polities. States have never been, however, responsible to all of humanity. To be sure, the United Nations, the International Court of Justice at the Hague, and numerous international organizations represent an external form of accountability and serve as imperfect arenas for articulating the so-called global interest. Notwithstanding the ability of such institutions to represent views that are not strictly national in scope, they themselves often struggle to work in the interest of all of humanity. This is partly because it is difficult to identify what such an interest would, in fact, be and partly because of the territorial perspective of member states.[69] The accountability efforts of transnational environmental groups are related but different in this regard in that activist members are not nation-states and these groups do not rely upon the financial contribution of states to carry out their operations. This gives environmental groups more autonomy in their actions and allows them to assume a more globalist perspective on world affairs.

As Richard Falk puts it, a global perspective is one that is "as liberated as possible from the interests, biases, and habitual attitudes of any particular place or nation in the world."[70] Transnational environmental groups work to assume a genuinely global perspective on world affairs and try to bring this perspective to bear on international relations by lacing it through the nettings of world political life. In doing so, transnational groups establish a thin but increasingly present form of global environmental accountability.

To acknowledge such a mechanism of accountability is not to claim that activist groups have taken over world politics—that is, that they have changed fundamentally the basic dynamics of international relations. Nor is it, for that matter, to suggest that activists genuinely represent the common good or even that they have the best insights on environmental protection. It *is* to suggest, however, that as environmental activists infiltrate and "colonize" increasing dimensions of global political life, they will create a denser, stickier viscosity to international environmental affairs, and this will force states to be more sensitive to environmental issues as activists understand them. It will, in other words, lend more weight, scope, and effectiveness to global environmental accountability. As this happens, the work of transnational environmental activist groups will become more clearly political to even the staunchest skeptic. For the interdependencies themselves will play a more powerful role in determining world affairs. The nettings of global political life will increasingly condition state actions, and thus it will be the movers and shakers of these entanglements who will increasingly influence world politics.

Having said this, it is important to remember that transnational activists themselves have an accountability problem. Directors and staff of these organizations are rarely elected and, more often than not, are appointed by the organization itself. This allows them to pursue activities based on their own understandings of what is worthwhile. Moreover, to the degree that activists are accountable to anyone, it is usually to their own members who are environmentalists rather than citizens at large.[71] Unlike elected officials of government who are responsible to citizens of all ideological persuasions, activist groups must please only those concerned with environmental issues, and this raises questions about their overall accountability to society. Taken together, this does not categorically dismiss transnational groups as playing an important role as mechanisms of accountability, but it should be kept in mind as a qualification of the entire effort.

A second aspect of accountability relevant here has to do with the notion of giving an "account" of certain circumstances. It entails telling the truth about one's experience. Transnational environmental groups are constantly putting forth an interpretation of environmental challenges. What is curious is that when they do so they are being taken seriously. People are listening. Their voices speak with authority. Throughout the past few decades, environmental groups have enjoyed a sense of authority within domestic regimes. Citizens turn to activist organizations for information and insight into contemporary environmental affairs. At present, this is starting to happen internationally. Governments are now starting to look to activists for guidance in world environmental politics. For example, countries that cannot carry out their own scientific research rely on environmental groups for information. These countries see activist groups as independent and thus partially neutral sources of information.[72] In addition, some countries defer to activists' political judgments. They seek and take advice from activists on particular positions, negotiating stances and voting recommendations. Finally, transnational environmental groups have become international environmental authorities due to the exposés they carry out. Through investigative reporting and monitoring teams, activists reveal international ecologically abusive practices that would otherwise go unnoticed. This heightened expert status suggests that transnational environmental groups play an important role as worldwide "accountants" of environmental conditions. This complements and enhances the way they provide a mechanism of accountability for global international affairs in general.

Building a system of global accountability in environmental affairs is, obviously, no small undertaking, especially for a nonstate actor. It is the enormity of the task, however, that makes it necessary for groups such as FOE to cast their nets wide and work through multiple channels and levels of world political life to do so. Because of their relative weakness compared to other actors, transnational environmental groups seek to create as many checks and oversights as possible and use them to influence states and thus scramble the often anti-environmental imperatives of the state system.

Internationalism Versus Statism

In chapter 2, I claimed that there are three traditional political approaches to global environmental governance: statism, supra-statism, and sub-statism. I also suggested that, because each of these has significant difficulties for coming to terms with global environmental threats, we should look to transnational environmental groups for alternative and perhaps more promising forms of politics. In this chapter I have been examining the way transnational environmental activist groups engage states to restore and protect the environment. I described how they work through the intricacies and nettings of world politics to force states to be more sensitive and responsive to global environmental issues. If one thinks about statism, supra-statism, and sub-statism as the primary avenues for addressing global ecological threats, this strategy represents an alternative to the statist option. It is a practice that, while not reinforcing the parochialism and obstacles to cooperative action in the state system, is directed at the international level of politics. The idea behind constraining states via transnational interdependencies is not necessarily to make the state system, as a configuration of separate nation-states, work better. Rather, it is to create and empower a form of accountability that will hold states responsible to those who care about the environmental quality of the earth. In other words, it seeks to modify state behavior toward ecologically sound practices.

Statism is the notion that the state system, as it currently exists, provides the best response to global environmental problems. It suggests that states are willing and able to solve the threats of ozone depletion, the greenhouse effect, species extinction, and so forth without major modifications to the present character of intergovernmental relations. It praises the existence of sovereignty, the importance of national interest, and even interstate competition, and sees these as contributing—to be sure, in complicated ways—to the alleviation of global environmental problems. Additionally, statism holds that even if environmental protection requires significant changes in the character of world politics, governments are the only ones able to initiate and bring about such changes. Put differently, states are the only *realistic* agents of environmental renewal and protection. States are the most powerful and predominant actors in world affairs and thus the most capable of carrying out environmental protection. Indeed, if states fail to solve global environmental problems, we are truly doomed for there is no one else around to do so.

While governments can address many worldwide dilemmas, there are many processes that encourage them to focus on their own well-being to the exclusion of others. For this reason transnational environmental activist groups do not trust governments to act on their own for environmental protection. States must be pushed or cornered into caring about the earth. An important way to move the world toward ecological balance then, is to create globalist constraints on states. This will stem states' parochial and anti-ecological tendencies. Transnational environmental groups create such constraints by making international interdependencies work in the service of global environmental well-being.

In the vocabulary of politics, there is a word that comes close to describing the strategy of transnational environmental groups as I have been discussing it in this chapter: *internationalism*. Internationalism is the notion that "political activity should define its objectives not in terms of constitution, history, or geographical boundaries of any particular nation, but in terms of a universal human condition."[73] Transnational environmental organizations pursue a type of internationalist politics to the degree that they are more concerned with the fate of the entire earth than with state entities. Furthermore, while aiming at ends that go beyond the nation-state, most internationalist doctrines consciously recognize that states are unavoidably involved in larger international endeavors and must be engaged in one form or another in pursuing these higher aims. That is, internationalism traditionally aspires to universal aims higher than those embodied in state action yet prescribes enlisting states in the realization of this larger project. Transnational environmental groups share this sensitivity insofar as they use states in their pursuit of global ecological restoration and protection. To appreciate the utility of the term internationalism in the present context, it is useful to compare briefly the politics of transnational environmental groups with the two most significant forms of internationalism, Marxism and Kantianism.

Marxism espouses an internationalist doctrine insofar as it sees the means of political action in terms of class struggle and the ends in terms of nonnational, classless societies—*international socialism*. Kantianism conceives of politics in terms of moral individuals and promotes the concept of nonnationalistic, objectively determined, universally applicable law—*universal right*.[74] While their aims are beyond nation-states, both Marxism and Kantianism accept that states are key actors in world political life and must be reckoned with. What is interesting is that states are not merely things to work around but can actually be enlisted in advancing the Marxist and Kantian projects. Marx himself and later Marxists, for example, talk about establishing socialism in one state as a precursor to international socialism.[75] Some strands of Kantianism see the need to establish republican states as a precursor to a body of universally applicable law.[76] This is the central theoretical insight of arguments that see the expansion of democratic regimes leading to world peace.[77] In both doctrines, states are strategic targets, although the seizure of state power or reforming states is not the end in itself.

What is also significant about Marxism and Kantianism is that, in their efforts to engage states, nonstate actors are the key political players and the essential engines for transforming social and political conditions. For traditional Marxists, the proletariat throughout the world plays the central role in the overthrow of capitalism and establishment of international socialism.[78] For Kantians, liberal economic practices—or the "spirit of commerce—contribute to more pacific conditions and enhance the applicability of universal right.[79] Both sets of factors will have an impact on existing states, although they are not themselves part of the governmental arena.

The politics of transnational environmental groups share much with the internationalist strain to the degree that they recognize states as important actors in world politics and try to enlist them in the project of ecological well-being.[80] That is, they understand both the strategic importance of states and their ultimate secondary significance. Additionally, transnational environmental groups share this orientation insofar as they go beyond governmental forces to move states. They target and rally behind nongovernmental mechanisms to nudge states toward more environmentally responsible actions.

From an ecological standpoint, the state system is not an answer to global environmental problems. In fact, in many ways it impedes appropriate political responses to threats such as ozone depletion, the greenhouse effect, and species extinction. Nonetheless, the vast majority of people look to states to solve our ecological woes. They subscribe to some form of statism. For many activists, as long as people keep merely looking to states, they will only reinforce the major dilemmas that plague global environmental restoration and protection. States, left to themselves, will never undertake the kinds of actions necessary to respond appropriately. The internationalism of transnational environmental groups goes a long way toward moving beyond statism. Its strategy to entangle states, to not leave them alone, reveals a sensitivity to the problems involved with a project that transcends states per se, yet one whose success requires grappling with the existence of states in a fundamental way. Because the term *internationalism* highlights this dual sensitivity, I think it is helpful in conceptualizing the politics of transnational environmental activist groups.

To tie this chapter into the larger arguments of the book, internationalism is another example of how transnational environmental activist groups use the realm of global civil society to alter human behavior on the planet. In chapter 3, I showed how activists work within this domain to disseminate an ecological sensibility. I demonstrated how they manipulate ideational factors on a world scale to force people to undertake ecologically sound activities. In chapter 4, I demonstrated how transnational activist groups empower local communities with the aim of structuring successive levels of institutions to advance environmental protection. This chapter, although it focuses on the government-oriented aspect of activists, follows this line of analysis. Interdependencies are not strictly governmental in nature. Rather, they are a mix of governmental and nongovernmental processes. They are intersections of social, cultural, economic, and governmental factors. When transnational environmental activist groups work through these meshes they are pinpointing those interconnections that they themselves have some affect upon, and forge them into levers of power that will force states to act in environmentally sound ways.

In the Introduction, I suggested that one way to look at this kind of activism is the politicization of global civil society. This is an activity that makes global civil society—that slice of collective activity that takes place above the individual and below the state yet across national borders—a political arena. It consists of experimenting with numerous activities undertaken in the economic, social, and cultural spheres of life, with the intention of finding unconventional channels and mechanisms of political engagement. This chapter can be understood as presenting another aspect of politicizing global civil society although I think one can appreciate the work of transnational groups more accurately if one switches the wording. That is, certainly transnational environmental groups are politicizing global civil society in their attempts to modify state behavior. Yet, I would suggest that in this case, for conceptual reasons, it makes more sense to say that they are *civilizing* international politics. They are tying down intergovernmental politics to the constraints of global civil society. The emphasis is still on exploring the political efficacy of global civil processes although, because the discussion in this chapter focuses on the way activists engage states, it may be more fruitful to highlight the civilizing, constraining impact of environmental groups.

6   Environmental Activism and World Civic Politics

Rarer by far than originality in science or art is original-
ity in political action. And rarer still is original political
action that enlarges, rather than blights or destroys,
human possibilities.

—Jonathan Schell

Nation-states are so important in world affairs that we tend to associate their activities with the meaning of world politics itself. States enjoy the ability to reach into and influence the lives of their citizens, and thus it makes sense to see them as fundamental to international political life. Nonetheless, as this study of transnational environmental activist groups demonstrates, states do not monopolize world political activity. They share the international stage with other actors. While not as powerful as states, transnational environmental groups significantly shape widespread behavior as it relates to environmental issues. They play an important role in contemporary world environmental politics.

For most people, this is no surprise. Transnational groups such as Greenpeace—with an operating budget of over $100 million, 6 million members and offices worldwide—*must* play a part in shaping the way people interact with the natural environment; they must change the way people act toward the environment. Problems arise, however, when one seeks to understand exactly *how* activists effect change. The conventional understanding is that environmental activists are politically effective when they influence state behavior. That is, they bring about change by lobbying states to enact environmental policies. According to this view, widespread human behavior shifts because of states. They are the political agents; activists serve only as pressure groups that shape governmental policy.

A central aim of this book has been to show that this view is not so much wrong as incomplete. Transnational environmental groups not only lobby states but also directly shape the activities of other institutions, collectivities, and individuals. They do so by manipulating mechanisms of power that exist outside the realm of state-to-state relations. These include economic, social, and cultural practices that traverse countries and have an impact on public life. To use the conceptual language that is at the core of this book, Greenpeace, Friends of the Earth, and World Wildlife Fund politicize global civil society and thus engage in world civic politics.

The practice of world civic politics represents a distinct approach to global environmental governance. Most people look to states and the regimes states create to address environmental issues. They recognize that states are the primary actors in world affairs and count on them to pursue actions that advance environmental well-being. In earlier chapters I referred to this perspective as *statism* because it sees environmental governance strictly as a matter of state action. While statism has many advocates, it is not the only form or scenario of global environmental governance. For some thinkers, statism possesses inherent problems that compromise its ability to address appropriately environmental issues. For these thinkers, effective environmental governance necessitates moving political authority beyond the level of the state and shifting it upward or downward, as it were, to protect the earth's ecosystem. The two most important schools of thought along these lines are supra-statism and sub-statism, with the first calling for some form of world government and the second arguing for decentralizing governmental power.

For transnational environmental activists, statism, supra-statism and sub-statism represent, at best, partial approaches to global environmental governance. Each perspective sees the state as playing a central role—as either the answer to environmental problems or the foil against which alternative responses must be explored. Each reifies the governmental dimension of politics and sees it as the overriding focus of a sound environmental strategy. This is unfortunate because such a view bleaches out the potential of other forms of world political activity that can be and are being enlisted in the service of environmental protection. World civic politics, which takes place in global civil society, has its own role to play and has already brought about changes with regard to environmental issues that are outside the capacity of nation-states. World civic politics, then, is a parallel type of activity. It does not replace statism nor categorically dismiss supra-statism and sub-statism. Rather, it represents a qualitatively different approach to global environmental governance.

In this book I have tried to delineate the distinct approach of world civic politics by differentiating it from statism, supra-statism, and sub-statism and by describing its quality as a particular form of political practice. In this concluding chapter, I want to pull together the diverse themes presented along these lines in the empirical chapters and explore their meaning for scholarship in international relations and for attempts to address global or transboundary environmental issues. This involves, foremost, reflecting upon the notion of agency in world affairs and arguing that proper appreciation for its diverse forms—especially its civic mode—calls upon one to expand one's notion and practice of world politics itself.

NON STATE-ORIENTED
WORLD POLITICAL ACTIVITY

One alternative conceptualization to the state system as a mechanism for solving global problems is supra-statism. This scheme seeks to create some sort of world government. It suggests an institutional presence at the global level that will determine worldwide environmental policy and enforce it through law backed by force. The central notion is that the present world of sovereign states is too fragmented and competitive to address global ecological problems successfully and thus some meta-institutional presence is necessary to do the job.

Earlier I contrasted this with the work of Greenpeace. Greenpeace pitches its efforts toward the global arena, although its orientation is not to create an institutional presence. Rather, it tries to change consciousness. Its work is process rather than institutionally oriented. It seeks to alter people's minds and actions throughout the world by disseminating an ecological sensibility. For Greenpeace, consciousness itself can be a form of governance. It can modify human practices and thus represents an important avenue for creating conditions that will direct the behavior of others. Greenpeace targets this dimension of collective life. To highlight the distinction between Greenpeace's work and the supra-statist approach, I suggested we think of Greenpeace's politics as a form of globalism rather than supra-statism.

The same contrast exists between sub-statism and the political efficacy of World Wildlife Fund. Sub-statists feel the problem with the present state system is that the nation-state is too big to address environmental dangers successfully. It is too insensitive to the local dynamics of environmental harm and thus unable to achieve genuine environmental protection. Instead, sub-statists prescribe breaking it into smaller units within which people can be more aware of and responsive to the environmental consequences of their actions. In one formulation, sub-statists call for establishing bioregions that forge communities around ecological rather than formally governmental boundaries.

World Wildlife Fund also works at the local level insofar as it undertakes many of its projects within Third World villages but pursues a fundamentally different strategy than sub-statism. WWF is not concerned with constructing an institutional, administrative presence at the local level that would replace the nation-state or even refashion communities in a way that would necessarily shift citizen's loyalty. Rather, it seeks to carry out ecological work at this level with the hope of empowering local people to protect their own environments and, in turn, to exert pressure upward through the international system for more ecologically sound practices worldwide. The emphasis is on just that, *practices*, not institutional arrangements. Like Greenpeace, WWF is committed to a process approach to ecological restoration and protection, not an institutional one. To accentuate the difference between the work of WWF and sub-statist approaches, I referred to WWF's efforts as a form of localism versus sub-statism.

Finally, the same sort of contrast exists between statism and the orientation of Friends of the Earth. Statism assumes that because states are the main actors in world affairs, they themselves will undertake or at least orchestrate all significant political activity directed at environmental protection. Domestically, states will pass legislation and work nationally for environmental well-being; transnationally and globally, they will create regimes to coordinate international environmental efforts. Statism, in other words, sees state action as central to environmental protection and trusts that states will effectively respond to environmental challenges.

FOE works at the level of states, as it were, but is less confident about states' ability to address environmental problems on their own. While it understands that states can do much to protect the environment, it nevertheless feels that such effort can go only so far. Operating within a self-help, relatively competitive system, states have difficulty fashioning long-term, promising responses to environmental issues. According to FOE, states must be forced, from the outside, to undertake environmental protection. This involves, to be sure, lobbying— that is, directly pressuring governments to adopt environmentalist objectives—and FOE, like other transnational groups, engages in such effort. Additionally, however, because of limitations associated with lobbying, FOE also mobilizes other pressures on states. Foremost, it turns the interdependencies of world affairs into mechanisms that promote environmental protection. As state activity intersects with these interdependencies, states are forced, often unwittingly, to pursue environmentally sound practices. The difference between statism and FOE's orientation, then, turns on where political activity is located. Statism places it in the state; world politics is about interstate relations and thus focusing on the institution of the nation-state is the key to environmental protection. Alternatively, FOE locates it outside the state, at the intersections of transnational economic, social, and cultural activities. It understands that the processes of world collective life are themselves forms of governance and can be enlisted in the service of environmental protection. To highlight this approach, I called it *internationalism* to distinguish it from *statism*.

What is important to recognize in all these transnational, process-oriented efforts is that the mechanisms environmental groups activate are forms of governance. They have control over people's lives. Put differently, they represent ways of ordering widespread human action. For this reason, it is important to see the work of transnational groups as genuinely political even though their efforts do not emanate from a state or take on the coercive character of its policies and instrumentalities.

WORLD CIVIC POLITICS

In his book, *Green Political Thought*, Andrew Dobson outlines the degrees to which activists engage in what he calls *extra-parliamentary* activities. In doing so, he points out how the situations of their political work and modes of expression are often outside formal channels of state power.[1] While Dobson refers predominantly to domestic activists, his insight is helpful for understanding the politics of transnational environmental groups.

Greenpeace's most significant form of political activity is disseminating an ecological sensibility. It works to spread an appreciation for the dangers of ecological destruction to communities throughout the world and to inspire as many people as possible to adopt practices that are "kind" to the planet. Its target, then, is the thin but increasingly emerging global cultural sphere. Through presenting alternative images of the environment, bearing witness, criticizing predominant modes of conduct, and exposing ecological atrocities, Greenpeace tries to express itself through communication technologies to joggle the minds of the world. It literally speaks through the air waves spanning the globe. Satellite dishes, fax machines, video cameras, and electronic mail services are the tools of Greenpeace's political action. And these are, essentially, entry ways into the world media network. Global communication systems are the sites for disseminating an ecological sensibility.

World Wildlife Fund targets particular spaces for its activities. WWF applies itself, in many of its projects, to villages in the Third World. These can be thought of as the capillaries of anti-ecological practices; they sit at the most local of levels of ecological destruction. WWF focuses on this level because even though the actions of villagers reflect a response to global pressures to exploit the environment, power relations in these local circumstances are much different than at the heights of global political, economic, and social structures; these areas represent the extremities of global power relations and as such are more fragile and thus amenable to alternative practices. Third World, local situations represent the arena of WWF's politics.

Friends of the Earth also targets a particular site for its activities. It focuses on the intersections of collective life. Local, national, and international processes represent different spheres of political experience; likewise corporate, social, and governmental arenas represent different areas of collective activity. In between these spheres there are "switching points." These are places where one type of social life interacts with another. When a company sells a product, for example, it does so in numerous settings that span municipal, regional, and at times international jurisdictions. Similarly, when a multilateral bank loans money abroad it works through different state and corporate agencies in a number of countries. At each step a type of translation takes place where one discourse meets another, where different sets of rules apply. At these intersections there is an "opening" for political manipulation and expression. To be sure, Friends of the Earth focuses on these with the aim of cornering states, but the quality and location of the site is outside, as it were, the state system per se.

The predominant aspect of all these sites is that they sit outside the formal control of states. They are far from the halls of parliaments, offices of congresspeople, residences of world leaders. To be sure, states compete for control of these arenas. They have not yet, and seemingly cannot, however, monopolize the dynamics of these regions. These arenas are, then, semiautonomous. They represent domains that can be co-opted or colonized by different actors. Transnational ecological groups work to win control of these openings.

In addition to extra-parliamentary sites of activity, transnational groups use modes of effectiveness that are not informed by the predominant type of power exercised by the state. The main efficacy of state power emanates from its ability to set-up laws and ensure compliance through force. Activists use a different type of power. When Greenpeace disseminates an ecological sensibility, WWF empowers local residents, and Friends of the Earth entangles states in interdependencies, they enlist the instrumentalities of information, image-making, exposés, hands-on ecological restoration and protection, and corporate education. These aim to change consciousness, empower local residents, and create mechanisms of accountability. What is important to notice is that these actions have their own "pull" on people. They involve channeling human behavior in significant ways.

An important characteristic of these forms of power is that they do not work against the will of others but rather in tandem with it. Another way of saying this is that they work through persuasion rather than coercion; they enlist subjects in their own subjectification rather than bringing physical force to bear on them. This form of power will be familiar to readers acquainted with the thought of people such as Russell, Foucault, or Lukes.[2] These authors emphasize the constitutive character of dominant discourses, norms, moral codes, and knowledge. These conditions exert pressure on people and, by instilling certain understandings, determine human practices. Transnational ecological groups implicitly recognize the dynamics of these forms of power and devise strategies for enlisting them.

When one discusses extra-parliamentary sites and modes of political activity, one implicitly suggests that there is an arena of collective life that sits outside of state constraints yet that plays a part in political affairs. In domestic regimes this is increasingly recognized as the sphere of civil society. Civil society is that slice of collective life that takes place above the individual yet below the state. It is the sphere of economic, cultural, and social interaction as opposed to state activity. Contemporary usage stems in large part from Hegel insofar as he defined civil society in contrast to the state.[3] For Hegel, civil society is an arena wherein people pursue their particular private interests in common independent from, and in fact prior to, the state.[4] Many contemporary theorists also understand civil society in contrast to the state and identify it with forms of collective interaction that are voluntary, spontaneous, customary, and nonlegalistic in nature. The state, on the other hand, is a complex network of governmental institutions that operate formally and legalistically.

This distinction, while overly formulaic, is helpful for conceptualizing a politically relevant sphere of collective life that is separate from the state. When transnational groups manipulate cultural symbols to disseminate an ecological sensibility, or work with and empower local inhabitants, or carry out protests, boycotts, and educational campaigns at the intersections of collective life, they undertake activities outside of formal statist structures. At these times they operate in the sphere of customary, spontaneous, and voluntary collective life and not within the governmental, legalistic one. In fact, it is only because such activities can be undertaken in this sphere that environmental groups even have a chance to utilize them. They are forms of activity that are not already monopolized by the state. (To be sure, states engage in similar activities and thus vie for control of civil society. Short of totalitarian regimes, however, they have been unsuccessful at capturing all the dynamics of civil life).[5]

When environmental activist groups work in this realm they are deliberately politicizing the social, economic, and cultural spheres of transnational life. They are constituting global civil society in a way that makes it an explicit arena of political activity. The idea is to discover unconventional levers of power and employ nontraditional modes of action that can affect, if only unevenly and imperfectly, the global community. This involves teasing out and utilizing nonformal channels and mechanisms of political engagement or, put differently, manipulating forms of power that are generally considered ineffectual in the larger context of so-called genuine politics.

One of the best articulations of this form of politics comes out of the theoretical work on new social movements. In the early 1980s, German sociologists coined the phrase, *Neue soziale Bewegungen*, to describe the activities of contemporary human rights, peace, feminist and environmental activist groups operating in Western democracies. They claimed that these organizations represented qualitatively new forms of political activity and therefore needed to be distinguished from interest groups, political parties, and traditional labor movements.[6]

The literature is heterogeneous on what exactly constitutes the novelty of these movements. Some theorists suggest that new movements are ideologically distinct from their predecessors. New movements are preoccupied less with issues of economic growth, distribution of resources, and security, and more with "quality of life" concerns.⁷ Others identify the novelty in the organizational structure of activist groups. They point out that many groups stress participatory decision making, a decentralized structure and opposition to bureaucratic procedures.⁸ Still others contend that new movements are qualitatively distinct because they arise in response to fundamentally new challenges facing postindustrial societies. Contradictions in the welfare state, extensive colonization of the "life world" by governments, and global threats such as large-scale ecological collapse are overwhelming governmental capabilities and therefore give way to social movement activity.⁹

In addition to these insights, a number of theorists point to the tactics new movements use to induce change as the distinguishing characteristic of new social movements. Instead of merely lobbying government officials, participating in governmental commissions and supporting candidates for office, new movements employ a wide repertoire of actions. These include activities such as nature walks, film showings, conferences, and citizen tribunals.¹⁰ The important aspect of these types of activities is their unofficial, extra-parliamentary character. It is this last characteristic of new movements that signals the civil dimension of their politics.

To date, most of the literature on new social movements focuses on domestic polities. It examines the politicization of civil society within, for example, Germany, France, Poland, or the United States.¹¹ In my view, and as I hope the case studies discussed earlier demonstrate, it is possible to witness and theorize about *world* civic politics. In fact, this is exactly the kind of activity transnational ecological groups undertake. Greenpeace, World Wildlife Fund, and Friends of the Earth have offices in more than one country and pursue actions across state boundaries. They work literally worldwide. In addition to lobbying diverse governments, they work through global civil society to shape widespread practices. Activists see the political world as an expansive field of activity populated by a host of potential and actual mechanisms able to change human behavior. The state system is only one among many of such mechanisms.

TRANSNATIONAL ENVIRONMENTAL GROUPS AND WORLD POLITICS

Throughout this book I have been emphasizing how scholars privilege the state in their analysis of world political events. This is particularly true of political realists but is also the case with other intellectual traditions within international relations. I am obviously not the first to question such an approach to world politics. As mentioned in the Introduction, in the 1970s numerous scholars in the field did so. My work differs significantly, however, from this earlier critique. The key argument of people like Keohane, Nye, Mansbach, Ferguson, Lampert, Vernon, and Feld was that nonstate actors were growing in number and importance and that some of their actions were having an equal or larger impact on world affairs than nation-states. At a minimum, they claimed that transnational relations play into the calculations of states and force them to change their politics. At the extreme, they argued that NGOs, such as multinational corporations, would eventually eclipse the state as the preeminent political force in the world.[12]

In my view, this early work got off to a good start. One of its most significant contributions was to raise the issue of the meaning of politics itself. In their edited volume, *Transnational Relations and World Politics*, Keohane and Nye offer the following definition of politics, which reflects their sensitivity to transnational actors. Politics "refers to relationships in which at least one actor consciously employs resources, both material and symbolic, including the threat or exercise of punishment, to induce other actors to behave differently than they would otherwise behave."[13] They go on to emphasize that such actors need not be states.[14] While this is significant and commendable in that it raises the issue of politics itself, Keohane and Nye quickly skirt a frontal attack on the predominant view in the way they formulate the importance of this notion of politics. In the introductory essay, Keohane and Nye pose themes for the entire volume. The first and most important one is to assess the net effect of transnational relations on the ability of governments to operate. That is, transnationalism must be understood in terms of its effects on state behavior. Like much of the early transnational work, then, Keohane and Nye raise the minimalist position, viz., transnationalism is meaningful to the degree it plays into the calculations of states and induces them to modify policy. Furthermore, their second thematic question has to do with the influence of transnationalism for the study of international relations. Keohane and Nye want to know if an increase in transnational activity calls sufficient attention away from the state as the primary unit of analysis. Should scholars shift from a focus on states to multinational corporations, the Catholic Church, and so forth? Here the problem is less one of privileging the state so much as willing to set up the debate in either/or terms: either the state is the primary mover and shaker of world affairs or not.[15] This reflects the maximalist position, viz., that NGOs have replaced the state as the most important actor in world affairs.

By raising the issue of transnationalism in terms of minimalist and maximalist positions, scholars in general, and Keohane and Nye in particular, unnecessarily restrict their understanding of politics. In the first instance, they treat the state as a giant cash register: everything that happens politically must be paid for in its terms. Consequently, all other activities that could be politically relevant, although not having to do with the state per se, get bleached out of observation and analysis. In the second instance, setting up the debate in terms of the unit of analysis issue is problematic because it fashioned the controversy in a way that the transnationalist critique could be easily beaten back by state-centric thinkers. Indeed, people only had to prove the superior efficacy of the state to dismiss the transnationalist challenge. As I mentioned in the first chapter, this is exactly what happened. Gilpin, Waltz, Sullivan, and others argued successfully that the state was not going away as the central unit of analysis and still very much dictates world politics. This took a tremendous amount of wind out of the transnationalists' sails.

My own work uses the transnationalist critique as a point of departure but asks a different set of questions about world politics. Instead of getting into a debate about relative impact, I essentially bracket the role of states in world politics and examine nonstatist activities for their own richness and effectiveness. In 1970, commenting on recent scholarship on transnationalism, Peter Evans claimed that, "It is not interesting to exclude traditional state behavior and then study the residual only."[16] I disagree. I think it is extremely interesting to put questions of state activity in parentheses and explore the actual work of nonstate actors to appreciate the full spectrum of world politically relevant activity. Otherwise, all activity becomes obscured in the shadow of the state. This is important not to "knock off" the primary unit of analysis but to allow for fuller accounts of world political events and to introduce people to alternative forms of political activity that will expand and deepen the repertoire of responses to global problems. In short, while I appreciate the transnationalist critique and use it as a springboard for inquiry, I assume a different orientation. I utilize it to give voice to nonstatist forms of world politics and to emphasize their efficacy. I use it to illuminate world civic politics.

My hope is that an appreciation for this dimension of global experience will sensitize people to the limitations of the traditional understanding of *world politics*. First, it should cast into doubt the equation of *world* with *state system*. The world, in a political context, is more than the existence of nation-states. States represent only the most obvious components. Indeed, understanding *world* simply as a configuration of states is like believing a university is made up solely of students and professors. Such an understanding may reveal much about a university; it certainly will not provide a full or even accurate account of the dynamics at work or the institution's overall character. Emphasizing world civic politics, then, highlights the importance of nonstate actors and thus complicates the view that the word *world*, in the phrase *world politics*, refers simply to states or, as it is traditionally understood, international.

Second, an appreciation for nonstate forces adds depth to the notion of *politics*. Traditionally, politics is associated with the governing capabilities of government. Insofar as governments are those institutions endowed with the authority to make binding decisions applicable to the whole community, politics—as the use of power in a public context—is understood as the way governments implement such decisions. This view is problematic insofar as it equates authority with a particular notion of governance, viz., law backed by force. Governance entails more than this. As Lukes, Foucault, and others remind us, there are forms of power associated with norms, rules, and discourses that actually shape people's desires, conceptions, understandings of the self, and, ultimately, behavior without recourse to law or the threat of physical coercion. My emphasis on nonstate forces in world affairs borrows from these conceptions of power and extends them to the realm of world collective life. These more subtle forms of power have political consequences, and we should take them seriously if for no other reason than they can and are being used to create conditions that order the actions of people within a world context. Thus, it is imperative to expand our notion of politics itself (in the phrase *world politics*) to include nonstatist modes of governance.

The field of international relations is not blind to the importance of redefining world politics. An appreciation for the host of nonstate activities has led to a spate of formulations that try to capture such a sensitivity. Rosenau suggests referring to the field as *post–international relations*; Ashley offers the term *post–modern world politics*; Richard Falk talks, at times, of *postrealism*. I support these efforts. My own contribution to them is in putting the processes and activities involved in world civic politics into sharp relief. I give voice to a politics that is relevant in a world context but that takes place outside the grasp of states.

CONCLUSION

Expanding the concept of world politics is important for scholarly inquiry. I wish I could say, however, that the stakes involved were of such limited scope. Unfortunately, the problems of the globe do not turn merely on academic debate or the refinement of intellectual categories. The world faces dangers that threaten all living beings on earth. The greenhouse effect, ozone depletion, species extinction, and so forth are threats to the very infrastructure that supports life on earth. Addressing them properly is one of the most considerable responsibilities currently facing human beings. The task at hand involves changing widespread behavior. It is a first order challenge of politics.

By expanding the notion of world politics through an appreciation of its civil dimension, my hope is that I have not only provided an accurate understanding of transnational environmental activism but have also offered intellectual support for further fashioning global civil society into an arena within which people can advance the project of environmental protection. In many ways, transnational environmental groups work in global civil society without really knowing it. (One is reminded of Molière's remark that for forty years he did not know that he was speaking in prose.) They engage in world civic politics often unaware of the dynamics involved or the promise of more sustained effort directed immediately at global civil society. My work tries to provide some insight along these lines. It delineates the quality of agency at work and reflects upon the practice of world civic politics as an approach to global environmental governance. It suggests that, in addition to existing efforts, the dynamics of global civil society can be further explored and engaged to address environmental dangers. The instruments of power available in this realm can operate in places where states cannot go, and the quality of governance thus enlisted can shape widespread behavior in a different mode than the instrumentalities of states. To be sure, in itself, world civic politics is not an answer to environmental issues—there is no single answer. It represents, however, a significant contribution to environmental protection efforts. It can work at the local, international, and global levels of collective life to steer humanity toward more ecologically sensitive ways of living with, enjoying, and sustaining our blue-green planet.

Notes

CHAPTER 1

1. William Ophuls, *Ecology and the Politics of Scarcity: Prologue to a Political Theory of the Steady State* (San Francisco: W.H. Freeman, 1977), 1.

2. Julie Fisher, *The Road From Rio: Sustainable Development and the Nongovernmental Movement in the Third World* (Westport, CT: Praeger, 1993): xi; Alan Durning, "Action at the Grassroots: Fighting Poverty and Environmental Decline," *Worldwatch Paper 88* (Washington, DC: 1989): 10.

3. In 1994, the budgets of Greenpeace International and World Wildlife Fund were roughly $100 and $200 million, respectively. UNEP's budget was roughly $75 million.

4. In 1994, WWF had over 6 million members worldwide, Greenpeace had 4.8 million, and FOE had roughly 500,000.

5. Important exceptions include Thomas Princen and Matthias Finger, *Environmental NGOs and World Politics: Linking the Local and the Global* (London: Routledge 1994) and R. B. J. Walker, *One World/Many Worlds* (Boulder, CO: Lynne Rienner Publishers, 1988).

6. Kevin Stairs and Peter Taylor, "Non-Governmental Organizations and the Legal Protection of the Oceans: A Case Study," in Andrew Hurrell and Benedict Kingsbury, eds., *The International Politics of the Environment* (Oxford: Oxford University Press, 1992).

7. P. J. Sands, "The Role of Non-Governmental Organizations in Enforcing International Environmental Law," in W. E. Butler, ed., *Control over Compliance with International Law* (Netherlands: Kluer Academic Publishers, 1991).

8. Oran Young, *International Cooperation: Building Regimes for Natural Resources and the Environment* (Ithaca, NY: Cornell University Press, 1989): 41.

9. On the concept of global civil society, see Richard Falk, *Explorations at the Edge of Time: The Prospects for World Order* (Philadelphia: Temple University Press, 1992); Ronnie Lipschutz, "Restructuring World Politics: The Emergence of Global Civil Society," *Millennium 21*, no. 3 (Winter 1992).

10. According to Hegel, the thinker most associated with distinguishing the state and civil society, civil society exists above the family and below the state. (T. M. Knox, trans., *Hegel's The Philosophy of Right* (London: Oxford University Press, 1967) I deliberately amend this formulation because I am persuaded by thinkers such as Pateman that the family is an arena of political and social life. (Carole Pateman, "Feminist Critiques of the Public/Private Dichotomy," in S. Benn and G. Gauss, eds., *Public and Private in Social Life*, Canberra and London: Croom Helm, 1983.)

11. I follow a Hegelian understanding of civil society that includes the economy within its domain. Later formulations, most notably those offered by Gramsci and Parsons, introduce a three-part model that differentiates civil society from both the state and the economy. See Talcott Parsons, *The System of Modern Societies* (Englewood Cliffs, NJ: Prentice-Hall, 1971); and Antonio Gramsci, *Prison Notebooks* (New York: International Publishers, 1971). For an extensive argument to exclude the economy from civil society, see Jean Cohen and Andrew Arato, *Civil Society and Political Theory* (Cambridge, MA: MIT Press, 1992).

12. There is no single, static definition of civil society. The term has a long, continually evolving, if not contestable, conceptual history. For an appreciation of the historical roots of the term and usage in various contexts, see Cohen and Arato, *Civil Society and Political Theory*; and John Keane, "Despotism and Democracy: The Origins and Development of the Distinction Between Civil Society and the State 1750–1850," in John Keane, ed., *Civil Society and the State: New European Perspectives* (London: Verso, 1988).

13. See, for example, Alberto Melucci, "The Symbolic Challenge of Contemporary Movements," *Social Research 52*, No. 4 (Winter 1985); Jurgen Habermas, "What Does a Crisis Mean Today? Legitimation Problems in Late Capitalism," in Steven Seidman, ed., *Jurgen Habermas on Society and Politics*, Boston: Beacon Press 1989; Claus Offe, "Challenging the Boundaries of the Institutional Politics: Social Movements Since the 1960s," in Charles Maier, ed., *Changing Boundaries of the Political*, Cambridge: Cambridge University Press, 1987.

14. Alain Touraine, *Anti-Nuclear Protest: The Opposition to Nuclear Energy in France* (Cambridge: Cambridge University Press, 1983); Fritjof Capra, Charlene Spretnak and Wulf-Rudiger Lutz, *Green Politics* (New York: Duffon, 1984); Joyce Gelb, "Feminism and Political Action," in

Russell Dalton and Manfred Kuechler, eds., *Challenging the Political Order: New Social and Political Movements in Western Democracies* (New York: Oxford University Press, 1990).

15. Harry Boyte, "The Pragmatic Ends of Popular Politics," in Craig Calhoun, ed., *Habermas and the Public Sphere* (Cambridge, MA: MIT Press, 1992); Richard Shaull, *Heralds of a New Reformation: The Poor of South and North America* (New York: Orbis Books, 1984) especially chapter 8; Anil Agarwal, "Ecological Destruction and the Emerging Patterns of Poverty and People's Protests in Rural India," *Social Action* 35, no. 1 (Jan./Mar. 1985); Ponna Wignaraja, ed., *New Social Movements in the South* (London: Zed Books, 1992).

16. See Adam Michnik, *Letters from Prison and Other Essays*, trans. Maya Latynski (Berkeley: University of California Press, 1985); Vaclav Havel, *Open Letters: Selected Writings 1965–1990*, ed. Paul Wilson (New York: Knopf, 1991).

17. As a moment of social organization, civil society sits at an intermediate stage of collective development that finds its apex at the state. The state, however, does not supersede civil society but rather contains and preserves it in order to transform it into a higher level of social expression. The state's job, as it were, is to enable universal interest—in contrast to private interest—to prevail. In Hegelian terminology, it allows for the realization of ethical life in contrast to the abstract morality available in civil society. See T. M. Knox, trans., *Hegel's Philosophy of Right.*

18. Alexis de Tocqueville, *Democracy in America*, ed. J. P. Mayer (New York: Doubleday, 1969), 520.

19. David Held, "Introduction: Central Perspectives on the Modern State," in David Held, ed., *States and Societies* (New York: New York University Press, 1983).

20. Antonio Gramsci, *Prison Notebooks*, 238ff.

21. Timothy Mitchell, "The Limits of the State: Beyond Statist Approaches and Their Critics," *American Political Science Review* 85, no. 1 (March 1991); See also, Craig Calhoun, "Introduction: Habermas and the Public Sphere," in Craig Calhoun, ed., *Habermas and the Public Sphere*, Cambridge, MA: MIT Press, 1992. 21ff.

22. Much of my thinking about the application of Gramscian categories to international relations, and the distinction between the state-system and global civil society was influenced by Stephen Gill, ed., *Gramsci, Historical Materialism and International Relations* (Cambridge: Cambridge University Press, 1993).

23. Chapter 5 specifically focuses on the interface between global civil society and the state system and describes how transnational activist groups specifically manipulate global civil society to influence the conditions of interstate relations.

24. Cicero calls the commonwealth *res publica* meaning that it is the property of the people. See Sheldon Wolin, *Politics and Vision: Continuity and Innovation in Western Political Thought* (Boston: Little, Brown and Company, 1960), 2.

25. On the distinction between governance and government, see Oran Young, George Demko, and Kilaparti Ramakrishna, "Global Environmental Change and International Governance," pamphlet, Dartmouth College, 1991. See also, James Rosenau, "Governance, Order and Change in World Politics," in James Rosenau and Ernst-Otto Czempiel, eds., *Governance Without Government* (Cambridge: Cambridge University Press, 1992).

26. My categorization of world order reforms into supra-statism and sub-statism borrows significantly from David Orr and Stuart Hill, "Leviathan, the Open Society and the Crisis of Ecology," in David Orr and Marvin Soroos, eds., *The Global Predicament: Ecological Perspectives on World Order* (Chapel Hill: University of North Carolina Press, 1979). While these authors concentrate on domestic environmental politics, their discussion of the centralizing and decentralizing tendencies in environmental thinking provides a helpful framework to think about world order reforms in the service of the environment.

27. Further explication of how world civic politics differs from statism, supra-statism, and sub-statism is provided in chapter 2.

28. For examples using human rights NGOs, see David Forsythe, *Human Rights and World Politics*, 2nd ed. (Lincoln: University of Nebraska Press, 1989); Kathryn Sikkink, "Human Rights Issue–Networks in Latin America," *International Organization* 47, no. 3 (Summer 1993); Robert Goldman, "International Humanitarian Law: Americas Watch's Experience in Monitoring Internal Armed Conflict," *The American University Journal of International Law and Policy* 9, no. 1 (Fall 1993). For studies along these lines using environmental NGOs, see Kevin Stairs and Peter Taylor, "Non-Governmental Organizations and the Legal Protection of the Oceans: A Case Study," in Hurrell and Kingsbury, eds., *International Politics*; Barbara Bramble and Gareth Porter, "Non-Governmental Organizations and the Making of U.S. International Environmental Policy," in Hurrell and Kingsbury, eds., *International Politics*; Lee Kimble, "The Role of Non-Governmental Organizations in Antarctic Affairs," in Christopher Joyner and Sudhir Chopra, eds., *The Antarctica Legal Regime* (Dordrecht: Martinus Nijhoff Publishers, 1988); Gareth Porter and Janet Brown, *Global*

Environmental Politics (Boulder, CO: Westview Press, 1991); P. J. Sands, "The Role of Non-Governmental Organizations in Enforcing International Environmental Law," in Butler, ed., *Control Over Compliance.* For examples using peace groups, see Thomas Rochon, *Mobilizing for Peace: Antinuclear Movements in Western Europe* (Princeton, NJ: Princeton University Press, 1988); David Cortright, *Peace Works: The Citizen's Role in Ending the Cold War* (Boulder, CO: Westview Press, 1993).

29. In 1967, for example, General Motors had production facilities in 24 countries and total sales of $20 billion. This total was greater than the GNP of all but 14 of the 124 members of the United Nations at the time. Also in 1967, Standard Oil of New Jersey had facilities in 45 countries and total sales of $13.3 billion. See Gerald Sumida, "Transnational Movements and Economic Structures," in Cyril Black and Richard Falk, eds., *The Future of the International Legal Order*, vol. 4 (Princeton, NJ: Princeton University Press, 1972), 553.

30. For example, see George Modelski, "The Corporation in World Society," London Institute of World Affairs, *The Year Book of World Affairs 1968* (New York: Praeger, 1968); Werner Feld, *Nongovernmental Forces and World Politics: A Study of Business, Labor and Political Groups* (New York: Praeger, 1972); Abdul A. Said and Luiz Simmons, eds., *The New Sovereigns: Multinational Corporations as World Powers* (Englewood Cliffs, NJ: Prentice-Hall, 1975).

31. Robert Angell, *Peace on the March: Transnational Participation* (New York: Van Nostrand Reinhold, 1969); Robert Keohane and Joseph Nye, eds., *Transnational Relations and World Politics* (Cambridge, MA: Harvard University Press, 1972), especially essays by J. Bowyer Bell, Ivan Vallier, and Donald Warwock; Seyom Brown, *New Forces in World Politics* (Washington, DC: Brookings Institution, 1974); Richard Mansbach, Yale Ferguson, and Donald Lampert, *The Web of World Politics: Non State Actors in the Global System* (Englewood Cliffs, NJ: Prentice-Hall, 1976).

32. For attempts to discuss the world political system with special emphasis on transnational activity, see Werner Feld, *International Relations: A Transnational Approach* (California: Alfred Publishing, 1979); Johan Galtung, *The True Worlds: A Transnational Perspective* (New York: The Free Press, 1980).

33. For an overview of the debate, see Ray Maghroori and Bennett Ramberg, eds., *Globalism Versus Realism: International Relations' Third Debate* (Boulder, CO: Westview Press, 1982); K. J. Holsti, *The Dividing Discipline: Hegemony and Diversity in International Theory* (Boston MA: Allen and Unwin, 1985).

34. Robert Gilpin, "The Politics of Transnational Economic Relations," in Keohane and Nye, eds., *Transnational Relations*; and Robert Gilpin, "Three Models of the Future," in George Modelski, ed., *Transnational Corporations and World Order* (San Francisco: W.H. Freeman, 1979).

35. Kenneth N. Waltz, *Theory of International Politics* (New York: Random House, 1979).

36. Michael Sullivan, "Transnationalism, Power Politics and the Realities of the Present System," in Maghroori and Ramberg, eds., *Globalism Versus Realism*.

37. See, for example, Werner Feld and Robert Jordan, *International Organizations: A Comparative Approach* (New York: Praeger, 1983); Harold Jacobson, *Networks of Interdependence: International Organizations and the Global Political System* (New York: Knopf, 1984).

38. The term *sovereignty at bay* comes from the title of Raymond Vernon's book of 1971 (New York: Basic Books). It is important to note that Vernon was not a proponent of the transnationalist challenge, although the title of his book provided a catchphrase to encapsulate the host of arguments put forward by thinkers who were part of that challenge. See Raymond Vernon, "*Sovereignty at Bay*: Ten Years After," *International Organization* 35, no. 3, 1981.

39. In the words of John Ruggie, it could be said that the debate died down because scholars studied NGOs with an eye toward "institutional substitutability." If NGOs could not substitute for the state as an institutional entity, then they become politically irrelevant. Ruggie argues that such a mind-set bleaches out much phenomena that is responsible for long-term political change. See John Gerald Ruggie, "Territoriality and Beyond: Problematizing Modernity in International Relations," *International Organization* 47, no. 1 (Winter 1993): 143.

40. See K. J. Holsti, "Mirror, Mirror on the Wall, Which are the Fairest Theories of All," *International Studies Quarterly* 37, no. 3 (September 1987); Yosef Lapid, "The Third Debate: On the Prospects of International Theory in a Post-Positivist Era," *International Studies Quarterly* 33, no. 3 (September 1989). For one of the more provocative books to emerge from reflection on the third debate see R. B. J. Walker, *Inside/Outside: International Relations as Political Theory* (Cambridge: Cambridge University Press, 1993).

41. James Rosenau, *Turbulence in World Politics* (Princeton, NJ: Princeton University Press, 1990).

42. R.B.J. Walker, *One World/Many Worlds* (Boulder, CO: Lynne Reinner, 1988).

43. Falk, *Explorations at the Edge of Time.*

44. Here it is relevant to point out that the phrase *nongovernmental organization* itself reveals a state-centric understanding of politics.

45. Greenpeace's headquarters are in the Netherlands, WWF's are in Switzerland, and FOE's are in the United States.

46. For a comprehensive study of environmental NGOs in the developing world, with important references to transnational ones, see Fisher, *Road From Rio.*

47. For examples of how earlier peoples, known for practicing sound ecological practices, often used unsustainable and degrading methods of agriculture, see J. Donald Hughes, *Ecology in Ancient Civilization* (Albuquerque: University of New Mexico Press, 1975) and Gordon M. Day, "The Indian as an Ecological Factor in the Northeastern Forest," *Ecology 34*, no. 2 (April 1953): 329–346.

CHAPTER 2

1. Told by Stephen Levine, *Who Dies! An Investigation of Conscious Living and Conscious Dying* (New York: Anchor Books, 1982), 68.

2. Jessica Tuchman Mathews, "Introduction and Overview," in Jessica Tuchman Mathews, ed., *Preserving the Global Environment: The Challenge of Shared Leadership* (New York: W. W. Norton, 1991) 25.

3. On the distinction between domestic, international, and global environmental problems, see Paul Wapner, "On the Global Dimension of Environmental Challenges," *Politics and the Life Sciences* 13, no. 2 (August 1994).

4. For a short but comprehensive description of UNEP's history and activities, see Peter Haas, *International Environmental Issues: An ACUNS Teaching Text* (New York: Academic Council on the United Nations, 1991), 6-10.

5. Hilary French, "After the Earth Summit: The Future of Environmental Governance," *Worldwatch Paper 107* (Washington, DC: Worldwatch Institute, 1992): 6.

6. For an overview of UNCED, see Peter Haas, Marc Levy, and Edward Parson, "How Should We Judge UNCED's Success?" *Environment 34*, no. 8 (October 1992); and idem, "A Summary of the Major Documents Signed at the Earth Summit and the Global Forum," *Environment 34*, no. 8 (October 1992).

7. For an extended discussion of the way the state system has responded positively to global ecological threats, see Linda Starke, *Signs of Hope: Working Toward Our Common Future* (New York: Oxford University Press, 1990), especially chapter 3. See also Peter Haas, Robert Keohane, and Marc Levy, eds., *Institutions for the Earth: Sources of Effective International Protection* (Cambridge, MA: MIT Press, 1993); Caroline Thomas, *The Environment in International Relations* (London: Royal Institute of International Affairs, 1992); Peter Haas, *Saving the Mediterranean: the Politics of International Environmental Protection* (New York: Columbia University Press, 1990); Oran Young, *International Cooperation: Building Regimes for Natural Resources and the Environment* (Ithaca, NY: Cornell University Press, 1989); and Daniel Barstow Magraw and James W. Nickel, "Can Today's International System Handle Transboundary Environmental Problems?" in *Upstream/Downstream: Issues in Environmental Ethics* (Philadelphia: Temple University Press, 1990).

8. Norman Myers, *The Sinking Ark: A New Look at the Problems of Disappearing Species* (New York: Pergamon, 1979), 307. Quoted in Ariel Lugo, "Estimating Reductions in the Diversity of Tropical Forest Species," in E. O. Wilson, ed., *Biodiversity* (Washington DC: National Academy Press, 1988).

9. John Ryan, "Conserving Biological Diversity," in Lester Brown et al., eds., *State of the World 1992* (New York: W. W. Norton, 1992), 9.

10. Christopher Flavin, "Carbon Emissions Steady," in Lester Brown et al., eds., *Vital Signs 1992: The Trends that are Shaping Our Future* (New York: W. W. Norton, 1992), 61.

11. Lester Brown, "The New World Order," in Brown et al., *State of the World 1992*, 3.

12. Evidence of global environmental decline can be found in an abundance of sources. Some of the most useful include World Resources Institute, *World Resources 1994–1995*, New York: Oxford University Press 1994; Lester Brown, Hal Kane, and David Roodman, *Vital Signs 1994: The Trends that are Shaping Our Future* (New York: W. W. Norton, 1994).

13. Barbara Jancar-Webster, "Eastern Europe and the Former Soviet Union," in Sheldon Kamieniecki, ed., *Environmental Politics in the International Arena: Movements, Parties, Organizations and Policy* (Albany: State University of New York Press, 1993).

14. Louise Schubert, "Environmental Politics in Asia," in Kamieniecki, *Environmental Politics in the International Arena*.

15. Lynton Caldwell, *International Environmental Policy* (Durham, NC: Duke University Press, 1992), 17.

16. Ibid.

17. Hilary French, "After the Earth Summit: The Future of Environmental Governance," *Worldwatch Paper 107* (Washington, DC: Worldwatch Institute, 1992); J. H. Asubel and D. G. Victor, "Verification of International Environmental Agreements," *Annual Review of Energy and Environment* no. 17 (1992); Abram Chayes and Antonia Chayes, "On Compliance," *International Organization* 47, no. 2 (Spring 1993).

18. Earth Island Institute, "On the Front Line of the Whale Wars," *Earth Island Journal* 9, no. 3 (September 1993): 6.

19. Marydele Donnelly, "Cayman Turtle Farm Cited for International Trade Infractions, *Marine Turtle Newsletter*, no. 58 (July 1992). See also Katherine Bishop, "Suit Seeks Ban on Shrimp from Nations Not Protecting Sea Turtles," *New York Times*, 25 March 1992.

20. Todd Steiner, Mark Heitchue, and Henry W. Ghriskey, "Banned Sea Turtle Products Still Exported from Mexico," in *Earth Island Journal* 9, no. 3 (Summer 1994): 9.

21. At present, there are a number of efforts trying to evaluate compliance. The most extensive is a three-year project supported by the International Institute for Applied Systems Analysis, which is studying the domestic implementation of international environmental agreements. For a short review of this research project, see David Victor, "Implementation and Effectiveness of International Environmental Commitments," *Options* (Spring 1994): 6–7.

22. "The Earth Summit Debacle," *The Ecologist* 22, no. 4 (July/August 1992): 122.

23. United Nations, *Survey of Existing Agreements and Instruments and Its Follow-up*, A/Conf.151/PC/103, 20 January 1992. See also Lawrence Susskind and Connie Ozawa, "Negotiating More Effective International Environmental Agreements," in Andrew Hurrell and Benedict Kingsbury, eds., *The International Politics of the Environment* (Oxford: Oxford University Press, 1992).

24. United Nations, *Survey of Existing Agreements*, 9.

25. John Stanley, "Treaty Compliance Can't Be Enforced," *Earth Summit Times*, 9 June 1992, p. 7. See also Lee Kimball, *Forging Internatonal Agreement: Strengthening Inter-Governmental Institutions for Environment and Development*, Washington DC: World Resources Institute, 1992, p 45. For an overall assessment of international reporting, see General Accounting Office, *International Environment: International Agree-*

ments are Not Being Well Monitored, CGAO/RCED-92-43, 27 January 1992.

26. Caldwell, *International Environmental Policy*, 18. Similar assessments are made by others. For example, Philip Shabecoff claims that, "The record of international cooperation to protect the environment is indeed a slender one, providing but a flimsy diplomatic and institutional foundation from which to confront the profound threats facing the planet." See Philip Shabecoff, *A Fierce Green Fire: The American Environmental Movement* (New York: Hill and Wang, 1993), 190. He also maintains that, "[T]he response of the international community remains inadequate to the gravity of the crisis." Ibid., 191.

27. World Commission on Environment and Development, *Our Common Future* (New York: Oxford University Press, 1987), 29.

28. Waltz refers to this characteristic as the ordering principle of the system. See Kenneth Waltz, *Theory of International Politics* (New York: Random House, 1979), 88.

29. One of the best sustained discussions about the conflict between the national interest and the well-being of the earth is Robert Johansen, *The National and the Human Interest* (Princeton, NJ: Princeton University Press, 1980). See also Gerald Mische and Patricia Mische, *Toward a Human Order: Beyond the National Security Straightjacket* (New York: Paulist Press, 1977).

30. Fred Pearce, "How Green Was Our Summit?" *New Scientist* 134, no. 1827 (27 June 1992): 13.

31. Quoted in Fred Pearce, "Earth at Mercy of National Interests, *New Scientist* 134, no. 1826 (20 June 1992): 4.

32. Robert Tucker, *Politics as Leadership* (New York: Columbia University Press, 1981), 129.

33. Garrett Hardin and Mancur Olson provide the best theoretical accounts of their mismatch. See Garrett Hardin, "The Tragedy of the Commons," in Garrett Hardin and John Baden, eds., *Managing the Commons* (San Francisco: W. H. Freeman, 1977); Mancur Olson, *The Logic of Collective Action* (Cambridge, MA: Harvard University Press, 1971); and Mancur Olson, *The Rise and Decline of Nations: Economic Growth, Stagflation and Social Rigidities* (New Haven, CT: Yale University Press, 1982).

34. George Modelski, *Principles of World Politics* (New York: The Free Press, 1972), 76.

35. W. Warren Wagar, *The City of Man* (New York: Penguin Books, 1963), 221.

36. Much of the following is informed by discussion with and reading papers written by Deudney. See especially Daniel Deudney, "Toward Planetary Republicanism" (unpublished manuscript, Princeton University, Princeton, NJ, 1988), 19ff.

37. See G. A. Borgese, *Foundations of a World Republic* (Chicago: University of Chicago Press, 1953). This was conceived as an explanation of the principles and purposes of the Committee's Preliminary Draft of a World Constitution that itself appears in the appendix. For a detailed discussion of the committee's proposal and a review of other maximalist schemes, see Wagar, *City of Man*, 225–228.

38. Grenville Clark and Louis Sohn, *World Peace Through World Law* (Cambridge, MA: Harvard University Press, 1966). A second important dispute among minimalists and maximalists was the relationship between world order community and world government. See Robert Hutchins, "Constitutional Foundations for World Order," in Richard Falk and Saul Mendlovitz, eds., *The Strategy of World Order*, vol. 1 (New York: World Law Fund, 1966). For a detailed discussion of this dispute, see Deudney, "Planetary Republicanism," 19ff.

39. David Mitrany, *A Working Peace System* (Chicago: University of Chicago Press, 1966).

40. Ernst Haas, *Beyond the Nation-State* (Stanford, CA: Stanford University Press, 1968).

41. Garrett Hardin, *Exploring New Ethics for Survival* (New York: Viking Press, 1972), 18.

42. Ibid., 129–130.

43. Ibid., 121.

44. Robert Heilbroner, *An Inquiry into the Human Prospect: Looked at Again for the 1990s* (New York: W.W. Norton, 1991), 164.

45. Ibid., 106.

46. Ibid., 179.

47. Interpreters understand, however, that Hardin and Heilbroner implicitly prescribe world government. See K. J. Walker, "The Environmental Crisis: A Critique of Neo-Hobbesian Responses," *Polity* 11, no. 3 (Fall 1988); and Marvin Soroos, "The Future of the Environment," in Kenneth Dahlberg et al., eds., *Environment and the Global Arena* (Durham, NC: Duke University Press, 1985).

48. William Ophuls and A. Stephen Boyan, *Ecology and the Politics of Scarcity Revisited: The Unraveling of the American Dream* (New York: W. H. Freeman, 1992), 210.

49. Ibid., 219.

50. For a detailed discussion of world government schemes, with special attention to questions of feasibility and theoretical validity, see Inis Claude, Jr., *Swords into Plowshares* (New York: Random House, 1964), especially chapter 18.

51. Many of these points are made by David Orr and Stuart Hill, "Leviathan, the Open Society and the Crisis of Ecology," in David Orr and Marvin Soroos, eds., *The Global Predicament: Ecological Perspectives on World Order* (Chapel Hill: University of North Carolina Press, 1979), 17–20. See also Robyn Eckersley, *Environmentalism and Political Theory: Toward an Ecocentric Approach* (Albany: State University of New York Press, 1992), 145-178.

52. Peter Kropotkin, "Selections from *Fields, Factories and Workshops Tomorrow*," in Robin Clark, ed., *Notes for the Future: An Alternative History of the Past Decade* (New York: Universe Books, 1975).

53. Robert Mason et al., "Comments on *Bioregionalism and Watershed Consciousness*," *Professional Geographer* 39, no. 1 (1987): 67. For an interesting discussion on Kropotkin's notion of "mutual aid" and its relation to contemporary environmental issues, see Theodore Roszak, *The Voice of the Earth* (New York: Simon & Schuster, 1992) 228ff.

54. It is significant to note that there has been little scholarly work done on the contribution of anarchist thought to world politics. An important exception is Richard Falk, *The End of World Order* (New York: Holmes and Meier, 1983).

55. Leopold Kohr, *The Breakdown of Nations* (London: Routledge and Kegan Paul, 1957), ix.

56. Ibid., 57.

57. Eckersley, *Environmentalism*, 145–146.

58. According to John Dryzek, those who advocate radical decentralization as a response to environmental challenges share an aversion to hierarchy, not necessarily the scale of political organization. They object to power relations that enable some people to dominate others—a form of exploitation that is morally problematic and that encourages the development of bureaucratic structures that operate according to instrumental rationality. To be sure, hierarchy is central to the eco-anarchist analysis;

nonetheless, even Dryzek links it to issues of scale insofar as he asserts that the experience of living in small-scale, self-sufficient societies provides a high sensitivity and responsiveness to environmental pressures and can promote practical reason (in contrast to instrumental rationality). See John Dryzek, *Rational Ecology: Environmental and Political Economy* (Oxford: Basil Blackwell, 1987), 217ff.

59. Theodore Roszak, *Person/Planet: The Creative Disintegration of Industrial Society* (New York: Anchor Press, 1978), 32.

60. Ibid., 37.

61. Ibid., 38.

62. It should be noted that Schumacher does not call for the dissolution of large organizations so much as advocate smallness within present large-scale structures. See, generally, E. F. Schumacher, *Small is Beautiful: Economics as if People Mattered* (New York: Harper & Row, 1973). See also George McRobie, *Small is Possible* (New York: Harper & Row, 1981).

63. See Kirkpatrick Sale, *Dwellers in the Land: The Bioregional Vision* (Philadelphia: New Society Publishers, 1991), 42. See also Lester Milbrath, *Envisioning a Sustainable Society: Learning Our Way Out* (Albany: State University of New York Press, 1989), 211–216.

64. Peter Berg, "Strategies for Reinhabiting the North California Bioregion," *Seriatim: Journal of Ecotopia* 1, no. 3 (1977): 2. Quoted in James Parsons, "On Bioregionalism and Watershed Consciousness," *The Professional Geographer* 37, no. 1 (February 1985).

65. Sale, *Dwellers in the Land*, 53.

66. Ibid., 118.

67. For a more poetic expression of bioregionalism, see Gary Snyder, *The Practice of the Wild* (Berkeley, CA: North Point Press, 1990).

68. Peter Berg, "Growing Bioregional Politics," *RAIN* (July/August 1985): 14. Quoted in Eckersley, *Environmentalism*, 168.

69. Carrying Capacity Network, "Check-up and Connections," *Clearinghouse Bulletin* 2, no. 8 (October 1992): 5.

70. Kohr, *Breakdown of Nations*, 197.

71. Ibid., 199.

72. See Eckersley, *Environmentalism*, 171–172.

CHAPTER 3

1. The role of norms, values, and discourse among states have been studied extensively by liberals and neo-liberals. See, for example, Judith Goldstein and Robert Keohane, eds., *Ideas and Foreign Policy: Beliefs, Institutions and Political Change* (Ithaca, NY: Cornell University Press, 1993); Peter Haas, Robert Keohane and Marc Levy, eds., *Institutions for the Earth: Sources of Effective International Protection* (Cambridge, MA: MIT Press, 1993); Oran Young, *International Cooperation: Building Regimes for Natural Resources and the Environment* (Ithaca, NY: Cornell University Press, 1989); Joseph Nye, "Nuclear Learning and U.S.-Soviet Security Regimes," *International Organization* 41 no. 3 (Summer 1987). For a comprehensive overview of international liberal theory, see Mark W. Zacher and Richard A. Matthew, "Liberal International Theory: Common Threads, Divergent Strands," in Charles W. Kegley, Jr., ed., *Controversies in International Relations Theory: Realism and the Neo-Liberal Challenge* (New York: St. Martins Press, 1995).

2. See, for example, Richard Falk, *Explorations at the Edge of Time: Prospects for World Order* (Philadelphia: Temple University Press, 1992); Elise Boulding, *Building a Global Civic Culture* (New York: Teachers College Press, 1988); Hedley Bull and Adam Watson, eds., *The Expansion of International Society* (Oxford: Clarendon, 1984); Harold Lasswell, Daniel Lerner, and Hans Speier, eds., *Propaganda and Communication in World History*, 3 vols. (Honolulu: University Press of Hawaii, 1979, 1980); Lyman Bryson et al., eds., *Foundations of World Organization: A Political and Cultural Appraisal* (New York: Harper and Brothers, 1952); F. Ernest Johnson, ed., *World Order: Its Intellectual and Cultural Foundations* (New York: Harper and Brothers, 1945). It is tempting to categorize this literature as a form of sociological liberalism that emphasizes the transformative effect of transnational contacts and coalitions. I choose not to, however, because most instances of sociological liberalism measure transformative effects in terms of changes in state behavior or in the formulation of state interest. See Joseph Nye, "Neorealism and Neoliberalism," *World Politics* 40 (January 1988).

3. Christopher Stone, "The Law as a Force in Shaping Cultural Norms Relating to War and the Environment," in Arthur Westing, ed., *Cultural Norms, War and the Environment* (New York: Oxford University Press, 1988), 79.

4. While recently awareness has spread significantly, ideas of environmental protection have been around for centuries. See David Lowenthal, "Awareness of Human Impacts: Changing Attitudes and Emphasis," in B. L. Turner et al., eds., *The Earth as Transformed by Human Action* (New York: Cambridge University Press, 1990).

5. Robert Hunter, *Warriors of the Rainbow: A Chronicle of the Greenpeace Movement* (New York: Holt, Rinehart and Winston, 1979), 7. On the origins of Greenpeace, see Michael Brown and John May, *The Greenpeace Story* (Ontario: Prentice-Hall Canada, 1989); Greenpeace, *Overview of Greenpeace Origins* [Pamphlet] (Vancouver, Canada: Greenpeace, 1988); Peter Dykstra, "Greenpeace," *Environment* 28, no. 6 (July/August 1986); The Sunday Times Insight Team, *Rainbow Warrior: The French Attempt to Sink Greenpeace* (London: Hutchinson, 1986), 112ff; Greenpeace, "Fifteen Years at the Front Lines," *Greenpeace Examiner* 11, no. 3 (October/December 1986).

6. Hunter, *Warriors of the Rainbow*, 96.

7. Ibid., 61.

8. Wallace Turner, "A.E.C. Dismantles Aleutian Test Site of Controversial '71 Underground Blast," *New York Times*, 5 August 1972, A29.

9. Harry Eckstein, "A Cultural Theory of Social Change," *American Political Science Review* 82, no. 3 (September 1988), 790.

10. J. Glenn Gray, *The Warriors: Reflections on Men in Battle* (New York: Harper & Row, 1970), 29.

11. See, Brown and May, *The Greenpeace Story*.

12. *Greenpeace Magazine* 14, no. 6 (Nov.-Dec. 1989): 19.

13. Quoted in Rik Scare, *Eco-Warriors: Understanding the Radical Environmental Movement* (Chicago: Noble Press, 1990), 104.

14. For a more extensive discussion of environmental politics and Antarctica, see chapter 5.

15. R. B. J. Walker, *One World/Many Worlds* (Boulder, CO: Lynne Rienner Publishers, 1988), 93.

16. "Time Passes, As Clinton Adopts Anti-Chlorine Stance," *Greenpeace* 2, no. 2 (March/April/May 1994): 1.

17. See, "Chlorine Protesters Scale Time Building," *New York Times*, 12 July 1994.

18. Hunter, *Warriors of the Rainbow*, 229.

19. Sociological perspectives on world politics have proliferated over the past few years. See, for example, Leslie Sklair, *Sociology of the Global System* (Baltimore: Johns Hopkins University Press, 1991); David Jacobson, "The States System in the Age of Rights" (Ph.D. dissertation, Princeton University, 1991).

20. Joseph Gusfield, "Social Movements and Social Change: Perspectives on Linearity and Fluidity," in vol. 4 of Louis Kriesberg, ed., *Research in Social Movements, Conflicts and Change* (Greenwich, CT: JAI Press, 1981), 326.

21. Paul Joseph, *Peace Politics* (Philadelphia: Temple University Press, 1993), 147–151; Johan Galtung, "The Peace Movement: An Exercise in Micro-Macro Linkages," *International Social Science Journal* 40, no. 117 (August 1989): 377–382.

22. Gusfield, "Social Movements and Social Change. . .," 326. It is interesting to note how Gusfield's formulation sounds dated in part because of the feminist movement's efforts since the time of his writing.

23. Herbert Blumer, "Social Movements," in Barry McLaughlin, ed., *Studies in Social Movements: A Social Psychological Perspective* (New York: The Free Press, 1969).

24. See Casey Miller and Kate Swift, *The Handbook of Nonsexist Writing,* (New York: Barnes & Noble, 1980).

25. See Michael Hanchard, "Identity, Meaning and the African-American," *Social Text* 24 (Winter 1990).

26. This list does not include environmental parties, such as the Costa Rican Ecology Party, which do not formally call themselves *green*.

27. For a comprehensive discussion of the meaning of the word *green*, see Jonathan Porritt, *Seeing Green: The Politics of Ecology Explained,* (Oxford: Basil Blackwell, 1984). See also, Wolfgang Rudig, "Green Party Politics Around the World," *Environment* 33, no. 8 (October 1991).

28. See, for example., Susie Orbach, *Fat is a Feminist Issue,* (New York: Berkley Books, 1978), 28.

29. See, for example, Susan Faludi, *Backlash: The Undeclared War Against American Women* (New York: Crown, 1991); and Naomi Wolf, *The Beauty Myth: How Images of Beauty are Used Against Women* (New York: William Morrow, 1991).

30. The politicization of hitherto private issues is also evident in the move by nonliberal feminist theorists to open up the family and the household to scholarly concern of students of international relations. For these theorists, women's activities in all domains have political significance. The problem is that, until recently, their activities were marginalized because they were private rather than public. See Cynthia Enloe, *Bananas, Beaches and Bases: Making Feminist Sense of International Politics* (Berkeley: University of California Press, 1990); and V. Spike Peterson, ed., *Gendered States: Feminist (Re)Visions of International Relations Theory*

(Boulder, CO: Lynne Reinner, 1992); Katharine H. S. Moon, "International Relations and Women: A Case-Study of U.S.–Korea Camptown Prostitution, 1971–1976" (Ph.D. dissertation, Princeton University, June 1994).

31. An important exception is in times of plagues, epidemics, and pandemics, such as AIDS.

32. Environmental Defense Fund and Robert Boyle, *Malignant Neglect* (New York: Knopf, 1979), ix.

33. Samuel Hays, *Beauty, Health, and Permanence: Environmental Politics in the U.S. 1955–1985*, (Cambridge: Cambridge University Press, 1987), 26. See also, Philip Shabecoff, *A Fierce Green Fire: The American Environmental Movement* (New York: Hill and Wang, 1993), 105–106.

34. Hays, *Beauty, Health, and Permanence*, 26ff. See also, Shabecoff, *A Fierce Green*, 105ff.

35. Ralph Turner, "The Theme of Contemporary Social Movements," in R. Serge Denisoff and Robert Merton, eds., *The Sociology of Dissent* (New York: Harcourt Brace Jovanovich, 1974).

36. Richard Falk, "The Special Challenge of Our Time: Cultural Norms Relating to Nuclearism," in Arthur Westing, ed., *Cultural Norms, War and the Environment* (Oxford: Oxford University Press, 1988), 59. See also, Falk, *Explorations at the Edge of Time*, 190.

37. Frederick Buttle, "Age and Environmental Concern: A Multivariate Analysis," *Youth and Society* 10, no. 3 (March 1979).

38. Kent Van Liere and Riley Dunlap, "The Social Bases of Environmental Concern: A Review of Hypotheses, Explanations and Empirical Evidence," *Public Opinion Quarterly* 44, no. 2 (Summer 1980).

39. John Gillroy and Robert Shapiro, "The Polls: Environmental Protection," *Public Opinion Quarterly* 50, no. 2 (Summer 1986). On concern for the environment in general, see Richard Niemi, John Mueller, and Tom Smith, *Trends in Public Opinion: A Compendium of Survey Data* (New York: Greenwood Press, 1989), 79. According to a 1992 Gallup poll, the average U.S. citizen considers himself or herself an environmentalist. Cited in "This is Your Life, In General," *New York Times*, 26 July 1992, E5. See also, Riley Dunlap, George Gallup, Jr. and Alec Gallup, "Of Global Concern: Results of the Health of the Planet Survey," *Environment* 53, no. 9 (November 1993).

40. See especially, *Time Magazine*, 2 January 1989; and *National Geographic* 174, no. 6 (December 1988).

41. Clyde Haberman, "Pope Harshly Rebukes Lands that Foster Ecological Crisis, *New York Times*, 12 December 1988. See also, Jessica Tuchman Mathews, "Introduction and Overview," Jessica Tuchman Mathews, ed., *Preserving the Global Environment: The Challenge of Shared Leadership*, New York: W. W. Norton, 1991.

42. See Nannelore Wass, "Editorial" [Commemorating ten years of publishing *Death Studies*], *Death Studies* 10, no. 1 (1986); and, Stephen Levine, *Who Dies? An Investigation of Conscious Living and Conscious Dying* (New York: Anchor Books, 1982).

43. Hays, *Beauty, Health, and Permanence*, 27.

44. There is a robust literature on the relationship between environmental protection and sustainable development in the South. See, for example, Shridath Ramphal, *Our Country, The Planet: Forging a Partnership for Survival* (Washington, DC: Island Press, 1992); and Anil Agarwal and Sunita Narain, *Towards a Green World*, New Delhi, India: Centre for Energy and Environment, 1992.

45. See, for example, Durwood Zaelke, Paul Orbuch, and Robert Housman, eds., *Trade and the Environment: Law, Economics and Policy* (Washington, DC: Island Press, 1993).

46. See, for example, Robert Bullard, ed., *Unequal Protection: Environmental Justice and Communities of Color* (San Francisco: Sierra Club, 1994).

47. On the evolution of environmental concern, with particular emphasis on early concern for litter and the aesthetic dimension, see Robert Paehlke, *Environmentalism and the Future of Progressive Politics* (New Haven, CT: Yale University Press, 1989). For a similar type of change within the environmental movement, see also Ronald Faich and Richard Gale, "The Environmental Movement From Recreation to Politics," *Pacific Sociological Review* 14, no. 3 (1971). For a general description of the broadening of environmental concern, see Shabecoff, *A Fierce Green Fire*.

48. At an international conference in October 1989, the major producers of CFCs pledged to eliminate the use of CFCs in their worldwide operations. This was before CFCs were formally banned in 1992 in association with the Montreal Protocol. See "More Companies to Phase Out Peril to Ozone," *New York Times*, 11 October 1989. See also Barbara Bramble and Gareth Porter, "Non-Governmental Organizations and the Making of U.S. International Environmental Policy," in Andrew Hurrell and Benedict Kingsbury, eds., *The International Politics of the Environment* (Oxford: Oxford University Press 1992). An electric utility company in Connecticut has pledged to plant 52 million trees in Guatemala to offset carbon dioxide that is being released by its new coal-burning plant. See "U.S. Utility Turns

to Guatemala to Aid Air," *New York Times*, 11 October 1988. For an extended discussion, see Mark Trexler, Paul Faeth, and John Kramer, *Forestry As A Response to Global Warming: An Analysis of the Guatemala Agroforestry and Carbon Sequestration Project* (Washington, DC: World Resources Institute, 1989).

49. Linda Starke, *Signs of Hope: Working Toward Our Common Future*, (New York: Oxford University Press, 1990), 2, 105.

50. Matthew Wald, "Guarding the Environment: A World of Challenges," *New York Times*, 22 April 1990, A1.

51. Dunlap, Gallup, and Gallup, "Of Global Concern . . .,".

52. David Day, *The Whale War* (San Francisco: Sierra Club Books, 1987), 157. For a somewhat critical view of "Operation Breakout," see Tom Rose, *Freeing the Whales: How the Media Created the World's Greatest Non-Event* (New York: Birch Lane Press, 1989). It is interesting to note that, according to Rose, technological innovations in media services enabled a billion people to watch "operation breakout." A little more than half this number watched Neil Armstrong walk on the moon. See Rose, *Freeing the Whales*, 299.

53. See, for example, Bruce Smart, *Beyond Compliance: A New Industry View of the Environment* (Washington, DC: World Resources Institute, 1992).

54. Jeremy Warford and Zeinab Partow, "Evolution of the World Bank's Environmental Policy," *Finance and Development* 26 (December 1989).

55. See Council on Economic Priorities, *Shopping for a Better World* (New York: Council on Economic Priorities, 1988); and Cynthia Pollock Shea, "Doing Well by Doing Good," *World Watch* 2, no. 6 (Nov./Dec. 1989). According to a 1991 Gallup poll, 28 percent of the U.S. public claimed to have "boycotted a company's products because of its record on the environment" and, according to Cambridge Reports, in 1990, 50 percent of respondents said that they were "avoiding the purchase of products by a company that pollutes the environment"—an increase of 28 percent since 1987. Quoted in Riley Dunlap, "Public Opinion in the 1980s: Clear Consensus: Ambiguous Commitment," *Environment* 33, no. 8 (October 1991): 36.

56. U.S. Bureau of the Census, *Statistical Abstract of the United States 1993* (Washington DC: Bureau of the Census, 1993), p. 227, table 372.

57. The average price per seal pup skin dropped from $23.09 in 1979 to $10.15 in 1983. By 1985, it dropped to $6.99, which reflects the EEC ban

of 1983. See George Wenzel, *Animal Rights, Human Rights* (Toronto: University of Toronto Press, 1991), p. 124, table 6.12.

58. Wenzel, *Animal Rights, Human Rights*, 52–53; "Baby Harp Seals Spared," *Oceans* 21 (March/April 1988); See generally, David Day, *The Environmental Wars* (New York: Ballantine Books, 1989), 60–64.

59. This example also demonstrates that environmental activists are not always accurate in assessing environmental threats and guaranteeing the ecological soundness of the sensibility they wish to impart. There is no evidence that harp seals were ever an endangered species and this is particularly troubling because the activities of Greenpeace, and others produced severe social dislocation and hardship for communities as far away as Greenland, Iceland, and the Faroe Islands, as well as the coastal communities of Newfoundland and Baffin Island. See Oran Young, *Arctic Politics: Conflict and Cooperation in the Circumpolar North* (Hanover, NH: University Press of New England, 1992), 128; J. Allen, "Anti-Sealing as an Industry," *Journal of Political Economy* 87 (April 1979); Leslie Spence et al., "The Not So Peaceful World of Greenpeace," *Forbes*, 11 November 1991; and Wenzel, *Animal Rights, Human Rights*.

60. David Elkins and Richard Simeon, "A Cause in Seach of its Effect, or What Does Political Culture Explain?" *Comparative Politics* 11, no. 2 (January 1979): 136.

61. See Peter Haas, "Introduction: Epistemic Communities and International Policy Coordination," *International Organization* 46, no. 1 (Winter 1992); and Peter Haas, *Saving the Mediterranean: The Politics of International Environmental Cooperation* (New York: Columbia University Press, 1990).

62. For a discussion of the relevance of communitarianism for international relations, see Chris Brown, *International Relations Theory: New Normative Approaches* (New York: Columbia University Press, 1992).

63. According to Lasswell, Lerner, and Speier, the crucial factor in innovations in communications technologies is the separation of the messenger from the message. This advancement increases the speed and scope of communication. See Lasswell, Lerner and Speier, "Introduction," *Propaganda and Communication in World History*, 1, 11.

64. UNESCO, *Statistical Yearbook 1988* (Paris: UNESCO, 1988), table 10–25.

65. UNESCO, *Statistical Yearbook 1991* (Paris: UNESCO, 1991), table 6–9.

66. In addition to television, the explosive proliferation of fax machines, electronic mail capabilities, and telephones is increasing cultural diffusion and greater contact between people throughout the world. For studies of how this is promoting greater capabilities for environmental and development activists in the South, see Sheldon Annis, "Evolving Connectedness Among Environmental Groups and Grassroots Organizations in Protected Areas of Central America," *World Development* 20, no. 4 (1992); and Sheldon Annis, "Giving Voice to the Poor," *Foreign Policy* 84 (Fall 1991).

67. The content of such diffusion is largely generated and dominated by the West. Thus, the ideas that whip around the planet today, including the mainstays of environmentalism, are significantly Western in origin and may represent cultural imperialism more than worldwide cultural expression. See, Vandana Shiva, "The Greening of Global Reach," *The Ecologist* 22, no. 6 (Nov./Dec. 1992). See also, Herbert Schiller, *Mass Communications and the American Empire* (Boulder, CO: Westview Press, 1992).

68. Ivo Duchacek, *The Territorial Dimension of Politics Within, Among and Across Nations* (Boulder, CO: Westview Press, 1986), xiii.

69. Walter Truett Anderson, *To Govern Evolution* (New York: Harcourt Brace Jovanich, 1987), 281.

70. See generally, Hamid Mowlana, *Global Information and World Communication: New Frontiers in International Relations* (White Plains, NY: Longman, 1986); and Howard Frederick, *Global Communications and International Relations* (Belmont, CA: Wadsworth Publishing Company, 1993).

71. Philippe de Seynes, "Prospects for a Future Whole World," *International Organization* 26, no. 1 (1972): 1.

72. Christopher Stone, "The Law as a Force in Shaping . . .," 67.

73. Andre Brink, *Writing in a State of Siege: Essays on Politics and Literature* (New York: Summit Books, 1983), 53.

74. Quoted in Ibid.

CHAPTER 4

1. Lester Brown et al., *Vital Signs: Trends That Are Shaping Our Future* (New York: W.W. Norton, 1992), 110.

2. Riley Dunlap, George Gallup, Jr., and Alec Gallup, "Of Global Concern: Results of the Health of the Planet Survey," *Environment* 53, no. 9 (November 1993).

3. Robin Broad, "The Poor and the Environment: Friends or Foes?" *World Development 22*, no. 6 (1994).

4. The IUCN is a hybrid of governmental and nongovernmental bodies. It was created in October 1948 with the task of promoting preservation of wildlife and the natural environment through research, education, legislation, and proposed legislation. (It was originally established as the International Union for the Protection of Nature (IUPN).)

5. On the early years of WWF see Peter Scott, ed., *The Launching of the Ark* (London: Collins, 1964); Peter King, *Protect Our Planet: An Anniversary View from the World Wildlife Fund* (London: Quiller Press, 1986); and John McCormick, *Reclaiming Paradise: The Global Environmental Movement* (Bloomington: Indiana University Press, 1989).

6. Outside the United States, Australia, and Canada, WWF is known as the World Wide Fund for Nature. This is apparently easier to translate into other languages.

7. There are a few WWF offices that cannot raise enough money to carry out domestic projects. WWF–U.S. and WWF–International subsidize these offices.

8. On the evolution of WWF's conception of conservation, see Charles de Haes, "Director General's Report," in *World Wildlife Fund Yearbook 1980–81* (Gland, Switzerland: WWF, 1981); and Chris Rose, "Over 25 years: A Review of WWF Projects 1961–1986," in *World Wildlife Fund Yearbook 1986–87* (Gland, Switzerland: WWF, 1987).

9. These figures were provided by Wildlife Foundation, Washington, DC, May 1990. They are all rough estimates.

10. Quoted in Roger Stone, "Zambia's Innovative Approach to Conservation," *World Wildlife Fund Letter* 7, 1989, 3.

11. For detailed descriptions of WWF's ADMADE program, see World Wildlife Fund, *The Africa and Madagascar Program*, [pamphlet] (Washington DC: WWF, 1994); Nyamaluma Conservation Camp Lupande Development Project, *Zambian Wildlands and Human Needs Newsletter*, Mfuwe, no. 5, March 1990; Gabrielle Walters, "Zambia's Game Plan," *Topic Magazine* [U.S. Information Agency], no. 187, 1989; Stone, "Zambia's Innovative Approach to Conservation"; World Wildlife Fund, *Project Folder* #6152.

12. For detailed descriptions of WWF's Kilum mountain project, see *Proceedings of the Workshop on Community Forest/Protected Area Man-*

agement, sponsored by the Ministry of Environment and Forests (Yaounde, Cameroon: 12–13 October 1993); International Council for Bird Preservation, *Interim Report to WWF–U.S.: January 1992–June 1992* (London: WWF, 1992); Roger Stone, "The View from Kilum Mountain," *WWF Letter,* no. 4, 1989; Michael Wright, "People-Centered Conservation: An Introduction," *Wildlands and Human Needs: A Program of World Wildlife Fund,* [pamphlet] (Washington, DC: WWF, 1989); World Wildlife Fund, *Project Folder* #6250; World Wildlife Fund, *1988–1988 Annual Report on the Matching Grant for a Program in Wildlands and Human Needs* (Washington, DC: WWF, 1989), U.S. AID Grant #OTR-0158-A-00-8160-00.

13. World Bank, *World Development Report 1992,* (New York: Oxford University Press, 1992), 196.

14. Brazil had a total of $121,110 million in external public and private debt in 1992. See World Bank, *World Development Report 1994* (New York: Oxford University Press, 1994), 200–201.

15. Thomas Lovejoy, "Aid Debtor Nation's Ecology," *New York Times,* 4 October 1984.

16. Debt-for-equity exchanges have only worked between countries and private creditors (i.e., they have not included debts owed to the World Bank or the International Monetary Fund). The bulk of Third World debt, especially in Latin America, however, is owed to private creditors.

17. There are a number of reasons debtor countries are willing to redeem secondary debt at face value for equity within their own countries. First, repayment will be used in domestic programs and not simply go toward foreign debt payments. Second, local currency debt does not accrue hard currency interest. It may, in fact, accrue domestic currency interest through bonds and so forth, but this is usually less severe than foreign, hard currency interest. Finally, local countries have more control over domestic interest rates, and thus debt converted into local currency is easier to manage. Redeeming secondary debt at face value, then, is a matter of debt alleviation not debt reduction. For advantages more generally, see Kathryn Fuller and Douglas Williamson, "Debt-for-Nature Swaps: A Means of Funding Conservation in Developing Countries," *International Environmental Reporter* 11, no. 5 (5 May 1988); Marjorie Sun, "Swapping Debt for Nature," *Science* 239 (March 1988).

18. In some cases, debtor nations will negotiate a discount on the debt when it is converted into local currency, although so far this has been the exception rather than the rule.

19. Debt-for-nature swaps have been so attractive that since 1989 the U.S. government, through its Enterprise for the Americas Initiative, and a number of European countries, have experimented with using it to relieve

trade debt. See Peter Passell, "Washington Offers Mountain of Debt to Save the Forests," *New York Times*, 22 January 1991, C 1, 9; and Fred Pearce, "Europe Discovers the Debt-for-Nature Swap," *New Scientist* 133, no. 1803 (11 January 1992).

20. On debt-for-nature swaps in general see Amin Sarkar and Karen Ebbs, "A Possible Solution to Tropical Troubles? Debt-for-Nature Swaps," *Futures* 24, no. 7 (September 1992); Fuller and Williamson, "Debt-for-Nature Swap."; Anant Sundaram, "Swapping Debt for Debt in Less-Developed Countries: A Case Study of a Debt-for-Nature Swap in Ecuador," *International Environmental Affairs* 2, no. 1 (Winter 1990); WWF, "Debt-for-Nature Swaps: A New Conservation Tool, *WWF Letter* 1, no. 1, 1988; Noel Gerson and Diana Page, eds., *Debt For Nature: An Opportunity* (Washington, DC: WWF, 1989). There are a number of significant criticisms of debt-for-nature swaps. These range from encroachments on sovereignty and stimulating inflation to eco-imperialism. See, for example, Jorge Barreiro, "Debt Swap Condemned by Latin American NGOs," *Earth Island Journal* 7, no. 3 (Summer 1992); Rhona Mahoney, "Debt-for-Nature Swaps: Who Really Benefits?" *The Ecologist* 22, no. 3 (May/June 1992).

21. Michael Wright, *The Wildlands and Human Needs Program: Program Statement and Framework* (Washington, DC: World Wildlife Fund, April 1990), 3.

22. Peter Evans, Dietrich Rueschemyer, and Theda Skocpol, eds., *Bringing the State Back In* (New York: Cambridge University Press, 1985). The state, in this literature, is generally understood as "a set of administrative, policy, and military organizations headed, and more or less coordinated by an executive authority." See Theda Skocpol, *States and Social Revolutions* (Cambridge: Cambridge University Press, 1979), 29.

23. As Skocpol puts it, "They [social theorists] examine states *in relation to* particular kinds of socioeconomic and political environments populated by actors with given interests and resources." See Theda Skocpol, "Bringing the State Back In: Strategies of Analysis in Current Research," in Peter Evans, Dietrich Rueschemyer, and Theda Skocpol, eds., *Bringing the State Back In* (New York: Cambridge University Press, 1985), 19.

24. See, for example, Alfred Stepan, *State and Society: Peru in Comparative Perspective* (Princeton, NJ: Princeton University Press, 1978); David Collier, ed., *The New Authoritarianism in Latin America* (Princeton, NJ: Princeton University Press, 1979); Atul Kohli, ed., *The State and Development in the Third World* (Princeton, NJ: Princeton University Press, 1986).

25. Naomi Chazan, Robert Mortimer, John Ravenhill, and Donald Rothchild, eds. *Politics and Society in Contemporary Africa* (Boulder, CO: Lynne Reinner, 1988); Donald Rothchild and Naomi Chazan, eds. *The Precarious Balance* (Boulder, CO: Westview Press, 1988); Thomas Callaghy, *The State-Society Struggle: Zaire in Contemporary Perspective* (New York: Columbia University Press, 1984); Michael Bratton, "Beyond the State: Civil Society and Associational Life in Africa," *World Politics* 44, no. 3 (1989).

26. Joel Migdal, *Strong Societies and Weak States: State-Society Relations and State Capabilities in the Third World* (Princeton, NJ: Princeton University Press, 1988).

27. Goran Hyden, "African Social Structure and Economic Development," in Robert Berg and Jenifer Whitaker, eds., *Strategies for African Development* (Berkeley: University of California Press, 1986).

28. For a discussion of the "economy of affections," see Goran Hyden, *No Shortcuts to Progress: Africa Development Management in Perspective* (London: Heinemann, 1983).

29. Migdal, *Strong Societies and Weak States.*

30. Such intervention can also splinter traditional associations causing economic and social dislocations. See James Mittelman, *Out from Underdevelopment: Prospects for the Third World* (New York: St. Martin's Press, 1988), 43–44.

31. Michael Bratton, "The Politics of Government–NGO Relations in Africa," *World Development* 17, no. 4 (1989): 574.

32. There is no word that describes active members of civil society. "Civilian," while used traditionally to distinguish the difference between military and nonmilitary personnel, seems to be the most descriptive.

33. Shridath Ramphal, *Our Country, Our Planet* (Washington, DC: Island Press, 1992), 94, 91, 101.

34. Organization for Economic Cooperation and Development (OECD), *Development Cooperation in the 1990s: Efforts and Policies of the Members of the Development Assistance Committee* (Paris, France: OECD, 1989), 120.

35. On the relationship between the core and periphery, see generally, Immanuel Wallerstein, *The Capitalist World-Economy* (New York: Cambridge University Press, 1979). For the ecological dimension, see Shridath Ramphal, *Our Country, Our Planet* The South Commission, *The Challenge of the South* (Geneva Switzerland: The South Commission, 1990); The Centre for Science and Environment, "Statement on Global Environmental Democracy," *Alternatives 17*, no. 2 (Spring 1992).

36. These pockets of the North in the South have led some to speak of the "global south." See Clovis Maksoud, "Introduction," *Environnental Challenges and the Global South: UNCED and Beyond* (Washington, DC: The American University, 1992).

37. This conception is an elaboration of the traditional question of whether the most effective political activity is to change oneself or world social and political processes. The classic, although not the most satisfying, discussion of this issue can be found in Arthur Keostler, "The Yogi and the Commissar," in *The Yogi and the Commissar and Other Essays* (New York: Macmillan, 1946).

38. On the varied relations between NGOs and governments in different settings, see John Farrington, et. al., *Reluctant Partners? Non-Governmental Organizations, the State and Sustainable Agricultural Development* (London: Routledge, 1993); Bratton, "The Politics of Government-NGO Relations in Africa," 584; Anne Drabek, "Editor's Preface," *World Development 15*, supplement (Autumn 1987): xiii; and Ponna Wignaraja, ed., *Governance in Africa: New Social Movements in the South* (London: Zed Books, 1992).

39. Anil Agarwal, "Politics of Empowerment II, " in Centre for Science and Energy, *The State of India's Environment: The Second Citizens Report* (New Delhi: Centre for Energy and Environment, 1985).

40. Hilary French, "Rebuilding the World Bank," in Lester Brown et al., eds., *State of the World 1994* (New York: W. W. Norton, 1994), 163.

41. See "Withdraw from Sardar Sarovar, Now: An Open Letter to Mr. Lewis T. Preston, President of the World Bank," *The Ecologist 22*, no. 5 (September/October 1992); Bruce Rich, "The Emperor's New Clothes: The World Bank and Environmental Reform," *World Policy Journal 7*, no. 2 (Spring 1990); Ann Misch, "Gandhian Greens Fight Big Dams," *World Watch, 3*, no. 4 (July/August 1990); Lori Udall, "Protesters in India: World Bank, Stop Funding Sardar Sarovar Dam," *Not Man Apart 19*, no. 1 (February/May 1989).

42. Bruce Rich, *Mortgaging the Earth: The World Bank, Environmental Impoverishment, and the Crisis of Development* (Boston: Beacon Press, 1994); Alan Durning, "Action at the Grassroots: Fighting Poverty and Environmental Decline," *Worldwatch Paper 88* (Washington, DC: Worldwatch Institute, 1989); Vandana Shiva, "People's Ecology: The Chipko Movement," in Saul Mendlovitz and R. B. J. Walker, eds., *Towards a Just World Peace: Perspectives from Social Movements* (London: Butterworths, 1987).

43. Rajni Kothari, "The NGOs, The State and World Capitalism," *Social Action 36*, no. 4 (October/December, 1986); Rama Reddy, "The Cooperative Sector and Government Control," *Social Action 36*, no. 4 (October/December, 1986). For a study of further state penetration using a class analysis of the state, see Robert Futton, Jr., *Predatory Rule: State and Civil Society in Africa* (Boulder, CO: Lynne Reinner, 1992).

44. Migdal, *Strong Societies and Weak States*, xv.

45. The theoretical background for my position is based on Michel Foucault's insights into "resistances" and "reversals" of certain power relations. See Michel Foucault, "Prison Talk," in Colin Gordon, ed., *Power/Knowledge* (New York: Pantheon Books, 1980); Michel Foucault, *Discpline and Punish: The Birth of the Prison* (New York: Vintage Books, 1977), 59–60, 204. See also, Leslie Paul Thiele, "Foucault's Triple Murder and the Modern Development of Power," *Canadian Journal of Political Science* 19, no. 2 (June 1986).

46. People are not always incorporated into interlocking structures; many choose the "exit" option and disengage from the state. See Victor Azarya, "Reordering State-Society Relations: Incorporation and Disengagement," and Naomi Chazan, "Patterns of State-Society Incorporation and Disengagement in Africa," in Donald Rothchild and Naomi Chazon, eds., *The Precarious Balance: State and Society in Africa* (Boulder, CO: Westview Press, 1988).

47. Robert Livernash, "The Growing Influence of NGOs in the Developing World," *Environment 34*, no. 5 (June 1992): 15.

48. Such funding was evident in the preparatory meetings organized for the United Nations Conference on Environment and Development (UNCED). Organizations such as WWF spent thousands of dollars to bring Third World NGOs to Nairobi, Geneva, New York, and eventually to Brazil to attend the proceedings.

49. Sheldon Annis, "Can Small-Scale Development be a Large-Scale Policy?" *World Development 15*, supplement (Autumn 1987).

50. Terrill Hyde, "U.S. Taxes: The Issues," and Christine Bogdanowicz-Binert, "Third World Debt: An Analysis, " in Noel Gerson and Diana

Page, eds., *Debt for Nature: An Opportunity* (Washington, DC: WWF, 1989).

51. This supports the view that grassroots development organizations are more effective if they are two-tiered (i.e., have formal organization at the local level and at the national or international one). This was argued in the 1970s by Norman Uphoff and Milton Esman, *Local Organization for Rural Development in Asia* (Ithaca, NY: Center for International Studies, Cornell University, November 1974), 67ff.

52. For a discussion of how NGOs chip away at the sovereignty of First World states, see David Jacobson, "The State System in the Age of Rights" (Ph.D. dissertation, Princeton University, 1991).

53. Michael Cernea, "Nongovernmental Organizations and Local Development," *Regional Development Dialogue* 10, no. 2 (Summer 1989), 117. One should note that while the overall trend is increasingly to fund local NGOs, in 1987 the amount of money going to local NGOs decreased. It increased, however, the following year.

54. Michael Cernea, "Nongovernmental Organizations and Local Development," table 1, 118. One should note that the reason for this shift in funding is a combination of the perceived failure of governments to promote development, the proven effectiveness of NGO response to recent famines throughout Africa, and donor's preference for private sector development. See Drabek, "Editor's Preface."

55. Paul Lewis, "Fixing World Crises Isn't Just a Job for Diplomats," *New York Times*, 4 April 1992.

56. Alan Cowell, "The Hidden Population Issue: Money," *New York Times*, 12 September 1994.

57. See, for example, Organization for Economic Cooperation and Development, *Development Cooperation in the 1990s*, 82–83.

58. That this is the larger issue is highlighted by the fact that rechanneling funds does not necessarily mean that state governments have less money to spend on development or environmental protection. If NGOs undertake successful projects, the holdings of national treasuries may be unaffected. In fact, if NGOs perform more efficiently than governments, there may actually be a net fiscal benefit. Nonetheless, state governments still feel threatened. As Michael Bratton points out, the problem is more political than economic. See Bratton, "The Politics of Government–NGO Relations in Africa," 573.

59. Organization for Economic Cooperation and Development, *Development Cooperation in the 1990s*, 82.

60. David Mitrany, *A Working Peace System* (Chicago: Quadrangle Books, 1966); Ernst Haas, *Beyond the Nation-State* (Stanford, CA: Stanford University Press, 1968).

61. According to Jim MacNeill and others, ever since the Club of Rome published *The Limits to Growth* in 1972, a sufficient amount of environmental debates have asserted that environmental concerns and development are irreconcilable. See Jim MacNeill, et al., *Beyond Interdependence: The Meshing of the World's Economy and the Earth's Ecology* (New York: Oxford University Press, 1991), 29.

62. Indira Gandhi claimed that extremely poor people and countries must make an explicit trade-off, accepting long-term environmental degradation to meet their immediate needs for food and shelter. On the changing relationship between environment and development, see H. Jeffrey Leonard, "Overview: Environment and the Poor: Development Strategies for a Common Agenda," in H. Jeffrey Leonard, ed., *Environment and the Poor: Development Strategies for a Common Agenda* (New Brunswick, NJ: Transaction Books, 1989).

63. Charles Pearson claims, for example, that, in addition to consciousness raising at international conferences, concrete evidence from pilot projects was key to the receptiveness of eco-development. See Charles Pearson, "Environment, Development and Multinational Enterprise," in Charles Pearson, ed., *Multinational Corporations, Environment and the Third World* (Durham, NC: Duke University Press, 1987), 5. See also Czech Conroy and Miles Litvinoff, eds., *The Greening of Aid: Sustainable Livelihoods in Practice* (London: International Institute for Environment and Development, 1988).

64. The work of local and transnational NGOs has altered conceptualizations of development in additional ways. For more exhaustive discussions see D. L. Sheth, "Alternative Development as Political Practice," in Saul Mendlovitz and R. B. J. Walker, eds., *Towards a Just World Peace: Perspectives from Social Movements*; Anne Drabek, "Developing Alternatives: The Challenge for NGOs—An Overview of the Issues," *World Development 15*, supplement (Autumn 1987); Anil Agarwal, "Ecological Destruction and the Emerging Patterns of Poverty and People's Protests in Rural India," *Social Action 35*, no. 1 (January-March 1985); R. B. J. Walker, *One World/Many Worlds* (Boulder, CO: Lynne Reinner Publishers, 1988); Kishmore Saint, "Development and People's Participation," *Social Action 30*, no. 3 (July-September 1980).

65. Ariel Dorfman, "Bread and Burnt Rice: Culture and Economic Survival in Latin America," *Grassroots Development 7*, no. 2 (1984), quoted in Durning, "Action at the Grassroots," 22.

CHAPTER 5

1. See Robert Keohane and Joseph Nye, *Power and Interdependence: World Politics in Transition* (Boston: Little, Brown, 1977), 8.

2. See Henry Kissinger, *Observations: Selected Speeches and Essays, 1982–1984* (Boston: Little, Brown, 1988), 39, 46, 175, 185; Peter Willets, "The Politics of Global Issues: Cognitive Actor Dependence and Issue Linkage," in Barry Jones and Peter Willets, eds., *Interdependence on Trial* (London: Francis Pinter, 1984); Keohane and Nye, *Power and Interdependence,* 8.

3. Jim MacNeill et al., *Beyond Interdependence: The Meshing of the World's Economy and the Earth's Ecology* (New York: Oxford University Press, 1991). See also, Gareth Porter and Janet Brown, *Global Environmental Politics* (Boulder, CO: Westview Press, 1991), 129.

4. On the notion of sovereignty-free actors, see James Rosenau, *Turbulence in World Politics* (Princeton, NJ: Princeton University Press, 1990).

5. For detailed descriptions of Brower's work with the Sierra Club, see Stephen Fox, *John Muir and his Legacy* (Boston: Little, Brown, 1981), 275–290; Michael Cohen, *The History of the Sierra Club 1892–1970* (San Francisco: Sierra Club Books, 1988); and David Brower, *For Earth's Sake: The Life and Times of David Brower* (Salt Lake City: Peregrine Smith Books, 1990).

6. Quoted in Philip Shabecoff, *A Fierce Green Fire: The American Environmental Movement* (New York: Hill and Wang, 1993), 101.

7. Brower's authoritative role in FOE led to his eventual dismissal in 1986. His handling of financial accounts, managerial style, and personal image of the organization's purpose brought him into conflict with many of the group's leaders. In 1986, Brower was forced to resign as chairman of the board of FOE. Within months he established Earth Island Institute, which has become a transnational ecological group in its own right. For accounts of the controversies that led to Brower's dismissal from FOE see, Philip Shabecoff, "Conservation Figure Ousted for Resisting Orders to Cut Staff," *New York Times,* 7 July 1984, A1; Larry Stammer, "Founder Quits Friends of the Earth, Says Situation Just Got Hopeless," *Los Angeles Times,* 11 October 1986, A27; Tom Tuner, *Friends of the Earth: The First Sixteen Years* (San Francisco: Earth Island Institute, 1986), 44ff.

8. For an extended reflection of Brower's early career and a poetic account of his ideas see, John McPhee, *Encounters with the Archdruid: Narratives about a Conservationist and Three of his Natural Enemies* (New York: Farrar, Straus & Giroux, 1971).

9. Local FOE offices sometimes represent conglomerates of activist groups. For example, in the late 1980s, FOE-U.S. merged with the Oceanic Society and the Environmental Policy Institute. In Sierra Leone, the Future is in Our Hands Movement and the Kenema Voluntary Health Workers Association merged to form FOE–Sierra Leone.

10. The Group of Ten originally included the chief executive officers of the Environmental Defense Fund, Environmental Policy Institute, Friends of the Earth, Izaak Walton League of America, Natural Resources Defense Council, National Audubon Society, National Parks and Conservation Association, National Wildlife Federation, Sierra Club, and the Wilderness Society. (Since the Group of Ten's original organization, Environmental Policy Institute and Friends of the Earth have merged.) See Robert Cahn, ed., *An Environmental Agenda for the Future* (Washington, DC: Island Press, 1985). For a critique of the Group of Ten, see Peter Borrelli, "Environmentalism at a Crossroads," *Amicus Journal* 9, no. 3 (Summer 1987).

11. Gary Soucie, "Interview," *Not Man Apart*, February 1971, 10.

12. Interstate interactions are the relations between nation-states conceived of as unitary actors. Transgovernmental interactions refer to relations between different parts of governments across state boundaries. Transnational interactions are the relations across borders where at least one actor is not a state. These distinctions were first made by Keohane and Nye, *Power and Interdependence*, 25.

13. See Michael Shuman, *Toward a Global Village: International Community Development Initiatives* (London: Pluto Press, 1994) and "Dateline Main Street: Courts vs. Local Foreign Policies," *Foreign Policy*, no. 86 (Spring 1992); Will Swain, "Making Foreign Policy at City Hall," *The Progressive* 52 (July 1988).

14. Janice Castro, "One Big Mac, Hold the Box," *Time*, 25 January 1990, 44. Castro also reports that Portland and Glen Cove also banned polystyrene.

15. Michael Shuman, *Toward a Global Village*, 33.

16. For background on this, see Friends of the Earth International, "North American Cities Sign Ozone Accord," *Atmosphere* 2, no. 3 (Fall 1989); and Elizabeth Cook, "Global Environmental Advocacy: Citizen Activism in Protecting the Ozone Layer," *Ambio*, no. 14 (October 1990).

17. For FOE initiatives at the municipal level, see Corinna Gilfillan, "Friends of the Earth Launches Halon Campaign in Takoma Park," *The Takoma Voice*, October 1994, 8; for initiatives at the state level, see "States Forge Ahead, Require Car CFC Recycling," *Not Man Apart*, (June-September 1989): 11. For municipal initiatives on global warming see, Nancy Skin-

ner, "Atmospheric Protection Update," *Bulletin of Municipal Foreign Policy* 4, no. 2 (Spring 1990).

18. See Matthew Wald, "Nine States in East Plan to Restrict Pollution by Cars," *New York Times*, 30 October 1991, A1; Matthew Wald, "Recharting War on Smog: States like California are Taking the Lead Over Washington in Pollution-Control Law," *New York Times*, 10 October 1989, A1. See also, Cynthia Wilson, "A View from the Trenches," in Peter Borrelli, ed., *Crossroads: Environmental Priorities for the Future* (Washington, DC: Island Press, 1989); D. Vera Cohn and Dan Beyers, "Clean Air Argument Hits Snag," *Washington Post*, 12 March 1992, B1, 6.

19. "A Flexible Approach to Ending Northeast Smog Pollution," *Environmental Defense Fund Letter*, Vol. 25, No. 6 (September 1994) 1.

20. Sharon Roan, *Ozone Crisis: The Fifteen Year Evolution of a Sudden Global Emergency* (New York: Wiley, 1989), 49–50.

21. See Gareth Porter and Janet Welsh Brown, *Global Environmental Politics* (Boulder, CO: Westview Press, 1991) 63–64; and Herman Verhagen, "Dutch Tropical Rainforest Campaign Successful," *FOE Link*, March 1989.

22. Michael Shuman, *Toward a Global Village*, 32.

23. The strategy to use municipalities in the service of national and international environmental political work reflects a more general trend of moving from smaller to larger governmental units to initiate change. See Wald, "Recharting War on Smog;" See also Wilson, "A View from the Trenches;" and Michael Shuman, *Toward a Global Village*.

24. For a comprehensive examination of the principles, see Valerie Ann-Zondorak, "A New Face in Corporate Environmental Responsibility: The Valdez Principles," *Boston College Environmental Affairs Law Review* 18 (Spring 1991).

25. See Ann-Zondorak, "A New Face in Corporate Environmental Responsibility"; CERES Coalition, *The 1990 Ceres Guide to the Valdez Principles* (Boston: Coalition for Environmentally Responsible Economies, 1990); Jack Doyle, "Valdez Principles: Corporate Code of Conduct," *Social Policy* 20 (Winter 1990).

26. Alan Miller and Irving Mintzer, *The Sky* Is *the Limit: Strategies for Protecting the Ozone Layer* (Washington, DC: World Resources Institute, 1986), 21.

27. U.S. Congress, Senate, Committee on the Environment and Public Works, *Ozone Depletion, the Global Effect, and Climate Change: Joint Hearings Before the Subcommittee on Environmental Protection and Hazardous Wastes and Toxic Substances*, Testimony of Richard Barnett, 100th

Cong., 1st sess., 1987. Cited in Peter Haas, "Banning Chlorofluorocarbons: Epistemic Community Efforts to Protect Stratospheric Ozone," *International Organization* 46, no. 1 (Winter 1992): 207. See also Porter and Brown, *Global Environmental Politics*.

28. Miller and Mintzer, *The Sky Is the Limit*, 21. For the interplay between U.S. unilateral and international efforts, see Haas, "Banning Chlorofluorocarbons," 200ff.

29. Richard Benedick, *Ozone Diplomacy: New Directions in Safeguarding the Planet* (Cambridge, MA: Harvard University Press, 1991), 30ff 54.

30. Also critical were widespread agreement among scientists and policy makers on the causal explanation of ozone depletion (see, Peter Haas, "Banning Chloroflourocarbons: Epistemic Community Efforts to Protect Stratospheric Ozone," *International Organization* 46, no. 1 (Winter 1992) and the development of acceptable industry substitutes for CFCs (see Detlef Sprinz and Tapani Vaahtoranta, "The Interest-Based Explanation of International Environmental Policy," *International Organization* 48, no. 1, (Winter 1994) 93–94). For a rich empirical account of events leading up to the Montreal Protocol, see Edward Parson, "Protecting the Ozone Layer," in Peter Haas, Robert Keohane, and Marc Levy, eds., *Institutions for the Earth: Sources of Effective International Environmental Protection* (Cambridge, MA: MIT Press, 1993).

31. Barbara Bramble and Gareth Porter, "Non-Governmental Organizations and the Making of U.S. International Environmental Policy," in Andrew Hurrell and Benedict Kingsbury, eds., *The International Politics of the Environment* (New York: Oxford University Press, 1992), 341.

32. Stephen Krasner, "Structural Causes and Regime Consequences: Regimes as Intervening Variables," in Stephen Krasner, ed., *International Regimes* (Ithaca, NY: Cornell University Press, 1983), 1.

33. Harold Jacobson, *Networks of Interdependence: International Organizations and the Global Politics System* (New York: Knopf, 1979), 109.

34. For an extended discussion of compliance with international regimes, see Oran Young, *Compliance and Public Authority: A Theory with International Applications* (Baltimore: The Johns Hopkins University Press, 1979). See also Oran Young, *International Cooperation: Building Regimes for National Resources and the Environment* (Ithaca, NY: Cornell University Press, 1989) and Abram Chayes and Antonia Chayes, "On Compliance," *International Organization* 47, no. 2 (Spring 1993).

35. It is worthwhile noting that a transnational NGO, the Women's International League for Peace and Freedom (WILPF), provided the original impetus to create the ATS. In 1947, it recommended that the UN administer an international regime for Antarctica. See Lee Kimble, "The Role of Non-Governmental Organizations in Antarctic Affairs," in Christopher Joyner and Sudhir Chopra, eds., *The Antarctic Legal Regime* (Dordrecht: Martinus Jijhoff Publishers, 1988).

36. Margaret Clark, "The Antarctica Environmental Protocol: NGOs in the Protection of Antarctica," in Thomas Princen and Matthias Finger, *Environmental NGOs in World Politics: Linking the Local and the Global* (London: Routledge, 1994), 176.

37. This is also one of FOE's main contributions to ASOC.

38. That *ECO* was important to the conference was signaled by the secretary of the conference, Maurice Strong, who called the *ECO* office after its second publication and complained that he did not receive his copy until 11 AM. He ordered messengers to deliver the news sheet immediately from the publication center from that time forward. See Tuner, *Friends of the Earth: The First Sixteen Years*, 13.

39. For arguments for and against CRAMRA, see Colin Deihl, "Antarctica: An International Laboratory," *Boston College Environmental Affairs Law Review* 18, no. 3 (Spring 1991).

40. See Alan Riding, "Pact Bans Oil Exploration in Antarctic," *New York Times*, 5 October 1991, A3; Malcolm Browne, "U.S. Agrees to Protect Minerals in Antarctica," *New York Times*, 6 July 1991, A5; and Deihl, "Antarctica: An International Laboratory."

41. *Protocol on Environmental Protection to the Antarctica Treaty*, Madrid, June 1991. Quoted in Daniel Jaffe, Elizabeth Leighton, and Mark Tumeo, "Environmental Impact on the Polar Regions," *Forum for Applied Research and Public Policy* 9, no. 1 (Spring 1994), 66.

42. See Margaret Clark, "The Antarctica Environmental Protocol;" Deihl, "Antarctica: An International Laboratory," 444–445; Riding, "Pact Bans Oil Exploration in Antarctic;" Porter and Brown, *Global Environmental Politics*, 88–92.

43. Quoted in Paul Larmer, "The Great White Heap," *Sierra* 75 (March/April 1990): 28.

44. James Barnes, "Legal Aspects of Environmental Protection in Antarctica," in Christopher Joyner and Sudhir Chopra, eds., *The Antarctic Legal Regime* (Dordrecht: Martinus Jijhoff Publishers, 1988), 257.

45. For example, ASOC distributed the "ASOC Report on Airstrip Construction at Dumont d'Urville" at the XI Antarctica Treaty Special Consultative Meetings in Spain in the spring of 1991. See Clark, "In the Green Corner: The Victory of Environmental NGOs in the Protection of Antarctica." Manuscript prepared for Seminar International NGOs: The Great Lakes and Beyond, Oct. 18–19, 1991, Ann Arbor: University of Michigan, 19.

46. Alan Hall, "The World's Frozen Clean Room," *Business Week*, 22 January 1990, 73.

47. On further roles of ASOC, see Barnes, "Legal Aspects of Environmental Protection in Antarctica," 259.

48. Bramble and Porter, "Non-Governmental Organizations and the Making of U.S. International Environmental Policy," 326.

49. Robin Broad, John Cavanaugh, and Walden Bello, "Development: The Market is Not Enough," *Foreign Policy*, no. 8 (Winter 1990–1991); and Richard Wallace, "Structural Adjustment and the Environment: An Analysis of Export Promotion, Market Liberalization and Reductions in Government Spending," *Swords and Ploughshares* 2, no. 1 (Fall 1992).

50. For a discussion of why the trade-offs may make sense, see Gregg Easterbrook, "Forget PCB's, Radon, Alar: The World's Greatest Environmental Dangers are Dung Smoke and Dirty Water," *New York Times Magazine*, 11 September 1994.

51. See Bruce Rich, *Mortgaging the Earth: The World Bank, Environmental Impoverishment and the Crisis of Development* (Boston: Beacon Press, 1994); Montague Yudelman, "The World Bank and Agricultural Development—An Insider's View," *World Resources Institute Papers*, no. 1 (December 1985); Robert Stein, *Banking on the Biosphere? Environmental Procedures and Practices of Nine Multilateral Development Agencies* (Lexington, MA: Lexington Books, 1979); Lee Talbot, "Helping Developing Countries Help Themselves," *World Resources Institute Working Paper* (January 1985); Friends of the Earth/Environmental Policy Institute/Oceanic Society, *An NGO Perspective on the IMF: The Need to Reform* (Washington, DC: Friends of the Earth, August 1989); and the World Commission on Environment and Development, *Our Common Future* (New York: Oxford University Press, 1987), 75ff.

52. Pat Aufderheide and Bruce Rich, "Environmental Reform and the Multilateral Banks," *World Policy Journal* 5, no. 2 (Spring 1988). See generally, Bruce Rich, *Mortgaging the Earth.*

53. See Barbara Conable, "Development and the Environment: A Global Balance," *International Environmental Affairs* 2, no. 1 (Winter

1990). See also Bramble and Porter, "Non-Governmental Organizations and the Making of U.S. International Environmental Policy," 333ff.

54. For insightful criticisms, see Hilary French, "Rebuilding the World Bank," *State of the World 1994* (New York: W.W. Norton, 1994); Bruce Rich, *Mortgaging the Earth* and "The Emperor's New Clothes: The World Bank and Environmental Reform," *World Policy Journal 7*, no. 2 (Spring 1990); the Bank Information Center, *Funding Ecological and Social Destruction: The World Bank and International Monetary Fund* (Washington, DC: The Bank Information Center, 1990).

55. Gareth Porter and Janet Welsh Brown, *Global Environmental Politics*, 53–56; French, "Rebuilding the World Bank," 160; Bramble and Porter, "Non-Governmental Organizations and the Making of U.S. International Environmental Policy," 325–336.

56. See generally, Marijke Torfs, *Effects of the IMF Structural Adjustment Programs on Social Sectors of Third World Countries* (Washington, DC: Friends of the Earth, Environmental Policy Institute, Oceanic Society, May 1991).

57. According to Bramble and Porter, "Thus, from the beginning, the MDB campaign [by NGOs] was conceived as a method of exposing the mistaken priorities of modern development theory, not just to modify specific projects, nor even to reform the MDBs themselves. The banks were targeted because they were seen as effective levers for eventually modifying development theory and practice around the world." Bramble and Porter, *Non-Governmental Organizations and the Making of U.S. International Environmental Policy*, 326.

58. Keohane and Nye, *Power and Interdependence*, 9.

59. See generally, Robert Keohane, *International Institutions and State Power: Essays in International Relations Theory* (Boulder, CO: Westview Press, 1989); and Young, *International Cooperation*.

60. Young, *International Cooperation*.

61. See Raymond Aron, *Peace and War: A Theory of International Relations* (New York: Doubleday, 1966), 92ff, 280ff. Hans Morgenthau also suggests that when it comes to everything short of national security, national interest is a function of domestic attributes, elite ideology, and domestic politics. See Hans Morgenthau, *Politics Among Nations: The Struggle for Power and Peace* (New York: Knopf, 1948), 441; and Hans Morgenthau, *In Defense of the National Interest: A Critical Examination of American Foreign Policy* (New York: Knopf, 1951). This view is also described well in Keohane and Nye, *Power and Interdependence*, 34–35. See also Deepa Ollapally, *Domestic Determinants and International Inter-*

vention: U.S. Foreign Policy in Third World Conflicts (Westport, CT: Greenwood Press, 1993).

62. Raymond Bauer, Ithiel de Sola Pool, and Lewis Dexter, *American Business and Public Policy: The Politics of Foreign Trade* (Chicago: Aldine-Atherton, 1972), 474.

63. Keohane, "Neoliberal Institutionalism: A Perspective on World Politics," in *International Institutions and State Power.*

64. All structural theories of international relations take this position in one form or another. One of the best articles on the relationship between international social structure and states is Alexander Wendt, "The Agent-Structure Problem in International Relations Theory," *International Organization* 41, no. 3 (Summer 1987).

65. See Antonio Gramsci, *Selections from the Prison Notebooks* (New York: International Publishers, 1985), 5–14, 144–147, 229–239.

66. See Alain Touraine et al., *Anti-Nuclear Protest: The Opposition to Nuclear Energy in France* (Cambridge: Cambridge University Press, 1983); and Alain Touraine et al., *Solidarity: Poland 1980–1981* (Cambridge: Cambridge University Press, 1983).

67. Adam Michnik, *Letters from Prison and Other Essays* (Berkeley: University of California Press, 1985).

68. See generally, the "new social movement" literature. See especially, *Social Research* 52, no. 4 (Winter 1985).

69. On the restricted autonomous nature of international organizations as they relate to environmental politics, see Konrad von Moltke, "International Commissions and Implementation of International Environmental Law," in John Carroll, ed., *International Environmental Diplomacy: The Management and Resolution of Transfrontier Environmental Problems* (Cambridge: Cambridge University Press, 1988); see more generally Richard Falk, "Normative Initiatives and Demilitarisation: A Third System Approach," in *The Promise of World Order: Essays in Normative International Relations* (Philadelphia: Temple University Press, 1987).

70. Richard Falk, *A Global Approach to Foreign Policy* (Cambridge, MA: Harvard University Press, 1975), 1.

71. Accountability within the environmental community can be quite effective in that rank-and-file members of activist groups can stop donating money and energy to activist efforts.

72. On the importance of nonnational sources of environmental information and how many states depend upon them, see Lester Brown et al., *The State of the World 1991* (New York: W.W. Norton, 1991), xv–xvii.

73. Roger Scruton, *Dictionary of Political Thought* (New York: Harper & Row, 1982), 233.

74. The central Marxist text on internationalism is Karl Marx and Frederick Engels, "The Manifesto of the Communist Party," in Robert Tucker, ed., *The Marx-Engels Reader* (New York: W. W. Norton, 1978). For Immanuel Kant, the key texts are, "Idea for a Universal History from a Cosmopolitan Point of View," and "Perpetual Peace," in Lewis Beck, ed., *On History* (New York: Bobbs-Merrill, 1963).

75. Marx writes, for example, "[T]he struggle of the proletariat with the bourgeoisie is at first a national struggle. The proletariat of each country must, of course, first of all settle matters with its own bourgeoisie." In Robert Tucker, ed., *The Marx-Engels Reader*, 482. And, "United action, of the leading civilized countries at least, is one of the first conditions for emancipation of the proletariat." Ibid., 488.

76. "The republican constitution, besides purity of its origin," writes Kant, ". . . also gives a favorable prospect for the desired consequence, i.e., perpetual peace." In Kant, "Perpetual Peace," 94. Republican states, according to Kant, can establish a "league of peace" that will "gradually spread to all states and thus lead to perpetual peace." Ibid., 100.

77. See, for example, Michael Doyle, "Kant, Liberal Legacies, and Foreign Affairs," [part one] *Philosophy and Public Affairs* 12, no. 3 (Summer 1983); Randall Schweller, "Domestic Structure and Preventive War," *World Politics* 44, no. 2 (January 1992).

78. See generally, Karl Marx, "The German Ideology," and Karl Marx and Frederick Engels, "The Manifesto of the Communist Party," in Robert Tucker, ed., *The Marx-Engels Reader*.

79. "The spirit of commerce," writes Kant, "which is incompatible with war, sooner or later gains the upper hand in every state. As the power of money is perhaps the most dependable of all the powers (means) included under the state power, states see themselves forced, without any moral urge, to promote honorable peace and by mediation to prevent war wherever it threatens to break out." In "Perpetual Peace," 144. See also Doyle, "Kant, Liberalism and Foreign Affairs."

80. On the general notion of internationalism and world affairs, see Fred Halliday, "Three Concepts of Internationalism," *International Affairs* 64, no. 2 (Spring 1988).

CHAPTER 6

1. Andrew Dobson, *Green Political Thought* (London: Unwin Hyman, 1990), 139ff.

2. For example, Bertrand Russell, *Power: A New Social Analysis* (New York: W. W. Norton, 1938); Michel Foucault, *Power/Knowledge: Selected Interviews and Other Writings, 1972–1977,* ed., Colin Gordon (New York: Pantheon, 1980); Steven Lukes, *Power: A Radical View* (London: Macmillan, 1974).

3. There are, of course, traditions that use the term *civil society* in ways that differ from Hegel's understanding. Hobbes, Locke, Kant, and Mill put forth various conceptions that suggest alternative types of formulations. See John Keane, *Democracy and Civil Society* (London: Verso, 1988), 35–64.

4. T.M. Knox, trans., *Hegel's Philosophy of Right* (London: Oxford University Press, 1967).

5. Gramsci, at times, disagrees with this. In fact, often he understands civil society itself as an array of religious, educational, and associational institutions that ensure the domination of the ruling class. In particular, it serves to guarantee the ideological hegemony of that class's interest. At other times, however, Gramsci sees strands of civil society able to be enlisted in a counter-hegemonic effort that can lead ultimately to capturing state control. See Antonio Gramsci, *The Prison Notebooks* (New York: International Publishers, 1985), 210–275. This latter emphasis by Gramsci, which he ascribes to certain societies at particular historical moments, is closer to my own understanding of civil society.

6. Russell Dalton, Manfred Kuechler, and Wilhelm Burklin, "The Challenge of New Movements," in Russell Dalton and Manfred Kuechler, eds., *Challenging the Political Order: New Social and Political Movements in Western Democracies* (New York: Oxford University Press, 1990), 4.

7. Ronald Inglehart, "Values, Ideology, and Cognitive Mobilization in New Social Movements," in Dalton and Kuechler, *Challenging the Political Order;* Alberto Mellucci, "The Symbolic Challenge of Contemporary Movements," *Social Research* 52, no. 4 (1985).

8. Claus Offe, "New Social Movements: Challenging the Boundaries of Institutional Politics," *Social Research* 52, no. 4 (1985); Fritjof Capra Charlene Spretnak and Wulf-Rudiger Lutz, *Green Politics* (New York: Dutton, 1984); Leslie Paul Thiele, "Social Movements and the Interface of Domestic and International Politics: A Study of Peace Activism,"

Paper presented at the annual meeting of the American Political Science Association, San Francisco, CA, 1990.

9. Jurgen Habermas, "What Does a Crisis Mean Today? Legitimation Problems in Late Capitalism," in Steven Seidman, ed., *Jurgen Habermas on Society and Politics* (Boston: Beacon Press, 1989); Andrew Buchwalter, "Translator's Introduction," in Jurgen Habermas, ed., *Observations on "The Spiritual Situation of the Age,": Contemporary German Perspectives* (Cambridge, MA: MIT Press, 1985).

10. Dorothy Nelkin and Michael Pollak, *The Atom Besieged: Extraparliamentary Dissent in France and Germany* (Cambridge, MA: MIT Press, 1981); Thomas Rochon, *Mobilizing for Peace: Antinuclear Movements in Western Europe* (Princeton, NJ: Princeton University Press, 1988); Dieter Rucht, "The Strategies and Action Repertoires of New Movements," in Dalton and Kuechler, *Challenging the Political Order.*

11. See Alain Touraine, *Anti-Nuclear Protest: The Opposition to Nuclear Energy in France* (New York: Cambridge University Press, 1983); Adam Michnik, *Letters From Prison and Other Essays*, trans. Maya Latynski, (Berkeley: University of California Press, 1987); Harry Boyte, *The Backyard Revolution: Understanding the New Citizen Movement* (Philadelphia: Temple University Press, 1980); Claus Offe, "Challenging the Boundaries of Institutional Politics: Social Movements Since the 1960s," in Charles Maier, ed., *Changing Boundaries of the Political* (Cambridge: Cambridge University Press, 1987).

12. For an extensive discussion of this literature, see chapter 1.

13. Robert Keohane and Joseph Nye, "Transnational Relations and World Politics: An Introduction," *Transnational Relations and World Politics* (Cambridge, MA: Harvard University Press, 1972), xxiv.

14. Ibid., xxv.

15. To be sure, Keohane and Nye had changed their focus by the time they wrote *Power and Interdependence*, but, by this time, their attention had shifted from NGOs to international regimes.

16. Quoted in Keohane and Nye, "Transnational Relations and World Politics," xxiv.

Bibliography

Agarwal, Anil. "Ecological Destruction and the Emerging Patterns of Poverty and People's Protests in Rural India." *Social Action* 35, no. 1 (January/March 1985).

Agarwal, Anil. "Politics of Empowerment II," in Centre for Science and Energy, *The State of India's Environment: The Second Citizens Report*. New Delhi: Centre for Energy and Environment, 1985.

Agarwal, Anil, and Narain, Sunita. *Towards a Green World*. New Delhi, India: Centre for Energy and Environment, 1992.

Allen, J. "Anti-Sealing as an Industry." *Journal of Political Economy* 87 (April 1979).

Anderson, Walter Truett. *To Govern Evolution*. New York: Harcourt Brace Jovanich, 1987.

Angell, Robert. *Peace on the March: Transnational Participation*. New York: Van Nostrand Reinhold, 1969.

Annis, Sheldon. "Can Small-Scale Development be a Large-Scale Policy?" *World Development* 15, supplement (Autumn 1987).

Annis, Sheldon. "Giving Voice to the Poor." *Foreign Policy* 84 (Fall 1991).

Annis, Sheldon. "Evolving Connectedness Among Environmental Groups and Grassroots Organizations in Protected Areas of Central America." *World Development 20*, no. 4 (1992).

Ann-Zondorak, Valerie. "A New Face in Corporate Environmental Responsibility: The Valdez Principles." *Boston College Environmental Affairs Law Review 18* (Spring 1991).

Aron, Raymond. *Peace and War: A Theory of International Relations*. New York: Doubleday, 1966.

Asubel, J. H., and D. G. Victor. "Verification of International Environmental Agreements." *Annual Review of Energy and Environment*, no. 17 (1992).

Aufderheide, Pat, and Bruce Rich. "Environmental Reform and the Multilateral Banks." *World Policy Journal 5*, no. 2 (Spring 1988).

Azarya, Victor. "Reordering State-Society Relations: Incorporation and Disengagement." In *The Precarious Balance: State and Society in Africa*, eds. Donald Rothchild and Naomi Chazon. Boulder, CO: Westview Press, 1988.

"Baby Harp Seals Spared." *Oceans* 21 (March/April 1988).

The Bank Information Center. *Funding Ecological and Social Destruction: The World Bank and International Monetary Fund*. Washington, DC: The Bank Information Center, 1990.

Barnes, James. "Legal Aspects of Environmental Protection in Antarctica." In *The Antarctic Legal Regime*, eds. Christopher Joyner and Sudhir Chopra. Dordrecht: Martinus Jijhoff Publishers, 1988.

Barreiro, Jorge. "Debt Swap Condemned by Latin American NGOs." *Earth Island Journal 7*, no. 3 (Summer 1992).

Bauer, Raymond, Ithiel de Sola Pool, and Lewis Dexter. *American Business and Public Policy: The Politics of Foreign Trade*. Chicago: Aldine-Atherton, 1972.

Benedick, Richard. *Ozone Diplomacy: New Directions in Safeguarding the Planet*. Cambridge, MA: Harvard University Press, 1991.

Berg, Peter. "Strategies for Reinhabiting the North California Bioregion." *Seriatim: Journal of Ecotopia 1*, no. 3 (1977).

Berg, Peter. "Growing Bioregional Politics." *RAIN* (July/August 1985).

Bishop, Katherine. "Suit Seeks Ban on Shrimp from Nations Not Protecting Sea Turtles." *New York Times*, 25 March 1992.

Blumer, Herbert. "Social Movements." In *Studies in Social Movements: A Social Psychological Perspective*, ed. Barry McLaughlin. New York: The Free Press, 1969.

Bogdanowicz-Binert, Christine. "Third World Debt: An Analysis." In *Debt for Nature: An Opportunity*, eds. Noel Gerson and Diana Page. Washington, DC: WWF, 1989.

Borgese, G. A. *Foundations of a World Republic*. Chicago,: University of Chicago Press, 1953.

Borrelli, Peter. "Environmentalism at a Crossroads." *Amicus Journal 9*, no. 3 (Summer 1987).

Boulding, Elise. *Building a Global Civic Culture.* New York: Teachers College Press 1988.

Boyte, Harry. *The Backyard Revolution: Understanding the New Citizen Movement.* Philadelphia: Temple University Press, 1980.

Boyte, Harry. "The Pragmatic Ends of Popular Politics," in Craig Calhoun, ed. *Habermas and the Public Sphere.* Cambridge, MA: MIT Press, 1992.

Bramble, Barbara, and Gareth Porter. "Non-Governmental Organizations and the Making of U.S. International Environmental Policy." In *The International Politics of the Environment,* eds. Andrew Hurrell and Benedict Kingsbury. New York: Oxford University Press, 1992.

Bratton, Michael. "Beyond the State: Civil Society and Associational Life in Africa." *World Politics 44,* no. 3 (1989).

Bratton, Michael. "The Politics of Government–NGO Relations in Africa." *World Development 17,* no. 4 (1989).

Brink, Andre. *Writing in a State of Siege: Essays on Politics and Literature.* New York: Summit Books, 1983.

Broad, Robin. "The Poor and the Environment: Friends or Foes?" *World Development 22,* no. 6 (1994).

Broad, Robin, John Cavanaugh, and Walden Bello. "Development: The Market is Not Enough." *Foreign Policy,* no. 8 (Winter 1990-1991).

Brower, David. *For Earth's Sake: The Life and Times of David Brower.* Salt Lake City: Peregrine Smith Books, 1990.

Brown, Chris. *International Relations Theory: New Normative Approaches.* New York: Columbia University Press, 1992.

Brown, Lester. "The New World Order." In *State of the World 1992,* eds. Lester Brown et al. New York: W.W. Norton Press, 1992.

Brown, Lester, et al. *The State of the World 1991.* New York: W.W. Norton and Co., 1991.

Brown, Lester, et al., eds. *State of the World 1994.* New York: W.W. Norton, 1994.

Brown, Lester, et al. *Vital Signs: Trends That Are Shaping Our Future.* New York: W.W. Norton, 1992.

Brown, Lester, Hal Kane, and David Roodman, eds. *Vital Signs 1994: The Trends that are Shaping Our Future.* New York: W.W. Norton, 1994.

Brown, Michael, and John May. *The Greenpeace Story*. Scarborough, Ontario: Prentice-Hall Canada, 1989.

Brown, Seyom. *New Forces in World Politics*. Washington, DC: Brookings Institution, 1974.

Browne, Malcolm. "U.S. Agrees to Protect Minerals in Antarctica." *New York Times*, 6 July 1991.

Bryson, Lyman, et al., eds. *Foundations of World Organization: A Political and Cultural Appraisal*. New York: Harper and Brothers, 1952.

Buchwalter, Andrew. "Translator's Introduction." In *Observations on "The Spiritual Situation of the Age,": Contemporary German Perspectives*, ed. Jurgen Habermas. Cambridge, MA: MIT Press, 1985.

Bull, Hedley, and Adam Watson, eds. *The Expansion of International Society*. Oxford: Clarendon, 1984.

Bullard, Robert, ed. *Unequal Protection: Environmental Justice and Communities of Color*. San Francisco: Sierra Club, 1994.

Buttle, Frederick. "Age and Environmental Concern: A Multivariate Analysis." *Youth and Society 10*, no. 3 (March 1979).

Cahn, Robert, ed. *An Environmental Agenda for the Future*. Washington, DC: Island Press, 1985.

Caldwell, Lynton. *International Environmental Policy*. Durham, NC: Duke University Press, 1992.

Calhoun, Craig, ed. *Habermas and the Public Sphere*. Cambridge, MA: MIT Press, 1992.

Callaghy, Thomas. *The State-Society Struggle: Zaire in Contemporary Perspective*. New York: Columbia University Press, 1984.

Capra, Fritjof, Charlene Spretnak, and Wulf-Rudiger Lutz. *Green Politics*. New York: Dutton, 1984.

Carrying Capacity Network. "Check-up and Connections." *Clearinghouse Bulletin 2*, no. 8 (October 1992).

Castro, Janice. "One Big Mac, Hold the Box." *Time*, 25 January 1990.

Centre for Science and Environment. "Statement on Global Environmental Democracy." *Alternatives 17*, no. 2 (Spring 1992).

CERES Coalition. *The 1990 Ceres Guide to the Valdez Principles*. Boston: Coalition for Environmentally Responsible Economies, 1990.

Cernea, Michael. "Nongovernmental Organizations and Local Development." *Regional Development Dialogue 10*, no. 2 (Summer 1989).

Chayes, Abram, and Antonia Chayes. "On Compliance." *International Organization 47*, no. 2 (Spring 1993).

Chazan, Naomi. "Patterns of State-Society Incorporation and Disengagement in Africa." In *The Precarious Balance: State and Society in Africa*, eds. Donald Rothchild and Naomi Chazon. Boulder, CO: Westview Press, 1988.

Chazan, Naomi, Robert Mortimer, John Ravenhill, and Donald Rothchild, eds. *Politics and Society in Contemporary Africa*. Boulder, CO: Lynne Reinner, 1988.

"Chlorine Protesters Scale Time Building." *New York Times*, 12 July 1994.

Clark, Grenville, and Louis Sohn. *World Peace Through World Law*. Cambridge, MA: Harvard University Press, 1966.

Clark, Margaret. "In the Green Corner: The Victory of Environmental NGOs in the Protection of Antarctica." Manuscript prepared for the seminar, International NGOs: The Great Lakes and Beyond, Oct. 18–19, 1991, Ann Arbor: University of Michigan.

Clark, Margaret. "The Antarctica Environmental Protocol: NGOs in the Protection of Antarctica." In *Environmental NGOs in World Politics: Linking the Local and the Global*, Thomas Princen and Matthias Finger, London: Routledge 1994

Claude, Inis Jr. *Swords into Plowshares*. New York: Random House, 1964.

Cohen, Jean, and Andrew Arato. *Civil Society and Political Theory*. Cambridge, MA: MIT Press, 1992.

Cohen, Michael. *The History of the Sierra Club 1892–1970*. San Francisco, CA: Sierra Club Books, 1988.

Cohn, D. Vera, and Dan Beyers. "Clean Air Argument Hits Snag." *Washington Post*, 12 March 1992.

Collier, David, ed. *The New Authoritarianism in Latin America*. Princeton, NJ: Princeton University Press, 1979.

Conable, Barbara. "Development and the Environment: A Global Balance." *International Environmental Affairs 2*, no. 1 (Winter 1990).

Conroy, Czech, and Miles Litvinoff, eds. *The Greening of Aid: Sustainable Livelihoods in Practice*. London: International Institute for Environment and Development, 1988.

Cook, Elizabeth. "Global Environmental Advocacy: Citizen Activism in Protecting the Ozone Layer." *Ambio*, no. 14 (October 1990).

Cortright, David. *Peace Works: The Citizen's Role in Ending the Cold War.* Boulder, CO: Westview Press, 1993.

Council on Economic Priorities. *Shopping for a Better World.* New York: Council on Economic Priorities, 1988.

Cowell, Alan. "The Hidden Population Issue: Money." *New York Times*, 12 September 1994, A6.

Dalton, Russell, Manfred Kuechler, and Wilhelm Burklin. "The Challenge of New Movements." In *Challenging the Political Order: New Social and Political Movements in Western Democracies*, eds. Russell Dalton and Manfred Kuechler. New York: Oxford University Press, 1990.

Day, David. *The Whale War.* San Francisco: Sierra Club Books, 1987.

Day, David. *The Environmental Wars.* New York: Ballantine Books, 1989.

Day, Gordon M. "The Indian as an Ecological Factor in the Northeastern Forest," *Ecology 34*, no. 2 (April 1953).

de Haes, Charles. "Director General's Report." In *World Wildlife Fund Yearbook 1980–81*. Gland, Switzerland: WWF, 1981.

Deihl, Colin. "Antarctica: An International Laboratory." *Boston College Environmental Affairs Law Review 18*, no. 3 (Spring 1991).

de Seynes, Philippe. "Prospects for a Future Whole World." *International Organization 26*, no. 1 (1972).

de Tocqueville, Alexis. *Democracy in America*, ed. J. P. Mayer. New York: Doubleday, 1969.

Deudney, Daniel. "Toward Planetary Republicanism." Unpublished manuscript, Princeton University, Princeton, New Jersey, 1988.

Dobson, Andrew. *Green Political Thought.* London: Unwin Hyman, 1990.

Donnelly, Marydele. "Cayman Turtle Farm Cited for International Trade Infractions." *Marine Turtle Newsletter*, no. 58 (July 1992).

Dorfman, Ariel. "Bread and Burnt Rice: Culture and Economic Survival in Latin America." *Grassroots Development 7*, no. 2 (1984).

Doyle, Jack. "Valdez Principles: Corporate Code of Conduct." *Social Policy 20* (Winter 1990).

Doyle, Michael. "Kant, Liberalism and Foreign Affairs." [part one] *Philosophy and Public Affairs 12*, no. 3.

Drabek, Anne. "Developing Alternatives: The Challenge for NGOs—An Overview of the Issues." *World Development 15*, supplement (Autumn 1987).

Drabek, Anne. "Editor's Preface." In *World Development* 15, supplement (Autumn 1987).

Dryzek, John. *Rational Ecology: Environmental and Political Economy.* Oxford: Basil Blackwell, 1987.

Duchacek, Ivo. *The Territorial Dimension of Politics Within, Among and Across Nations.* Boulder, CO: Westview Press, 1986.

Dunlap, Riley. "Public Opinion in the 1980s: Clear Consensus; Ambiguous Commitment." *Environment 33*, no. 8 (October 1991).

Dunlap, Riley, George Gallup Jr., and Alec Gallup. "Of Global Concern: Results of the Health of the Planet Survey." *Environment 53*, no. 9 (November 1993).

Durning, Alan. "Action at the Grassroots: Fighting Poverty and Environmental Decline." *Worldwatch Paper 88*, Washington, DC: Worldwatch Institute, 1989.

Dykstra, Peter. "Greenpeace." *Environment 28*, no. 6 (July/August 1986).

Earth Island Institute, "On the Front Line of the Whale Wars." *Earth Island Journal 9*, no. 3 (September 1993).

"The Earth Summit Debacle." *The Ecologist 22*, no. 4 (July/August 1992).

Easterbrook, Gregg. "Forget PCB's, Radon, Alar: The World's Greatest Environmental Dangers are Dung Smoke and Dirty Water." *New York Times Magazine*, 11 September 1994.

Eckersley, Robyn. *Environmentalism and Political Theory: Toward an Ecocentric Approach.* Albany: State University of New York Press, 1992.

Eckstein, Harry. "A Cultural Theory of Social Change." *American Political Science Review 82*, no. 3 (September 1988).

Elkins, David, and Richard Simeon. "A Cause in Seach of its Effect, or What Does Political Culture Explain?" *Comparative Politics 11*, no. 2 (January 1979).

Enloe, Cynthia. *Bananas, Beaches and Bases: Making Feminist Sense of International Politics.* Berkeley: University of California Press, 1990.

Environmental Defense Fund and Robert Boyle. *Malignant Neglect.* New York: Knopf, 1979.

Evans, Peter, Dietrich Rueschemyer, and Theda Skocpol, eds. *Bringing the State Back In.* New York: Cambridge University Press, 1985.

Faich, Richard and Richard, Gale. "The Environmental Movement From Recreation to Politics." *Pacific Sociological Review 14*, no. 3 (1971).

Falk, Richard. *A Global Approach to Foreign Policy.* Cambridge, MA: Harvard University Press, 1975.

Falk, Richard. *The End of World Order.* New York: Holmes and Meier, 1983.

Falk, Richard. "Normative Initiatives and Demilitarisation: A Third System Approach." In *The Promise of World Order: Essays in Normative International Relations.* Philadelphia: Temple University Press, 1987.

Falk, Richard. "The Special Challenge of Our Time: Cultural Norms Relating to Nuclearism." In *Cultural Norms, War and the Environment,* ed. Arthur Westing. Oxford: Oxford University Press, 1988.

Falk, Richard. *Explorations at the Edge of Time: Prospects for World Order.* Philadelphia, PA: Temple University Press, 1992.

Faludi, Susan. *Backlash: The Undeclared War Against American Women.* New York: Crown, 1991.

Farrington, John, and Anthony Bebbington. *Reluctant Partners? Non-Governmental Organizations, the State and Sustainable Agricultural Development.* London: Routledge, 1993.

Feld, Werner. *Nongovernmental Forces and World Politics: A Study of Business, Labor and Political Groups.* New York: Praeger, 1972.

Feld, Werner. *International Relations: A Transnational Approach.* Van Nuys, CA: Alfred Publishing, 1979.

Feld, Werner, and Robert Jordan. *International Organizations: A Comparative Approach.* New York: Praeger, 1983.

Fisher, Julie. *The Road From Rio: Sustainable Development and the Nongovernmental Movement in the Third World.* Westport, CT: Praeger, 1993.

Flavin, Christopher. "Carbon Emissions Steady." In *Vital Signs 1992: The Trends that are Shaping Our Future,* eds. Lester Brown et al. New York: W.W. Norton, 1992.

"A Flexible Approach to Ending Northeast Smog Pollution," *Environmental Defense Fund Letter* (September 1994).

Forsythe, David. *Human Rights and World Politics.* 2d ed. Lincoln: University of Nebraska Press, 1989.

Foucault, Michel. *Discipline and Punish: The Birth of the Prison.* New York: Vintage Books, 1977.

Foucault, Michel. *Power/Knowledge: Selected Interviews and Other Writings, 1972–1977.* ed., Colin Gordon. New York: Pantheon, 1980.

Fox, Stephen. *John Muir and his Legacy.* Boston: Little, Brown, 1981.

Frederick, Howard. *Global Communications and International Relations.* Belmont, CA: Wadsworth Publishing Company, 1993.

French, Hilary. "After the Earth Summit: The Future of Environmental Governance." *Worldwatch Paper 107,* Washington, DC: Worldwatch Institute, 1992.

French, Hilary. "Rebuilding the World Bank." In *State of the World 1994.* New York: W.W. Norton, 1994.

Friends of the Earth/Oceanic Society/Environmental Policy Institute. *An NGO Perspective on the IMF: The Need to Reform.* Washington, DC: August, 1989.

Friends of the Earth International. "North American Cities Sign Ozone Accord." *Atmosphere 2,* no. 3 (Fall 1989).

Fuller, Kathryn, and Douglas Williamson. "Debt-for-Nature Swaps: A Means of Funding Conservation in Developing Countries." *International Environmental Reporter 11,* no. 5 (5 May 1988).

Futton, Robert, Jr. *Predatory Rule: State and Civil Society in Africa.* Boulder, CO: Lynne Reinner, 1992.

Galtung, Johan. *The True Worlds: A Transnational Perspective.* New York: The Free Press, 1980.

Galtung, Johan. "The Peace Movement: An Exercise in Micro-Macro Linkages." *International Social Science Journal 40,* no. 117 (August 1989): 377–382.

Gelb, Joyce. "Feminism and Political Action." In *Challenging the Political Order: New Social and Political Movements in Western Democracies,* eds. Russell Dalton and Manfred Kuechler. New York: Oxford University Press, 1990.

General Accounting Office. *International Environment: International Agreements are Not Being Well Monitored.* 27 January 1992. CGAO/RCED-92-43.

Gerson, Noel, and Diana Page, eds. *Debt For Nature: An Opportunity.* Washington, DC: WWF, 1989.

Gilfillan, Corinna. "Friends of the Earth Launches Halon Campaign in Takoma Park." *The Takoma Voice,* October 1994.

Gill, Stephen, ed., *Gramsci, Historical Materialism and International Relations.* Cambridge: Cambridge University Press, 1993.

Gillroy, John, and Robert Shapiro. "The Polls: Environmental Protection." *Public Opinion Quarterly 50,* no. 2 (Summer 1986).

Gilpin, Robert. "The Politics of Transnational Economic Relations." In *Transnational Relations and World Politics,* ed., Robert Keohane and Joseph Nye. Cambridge, MA: Harvard University Press, 1972.

Gilpin, Robert. "Three Models of the Future." In *Transnational Corporations and World Order,* ed. George Modelski. San Francisco: W.H. Freeman, 1979.

Goldman, Robert. "International Humanitarian Law: Americas Watch's Experience in Monitoring Internal Armed Conflict." *The American University Journal of International Law and Policy 9,* no. 1 (Fall 1993).

Goldstein, Judith, and Robert Keohane, eds. *Ideas and Foreign Policy: Beliefs, Institutions and Political Change.* Ithaca, NY: Cornell University Press, 1993.

Gramsci, Antonio. *Prison Notebooks.* New York: International Publishers, 1971.

Gramsci, Antonio. *Selections from the Prison Notebooks.* New York: International Publishers, 1985.

Gray, J. Glenn. *The Warriors: Reflections on Men in Battle.* New York: Harper & Row, 1970.

Greenpeace. "Fifteen Years at the Front Lines." *Greenpeace Examiner 11,* no. 3 (October/December 1986).

Greenpeace. *Overview of Greenpeace Origins.* [Pamphlet] Vancouver, Canada: Greenpeace, 1988.

Greico, Joseph. "Anarchy and the Limits of Cooperation: A Realist Critique of the Newest Liberal Institutionalism." *International Organization* 42, no. 3 (Summer 1985).

Gusfield, Joseph. "Social Movements and Social Change: Perspectives on Linearity and Fluidity." In *Research in Social Movements, Conflicts and Change*, vol. 4, ed. Louis Kriesberg. Greenwich, CT: JAI Press, 1981.

Haas, Ernst. *Beyond the Nation-State*. Stanford, CA: Stanford University Press, 1968.

Haas, Peter. *Saving the Mediterranean: The Politics of International Environmental Cooperation*. New York: Columbia University Press, 1990.

Haas, Peter. *International Environmental Issues: An ACUNS Teaching Text*. New York: Academic Council on the U.N., 1991.

Haas, Peter. "Introduction: Epistemic Communities and International Policy Coordination." *International Organization* 46, no. 1 (Winter 1992).

Haas, Peter. "Banning Chlorofluorocarbons: Epistemic Community Efforts to Protect Stratospheric Ozone." *International Organization* 46, no. 1 (Winter 1992).

Haas, Peter, Robert Keohane, and Marc Levy, eds. *Institutions for the Earth: Sources of Effective international Protection*. Cambridge, MA: MIT Press, 1993.

Haas, Peter, Marc Levy, and Edward Parson. "How Should We Judge UNCED's Success?" *Environment 34*, no. 8 (October 1992).

Haberman, Clyde. "Pope Harshly Rebukes Lands that Foster Ecological Crisis." *New York Times*, 12 December 1988.

Habermas, Jurgen. "What Does a Crisis Mean Today? Legitimation Problems in Late Capitalism." In *Jurgen Habermas on Society and Politics*, ed. Steven Seidman. Boston: Beacon Press, 1989.

Hall, Alan. "The World's Frozen Clean Room." *Business Week*, 22 January 1990.

Halliday, Fred. "Three Concepts of Internationalism." *International Affairs 64*, no. 2 (Spring 1988).

Hanchard, Michael. "Identity, Meaning and the African-American." *Social Text 24* (Winter 1990).

Hardin, Garrett. *Exploring New Ethics for Survival.* New York: Viking Press, 1972.

Hardin, Garrett. "The Tragedy of the Commons." In *Managing the Commons,* eds. Garrett Hardin and John Baden. San Francisco: W.H. Freeman, 1977.

Havel, Vaclav. *Open Letters: Selected Writings 1965–1990,* ed. Paul Wilson. New York: Knopf, 1991.

Hays, Samuel. *Beauty, Health, and Permanence: Environmental Politics in the U.S. 1955–1985.* Cambridge: Cambridge University Press, 1987.

Heilbroner, Robert. *An Inquiry into the Human Prospect: Looked at Again for the 1990s.* New York: W.W. Norton, 1991.

Held, David. "Introduction: Central Perspectives on the Modern State." In *States and Societies,* ed. David Held New York: New York University Press, 1983.

Holsti, K. J. *The Dividing Discipline: Hegemony and Diversity in International Theory.* Boston, Massachusetts: Allen and Unwin, 1985.

Holsti, K. J. "Mirror, Mirror on the Wall, Which are the Fairest Theories of All." *International Studies Quarterly* 37, no. 3 (September 1987).

Hughes, J. Donald. *Ecology in Ancient Civilization.* Albuquerque: University of New Mexico Press, 1975.

Hunter, Robert. *Warriors of the Rainbow: A Chronicle of the Greenpeace Movement.* New York: Holt, Rinehart and Winston, 1979.

Hutchins, Robert. "Constitutional Foundations for World Order." In *The Strategy of World Order,* vol. 1, eds. Richard Falk and Saul Mendlovitz. New York: World Law Fund, 1966.

Hyde, Terrill. "U.S. Taxes: The Issues." In *Debt for Nature: An Opportunity,* eds. Noel Gerson and Diana Page. Washington, DC: WWF, 1989.

Hyden, Goran. *No Shortcuts to Progress: Africa Development Management in Perspective.* London: Heinemann, 1983.

Hyden, Goran. "African Social Structure and Economic Development." In *Strategies for African Development,* eds. Robert Berg and Jenifer Whitaker. Berkeley: University of California Press, 1986.

Inglehart, Ronald. "Values, Ideology, and Cognitive Mobilization in New Social Movements." In *Challenging the Political Order: New Social and Political Movements in Western Democracies,* eds. Russell Dalton and Manfred Kuechler. New York: Oxford University Press, 1990.

International Council for Bird Preservation. *Interim Report to WWF–US: January 1992–June 1992.* London: WWF, 1992.

Jacobson, David. "The State System in the Age of Rights." Ph.D. dissertation, Princeton University, 1991.

Jacobson, Harold. *Networks of Interdependence: International Organizations and the Global Political System.* New York: Knopf, 1979.

Jaffe, Daniel, Elizabeth Leighton, and Mark Tumeo. "Environmental Impact on the Polar Regions." *Forum for Applied Research and Public Policy 9,* no. 1 (Spring 1994).

Jancar-Webster, Barbara, "Eastern Europe and the Former Soviet Union." In *Environmental Politics in the International Arena: Movements, Parties, Organizations and Policy,* ed. Sheldon Kamieniecki. Albany: State University of New York Press, 1993.

Johansen, Robert. *The National and the Human Interest.* Princeton, NJ: Princeton University Press, 1980.

Johnson, F. Ernest, ed. *World Order: Its Intellectual and Cultural Foundations.* New York: Harper and Brothers, 1945.

Joseph, Paul. *Peace Politics.* Philadelphia: Temple University Press, 1993.

Kant, Immanuel. *On History,* ed. Lewis Beck. New York: Bobbs-Merrill, 1963.

Keane, John. *Democracy and Civil Society.* London: Verso, 1988.

Keane, John. "Despotism and Democracy: The Origins and Development of the Distinction Between Civil Society and the State 1750–1850." In *Civil Society and the State: New European Perspectives,* ed. John Keane. London: Verso, 1988.

Keohane, Robert. *International Institutions and State Power: Essays in International Relations Theory.* Boulder, CO: Westview Press, 1989.

Keohane, Robert, and Joseph Nye, eds. *Transnational Relations and World Politics.* Cambridge, MA: Harvard University Press, 1972.

Keohane, Robert, and Joseph Nye. *Power and Interdependence: World Politics in Transition.* Boston: Little, Brown, 1977.

Keostler, Arthur. "The Yogi and the Commissar." In *The Yogi and the Commissar and Other Essays.* New York: Macmillan, 1946.

Kimball, Lee. "The Role of Non-Governmental Organizations in Antarctic Affairs." In *The Antarctica Legal Regime*, eds. Christopher Joyner and Sudhir Chopra. Dordrecht: Martinus Nijhoff Publishers, 1988.

Kimball, Lee. *Forging International Agreement: Strengthening Inter-Governmental Institutions for Environment and Development*. Washington DC: World Resources Institute, 1992.

King, Peter. *Protect Our Planet: An Anniversary View from the World Wildlife Fund*. London: Quiller Press, 1986.

Kissinger, Henry. *Observations: Selected Speeches and Essays, 1982–1984*. Boston: Little, Brown, 1988.

Knox, T. M., trans. *Hegel's Philosophy of Right*. London: Oxford University Press, 1967.

Kohli, Atul, ed. *The State and Development in the Third World*. Princeton, NJ: Princeton University Press, 1986.

Kohr, Leopold. *The Breakdown of Nations*. London: Routledge and Kegan Paul, 1957.

Kothari, Rajni. "The NGOs, The State and World Capitalism." *Social Action 36*, no. 4 (October/December, 1986).

Krasner, Stephen. "Structural Causes and Regime Consequences: Regimes as Intervening Variables." In *International Regimes*, ed. Stephen Krasner. Ithaca, NY: Cornell University Press, 1983.

Kropotkin, Peter. "Selections from *Fields, Factories and Workshops Tomorrow*." In *Notes for the Future: An Alternative History of the Past Decade*, ed. Robin Clark. New York: Universe Books, 1975.

Lapid, Yosef. "The Third Debate: On the Prospects of International Theory in a Post-Positivist Era." *International Studies Quarterly 33*, no. 3 (September 1989).

Larmer, Paul. "The Great White Heap." *Sierra 75* (March/April 1990).

Lasswell, Harold, Daniel Lerner, and Hans Speier, eds. *Propaganda and Communication in World History*. Honolulu, HI: University Press of Hawaii, 1979, 1980.

Leonard, H. Jeffrey. "Overview: Environment and the Poor: Development Strategies for a Common Agenda." In *Environment and the Poor: Development Strategies for a Common Agenda*, ed. H. Jeffrey Leonard. New Brunswick, NJ: Transaction Books, 1989.

Levine, Stephen. *Who Dies? An Investigation of Conscious Living and Conscious Dying.* New York: Anchor Books, 1982.

Lewis, Paul. "Fixing World Crises Isn't Just a Job for Diplomats." *New York Times,* 4 April 1992.

Lipschutz, Ronnie. "Restructuring World Politics: The Emergence of Global Civil Society." *Millennium 21,* no. 3 (Winter 1992).

Livernash, Robert. "The Growing Influence of NGOs in the Developing World." *Environment 34,* no. 5 (June 1992).

Lovejoy, Thomas. "Aid Debtor Nation's Ecology." *New York Times,* 4 October 1984.

Lowenthal, David. "Awareness of Human Impacts: Changing Attitudes and Emphasis." In *The Earth as Transformed by Human Action,* eds. B. L. Turner et al. New York: Cambridge University Press, 1990.

Lugo, Ariel. "Estimating Reductions in the Diversity of Tropical Forest Species." In *Biodiversity,* ed. E. O. Wilson. Washington DC: National Academy Press, 1988.

Lukes, Steven. *Power: A Radical View.* London: Macmillan 1974.

MacNeill, Jim, Pieter Winsemius, and Taizo Yakushiji. *Beyond Interdependence: The Meshing of the World's Economy and the Earth's Ecology.* New York: Oxford University Press, 1991.

Maghroori, Ray, and Bennett Ramberg, eds. *Globalism Versus Realism: International Relations' Third Debate.* Boulder, CO: Westview Press, 1982.

Magraw, Daniel Barstow, and James W. Nickel. "Can Today's International System Handle Transboundary Environmental Problems?" In *Upstream/Downstream: Issues in Environmental Ethics,* ed. Donald Scherer. Philadelphia: Temple University Press, 1990.

Mahoney, Rhona. "Debt-for-Nature Swaps: Who Really Benefits?" *The Ecologist 22,* no. 3 (May/June 1992).

Maksoud, Clovis. "Introduction." In *Environmental Challenges and the Global South UNCED and Beyond.* Washington, DC: The American University, 1992.

Mansbach, Richard, Yale Ferguson, and Donald Lampert. *The Web of World Politics: Non State Actors in the Global System.* Englewood Cliffs, NJ: Prentice-Hall, 1976.

Marx, Karl. "The German Ideology." In *The Marx-Engels Reader*, ed. Robert Tucker. New York: Norton, 1978.

Marx, Karl, and Frederick Engels. "The Manifesto of the Communist Party." In *The Marx-Engels Reader*, ed. Robert Tucker. New York: Norton, 1978.

Mason, Robert, William Solecki, and Enid L. Lotstein. "Comments on *Bioregionalism and Watershed Consciousness.*" *Professional Geographer 39*, no. 1 (1987).

Mathews, Jessica Tuchman. "Introduction and Overview," in Jessica Tuchman Mathews, ed., *Preserving the Global Environment: The Challenge of Shared Leadership.* New York: W. W. Norton, 1991.

McCormick, John. *Reclaiming Paradise: The Global Environmental Movement.* Bloomington: Indiana University Press, 1989.

McPhee, John. *Encounters with the Archdruid: Narratives about a Conservationist and Three of his Natural Enemies.* New York: Farrar, Straus & Giroux, 1971.

McRobie, George. *Small is Possible.* New York: Harper & Row, 1981.

Mellucci, Alberto. "The Symbolic Challenge of Contemporary Movements." *Social Research 52*, no. 4 (1985).

Michnik, Adam. *Letters From Prison and Other Essays*, trans. Maya Latynski. Berkeley: University of California Press, 1987.

Migdal, Joel. *Strong Societies and Weak States: State-Society Relations and State Capabilities in the Third World.* Princeton, NJ: Princeton University Press, 1988.

Milbrath, Lester. *Envisioning a Sustainable Society: Learning Our Way Out.* Albany: State University of New York Press, 1989.

Miller, Alan, and Irving Mintzer. *The Sky Is the Limit: Strategies for Protecting the Ozone Layer.* Washington, DC: World Resources Institute, 1986.

Miller, Casey, and Kate Swift. *The Handbook of Nonsexist Writing.* New York: Barnes & Noble, 1980.

Misch, Ann. "Gandhian Greens Fight Big Dams." *World Watch, 3*, no. 4 (July/August 1990).

Mische, Gerald, and Patricia Mische. *Toward a Human Order: Beyond the National Security Straightjacket.* New York: Paulist Press, 1977.

Mitchell, Timothy. "The Limits of the State: Beyond Statist Approaches and Their Critics." *American Political Science Review* 85, no. 1 (March 1991).

Mitrany, David. *A Working Peace System*. Chicago: University of Chicago Press, 1966.

Mittelman, James. *Out from Underdevelopment: Prospects for the Third World*. New York: St. Martin's Press, 1988.

Modelski, George. "The Corporation in World Society." In *The Year Book of World Affairs* 1968, London Institute of World Affairs. New York: Praeger, 1968.

Modelski, George. *Principles of World Politics*. New York: The Free Press, 1972.

Moltke, Konrad von. "International Commissions and Implementation of International Environmental Law." In *International Environmental Diplomacy: The Management and Resolution of Transfrontier Environmental Problems*, ed. John Carroll. Cambridge: Cambridge University Press, 1988.

Moon, Katharine H. S. "International Relations and Women: A Case-Study of U.S.–Korea Camptown Prostitution, 1971–1976." Ph.D. dissertation, Princeton University, June 1994.

"More Companies to Phase Out Peril to Ozone." *New York Times*, 11 October 1989.

Morgenthau, Hans. *Politics Among Nations: The Struggle for Power and Peace*. New York: Knopf, 1948.

Morgenthau, Hans. *In Defense of the National Interest: A Critical Examination of American Foreign Policy*. New York: Alfred Knopf, 1951.

Mowlana, Hamid. *Global Information and World Communication: New Frontiers in International Relations*. New York: Longman, 1986.

Myers, Norman. *The Sinking Ark: A New Look at the Problems of Disappearing Species*. New York: Pergamon, 1979.

Nelkin, Dorothy, and Michael Pollak. *The Atom Besieged: Extraparliamentary Dissent in France and Germany*. Cambridge, MA: MIT Press, 1981.

Niemi, Richard, John Mueller, and Tom Smith. *Trends in Public Opinion: A Compendium of Survey Data*. Westport, CT: Greenwood Press, 1989.

Nyamaluma Conservation Camp Lupande Development Project. *Zambian Wildlands and Human Needs Newsletter.* March 1990.

Nye, Joseph. "Nuclear Learning and US-Soviet Security Regimes." *International Organization* 41, no. 3 (Summer 1987).

Nye, Joseph. "Neorealism and Neoliberalism." *World Politics 40* (January 1988).

Offe, Claus. "New Social Movements: Challenging the Boundaries of Institutional Politics." *Social Research 52*, no. 4 (1985).

Offe, Claus. "Challenging the Boundaries of Institutional Politics: Social Movements since the 1960s." In *Changing Boundaries of the Political*, ed. Charles Maier. Cambridge: Cambridge University Press, 1987.

Ollapally, Deepa. *Domestic Determinants and International Intervention: U.S. Foreign Policy in Third World Conflicts.* Westport, CT: Greenwood Press, 1993.

Olson, Mancur. *The Logic of Collective Action.* Cambridge, MA: Harvard University Press, 1971.

Olson, Mancur. *The Rise and Decline of Nations: Economic Growth, Stagflation and Social Rigidities.* New Haven, CT: Yale University Press, 1982.

Ophuls, William. *Ecology and the Politics of Scarcity: Prologue to a Political Theory of the Steady State.* San Francisco: W.H. Freeman, 1977.

Ophuls, William, and A. Stephen Boyan. *Ecology and the Politics of Scarcity Revisited: The Unraveling of the American Dream.* New York: W.H. Freeman, 1992.

Orbach, Susie. *Fat is a Feminist Issue.* New York: Berkley Books, 1978.

Organization for Economic Cooperation and Development (OECD). *Development Cooperation in the 1990s: Efforts and Policies of the Members of the Development Assistance Committee.* Paris, France: OECD, 1989.

Orr, David, and Stuart Hill. "Leviathan, the Open Society and the Crisis of Ecology." In *The Global Predicament: Ecological Perspectives on World Order*, eds. David Orr and Marvin Soroos. Chapel Hill: University of North Carolina Press, 1979.

Paehlke, Robert. *Environmentalism and the Future of Progressive Politics.* New Haven, CT: Yale University Press, 1989.

Parson, Edward. "Protecting the Ozone Layer," in Peter Haas, Robert Keohane, and Marc Levy, eds., *Institutions for the Earth: Sources of Effective International Environmental Protection.* Cambridge, MA: MIT Press, 1993.

Parsons, James. "On Bioregionalism and Watershed Consciousness." *The Professional Geographer 37,* no. 1 (February 1985).

Parsons, Talcott. *The System of Modern Societies.* Englewood Cliffs, NJ: Prentice-Hall, 1971.

Passell, Peter. "Washington Offers Mountain of Debt to Save the Forests." *New York Times,* 22 January 1991.

Pearce, Fred. "Europe Discovers the Debt-for-Nature Swap." *New Scientist 133,* no. 1803 (11 January 1992).

Pearce, Fred. "Earth at Mercy of National Interests." *New Scientist 134,* no. 1826 (20 June 1992).

Pearce, Fred. "How Green Was Our Summit?" *New Scientist 134,* no. 1827 (27 June 1992).

Pearson, Charles. "Environment, Development and Multinational Enterprise." In *Multinational Corporations, Environment and the Third World,* ed. Charles Pearson. Durham, NC: Duke University Press, 1987.

Peterson, V. Spike, ed. *Gendered States: Feminist (Re)Visions of International Relations Theory.* Boulder, CO: Lynne Reinner, 1992.

Pateman, Carole. "Feminist Critiques of the Public/Private Dichotomy." In *Public and Private in Social Life,* ed. S. Benn and G. Gauss. Canberra and London: Croom Helm, 1983.

Porritt, Jonathan. *Seeing Green: The Politics of Ecology Explained.* Oxford: Basil Blackwell, 1984.

Porter, Gareth, and Janet Welsh Brown. *Global Environmental Politics.* Boulder, CO: Westview Press, 1991.

Princen, Thomas and Matthias Finger. *Environmental NGOs and World Politics: Linking the Local and the Global.* London: Routledge, 1994.

Proceedings of the Workshop on Community Forest/Protected Area Management. Sponsored by the Ministry of Environment and Forests. Yaounde, Cameroon: 12–13 October 1993.

Ramphal, Shridath. *Our Country, The Planet: Forging a Partnership for Survival.* Washington, DC: Island Press, 1992.

Reddy, Rama. "The Cooperative Sector and Government Control." *Social Action 36*, no. 4 (October/December, 1986).

Rich, Bruce. "The Emperor's New Clothes: The World Bank and Environmental Reform." *World Policy Journal 7*, no. 2 (Spring 1990).

Rich, Bruce. *Mortgaging the Earth: The World Bank, Environmental Impoverishment and the Crisis of Development.* Boston: Beacon Press, 1994.

Riding, Alan. "Pact Bans Oil Exploration in Antarctic." *New York Times,* 5 October 1991.

Roan, Sharon. *Ozone Crisis: The Fifteen Year Evolution of a Sudden Global Emergency.* New York: Wiley, 1989.

Rochon, Thomas. *Mobilizing for Peace: Antinuclear Movements in Western Europe.* Princeton, NJ: Princeton University Press, 1988.

Rose, Chris. "Over 25 years: A Review of WWF Projects 1961–1986." In *World Wildlife Fund Yearbook 1986–87.* Gland, Switzerland: WWF, 1987.

Rose, Tom. *Freeing the Whales: How the Media Created the World's Greatest Non-Event.* New York: Birch Lane Press, 1989.

Rosenau, James. *Turbulence in World Politics.* Princeton, NJ: Princeton University Press, 1990.

Rosenau, James. "Governance, Order and Change in World Politics," in James Rosenau and Ernst-Otto Czempiel, eds., *Governance Without Government.* Cambridge: Cambridge University Press, 1992.

Roszak, Theodore. *Person/Planet: The Creative Disintegration of Industrial Society.* New York: Anchor Press, 1978.

Roszak, Theodore. *The Voice of the Earth.* New York: Simon & Schuster, 1992.

Rothchild, Donald, and Naomi Chazan, eds. *The Precarious Balance.* Boulder, CO: Westview Press, 1988.

Rucht, Dieter. "The Strategies and Action Repertoires of New Movements." In *Challenging the Political Order: New Social and Political Movements in Western Democracies,* eds. Russell Dalton and Manfred Kuechler. New York: Oxford University Press, 1990.

Rudig, Wolfgang. "Green Party Politics Around the World." *Environment 33*, no. 8 (October 1991).

Ruggie, John Gerald. "Territoriality and Beyond: Problematizing Modernity in International Relations." *International Organization 47*, no. 1 (Winter 1993).

Russell, Bertrand. *Power: A New Social Analysis*. New York: W.W. Norton, 1938.

Ryan, John. "Conserving Biological Diversity." In *State of the World 1992*, eds. Lester Brown et al. New York: W.W. Norton, 1992.

Said, Abdul A., and Luiz Simmons, eds. *The New Sovereigns: Multinational Corporations as World Powers*. Englewood Cliffs, NJ: Prentice–Hall, 1975.

Saint, Kishmore. "Development and People's Participation." *Social Action 30*, no. 3 (July-September 1980).

Sale, Kirkpatrick. *Dwellers in the Land: The Bioregional Vision*. Philadelphia: New Society Publishers, 1991.

Sands, P. J. "The Role of Non-Governmental Organizations in Enforcing International Environmental Law." In *Control over Compliance with International Law*, ed. W. E. Butler. Netherlands: Kluer Academic Publishers, 1991.

Sarkar, Amin, and Karen Ebbs. "A Possible Solution to Tropical Troubles? Debt-for-Nature Swaps." *Futures 24*, no. 7 (September 1992).

Scare, Rik. *Eco-Warriors: Understanding the Radical Environmental Movement*. Chicago: Noble Press, 1990.

Schiller, Herbert. *Mass Communication and American Empire*. Boulder, CO: Westview Press, 1992.

Schubert, Louise. "Environmental Politics in Asia." In *Environmental Politics in the International Arena: Movements, Parties, Organizations and Policy*, ed. Sheldon Kamieniecki. Albany: State University of New York Press, 1993.

Schumacher, E. F. *Small is Beautiful: Economics as if People Mattered*. New York: Harper & Row, 1973.

Schweller, Randall. "Domestic Structure and Preventive War." *World Politics 44*, no. 2 (January 1992).

Scott, Peter, ed. *The Launching of the Ark*. London: Collins, 1964.

Scruton, Roger. *Dictionary of Political Thought*. New York: Harper & Row, 1982.

Shabecoff, Philip. *A Fierce Green Fire: The American Environmental Move-ment*. New York: Hill and Wang, 1993.

Shabecoff, Philip. "Conservation Figure Ousted for Resisting Orders to Cut Staff." *New York Times*, 7 July 1984.

Shaull, Richard. *Heralds of a New Reformation: The Poor of South and North America*. New York: Orbis Books, 1984.

Shea, Cynthia Pollock. "Doing Well by Doing Good." *World Watch 2*, no. 6 (Nov./Dec. 1989).

Sheth, D. L. "Alternative Development as Political Practice." In *Towards a Just World Peace: Perspectives from Social Movements*, eds. Saul Mendlovitz and R. B. J. Walker. London: Butterworths, 1987.

Shiva, Vandana. "People's Ecology: The Chipko Movement." In *Towards a Just World Peace: Perspectives from Social Movements*, eds. Saul Mendlovitz and R. B. J. Walker London: Butterworths, 1987.

Shiva, Vandana. "The Greening of Global Reach." *The Ecologist 22*, no. 6 (November/December 1992.

Shuman, Michael. "Dateline Main Street: Courts vs. Local Foreign Poli-cies." *Foreign Policy*, no. 86 (Spring 1992).

Shuman, Michael *Toward a Global Village: International Community Development Initiatives*, London: Pluto Press 1994

Sikkink, Kathryn. "Human Rights Issue–Networks in Latin America." *International Organization 47*, no. 3 (Summer 1993).

Skinner, Nancy. "Atmospheric Protection Update." *Bulletin of Municipal Foreign Policy 4*, no. 2 (Spring 1990).

Sklair, Leslie. *Sociology of the Global System*. Baltimore: Johns Hopkins University Press, 1991.

Skocpol, Theda. "Bringing the State Back In: Strategies of Analysis in Cur-rent Research." In *Bringing the State Back In* eds. Peter Evans, Diet-rich Rueschemyer and Theda Skocpol. NY: Cambridge University Press 1985.

Skocpol, Theda. *States and Social Revolutions*. Cambridge: Cambridge University Press, 1979.

Smart, Bruce. *Beyond Compliance: A New Industry View of the Environ-ment*. Washington, DC: World Resources Institute, 1992.

Snyder, Gary. *The Practice of the Wild.* Berkeley, CA: North Point Press, 1990.

Soroos, Marvin. "The Future of the Environment." In *Environment and the Global Arena,* eds. Kenneth Dahlberg. Durham, NC: Duke University Press, 1985.

Soucie, Gary. "Interview." *Not Man Apart,* February 1971.

The South Commission. *The Challenge of the South.* Geneva Switzerland: The South Commission, 1990.

Spence, Leslie, Jan. Bollwerk, and Richard C. Morais. "The Not So Peaceful World of Greenpeace." *Forbes,* 11 November 1991.

Sprinz, Detlef, and Vaahtoranta, Tapani. "The Interest-Based Explanation of International Environmental Policy," *International Organization 48,* no. 1, (Winter 1994).

Stairs, Kevin, and Peter Taylor, "Non-Governmental Organizations and the Legal Protection of the Oceans: A Case Study." In *The International Politics of the Environment,* eds. Andrew Hurrell and Benedict Kingsbury. Oxford: Oxford University Press, 1992.

Stammer, Larry. "Founder Quits Friends of the Earth, Says Situation 'Just Got Hopeless'." *Los Angeles Times,* 11 October 1986.

Stanley, John. "Treaty Compliance Can't Be Enforced." *Earth Summit Times,* 9 June 1992.

Starke, Linda. *Signs of Hope: Working Toward Our Common Future.* New York: Oxford University Press, 1990.

"States Forge Ahead, Require Car CFC Recycling." *Not Man Apart,* June-September 1989.

Stein, Robert. *Banking on the Biosphere? Environmental Procedures and Practices of Nine Multilateral Development Agencies.* Lexington, MA: Lexington Books, 1979.

Steiner, Todd, Mark Heitchue, and Henry W. Ghriskey. "Banned Sea Turtle Products Still Exported from Mexico." In *Earth Island Journal 9,* no. 3 (Summer 1994).

Stepan, Alfred. *State and Society: Peru in Comparative Perspective.* Princeton, NJ: Princeton University Press, 1978.

Stone, Christopher. "The Law as a Force in Shaping Cultural Norms Relating to War and the Environment." In *Cultural Norms, War and the*

Environment, ed. Arthur Westing. New York: Oxford University Press, 1988.

Stone, Roger. "The View from Kilum Mountain." *World Wildlife Fund Letter,* no. 4, 1989.

Stone, Roger. "Zambia's Innovative Approach to Conservation." *World Wildlife Fund Letter,* no. 7, 1989.

Sullivan, Michael. "Transnationalism, Power Politics and the Realities of the Present System." In *Globalism Versus Realism: International Relations' Third Debate,* eds. Ray Maghroori and Bennett Ramberg. Boulder, CO: Westview Press, 1982.

Sumida Gerald, "Transnational Movements and Economic Structures." In *The Future of the International Legal Order,* vol. 4, eds. Cyril Black and Richard Falk. Princeton, NJ: Princeton University Press, 1972.

Sun, Marjorie. "Swapping Debt for Nature." *Science 239* (March 1988).

Sundaram, Anant. "Swapping Debt for Debt in Less-Developed Countries: A Case Study of a Debt-for-Nature Swap in Ecuador." *International Environmental Affairs 2,* no. 1 (Winter 1990).

The Sunday Times Insight Team. *Rainbow Warrior: The French Attempt to Sink Greenpeace.* London: Hutchinson, 1986.

Susskind, Lawrence, and Connie Ozawa, "Negotiating More Effective International Environmental Agreements." In *The International Politics of the Environment,* eds. Andrew Hurrell and Benedict Kingsbury. Oxford: Oxford University Press, 1992.

Swain, Will. "Making Foreign Policy at City Hall." *The Progressive 52* (July 1988).

Talbot, Lee. "Helping Development Countries Help Themselves." *World Resources Institute Working Paper,* January 1985.

Thiele, Leslie Paul. "Foucault's Triple Murder and the Modern Development of Power." *Canadian Journal of Political Science 19,* no. 2 (June 1986).

Thiele, Leslie Paul. "Social Movements and the Interface of Domestic and International Politics: A Study of Peace Activism." Presented at the 1990 Annual Meeting of the American Political Science Association, San Francisco, CA, 1990.

"This is Your Life, In General." *New York Times,* 26 July 1992.

Thomas, Caroline. *The Environment in International Relations*. London: Royal Institute of International Affairs, 1992.

"Time Passes, As Clinton Adopts Anti-Chlorine Stance." *Greenpeace* 2, no. 2 (March/April/May 1994).

Torfs, Marijke. *Effects of the IMF Structural Adjustment Programs on Social Sectors of Third World Countries*. Washington, DC: Friends of the Earth/Environmental Policy Institute/Oceanic Society, May 1991.

Touraine, Alain. *Anti-Nuclear Protest: The Opposition to Nuclear Energy in France*. Cambridge: Cambridge University Press, 1983.

Trexler, Mark, Paul Faeth, and John Kramer. *Forestry As A Response to Global Warming: An Analysis of the Guatemala Agroforestry and Carbon Sequestration Project*. Washington, DC: World Resources Institute, 1989.

Tucker, Robert, ed. *The Marx-Engels Reader*. New York: Norton, 1978.

Tucker, Robert. *Politics as Leadership*. New York: Columbia University Press, 1981.

Tuner, Tom. *Friends of the Earth: The First Sixteen Years*. San Francisco: Earth Island Institute, 1986.

Turner, Ralph. "The Theme of Contemporary Social Movements." In *The Sociology of Dissent*, eds. R. Serge Denisoff and Robert Merton. New York: Harcourt Brace Jovanovich, 1974.

Turner, Wallace. "A.E.C. Dismantles Aleutian Test Site of Controversial '71 Underground Blast." *New York Times*, 5 August 1972.

Udall, Lori. "Protesters in India: World Bank, Stop Funding Sardar Sarovar Dam." *Not Man Apart 19*, no. 1 (February/May 1989).

UNESCO. *Statistical Yearbook 1988*. Paris, France: UNESCO, 1988.

UNESCO. *Statistical Yearbook 1991*. Paris, France: UNESCO, 1991.

United Nations. *Survey of Existing Agreements and Instruments and Its Follow-up*. A/Conf.151/PC/103, 20 January 1992.

Uphoff, Norman, and Milton Esman. *Local Organization for Rural Development in Asia*. Ithaca, NY: Center for International Studies, Cornell University, November 1974.

U.S. Bureau of the Census. *Statistical Abstract of the United States 1993*. Washington DC: Bureau of the Census, 1993.

U.S. Congress. Senate. Committee on the Environment and Public Works. *Ozone Depletion, the Global Effect, and Climate Change: Joint Hearings Before the Subcommittee on Environmental Protection and Hazardous Wastes and Toxic Substances.* Testimony of Richard Barnett. 100th Cong., 1st sess., 1987.

"U.S. Utility Turns to Guatemala to Aid Air." *New York Times,* 11 October 1988.

Van Liere, Kent, and Riley Dunlap. "The Social Bases of Environmental Concern: A Review of Hypotheses, Explanations and Empirical Evidence." *Public Opinion Quarterly 44,* no. 2 (Summer 1980).

Verhagen, Herman. "Dutch Tropical Rainforest Campaign Successful." *FOE Link,* March 1989.

Vernon, Raymond. "*Sovereignty at Bay*: Ten Years After." *International Organization 35,* no. 3, 1981.

Victor, David. "Implementation and Effectiveness of International Environmental Commitments." *Options* (Spring 1994).

Wagar, Warren W. *The City of Man.* New York: Penguin Books 1963.

Wald, Matthew. "Recharting War on Smog: States like California are Taking the Lead Over Washington in Pollution-Control Law." *New York Times,* 10 October 1989.

Wald, Matthew. "Guarding the Environment: A World of Challenges." *New York Times,* 22 April 1990.

Wald, Matthew. "Nine States in East Plan to Restrict Pollution by Cars." *New York Times,* 30 October 1991.

Walker, K. J. "The Environmental Crisis: A Critique of Neo-Hobbesian Responses." *Polity 11,* no. 3 (Fall 1988).

Walker, R. B. J. *One World/Many Worlds.* Boulder, CO: Lynne Rienner Publishers, 1988.

Walker, R. B. J. *Inside/Outside: International Relations as Political Theory.* Cambridge: Cambridge University Press, 1993.

Wallace, Richard. "Structural Adjustment and the Environment: An Analysis of Export Promotion, Market Liberalization and Reductions in Government Spending." *Swords and Ploughshares 2,* no. 1 (Fall 1992).

Wallerstein, Immanuel. *The Capitalist World-Economy.* New York: Cambridge University Press, 1979.

Walters, Gabrielle. "Zambia's Game Plan." *Topic Magazine* [U.S. Information Agency], no. 187, 1989.

Waltz, Kenneth. *Theory of International Politics.* New York: Random House, 1979.

Wapner, Paul. "On the Global Dimension of Environmental Challenges." *Politics and the Life Sciences 13,* no. 2 (August 1994).

Warford, Jeremy, and Zeinab Partow. "Evolution of the World Bank's Environmental Policy." *Finance and Development* 26 (December 1989).

Wass, Nannelore. "Editorial." [Commemorating ten years of publishing *Death Studies*] *Death Studies 10,* no. 1 (1986).

Wendt, Alexander. "The Agent-Structure Problem in International Relations Theory." *International Organization 41,* no. 3 (Summer 1987).

Wenzel, George. *Animal Rights, Human Rights.* Toronto: University of Toronto Press, 1991.

Wignaraja, Ponna, ed. *New Social Movements in the South.* London: Zed Books, 1992.

Willets, Peter. "The Politics of Global Issues: Cognitive Actor Dependence and Issue Linkage." In *Interdependence on Trial,* eds. Barry Jones and Peter Willets. London: Francis Pinter, 1984.

Wilson, Cynthia. "A View from the Trenches." In *Crossroads: Environmental Priorities for the Future,* ed. Peter Borrelli. Washington, DC: Island Press, 1989.

"Withdraw from Sardar Sarovar, Now: An Open Letter to Mr. Lewis T. Preston, President of the World Bank." *The Ecologist 22,* no. 5 (September/October 1992).

Wolf, Naomi, *The Beauty Myth: How images of Beauty are Used Against Women.* New York: William Morrow, 1991.

Wolin, Sheldon. *Politics and Vision: Continuity and Innovation in Western Political Thought.* Boston: Little, Brown, 1960.

World Bank. *World Development Report 1992.* New York: Oxford University Press, 1992.

World Bank. *World Development Report 1994.* New York: Oxford University Press, 1994.

World Commission on Environment and Development. *Our Common Future.* New York: Oxford University Press, 1987.

World Wildlife Fund. "Debt-for-Nature Swaps: A New Conservation Tool." *World Wildlife Fund Letter 1*, no. 1, 1988.

World Wildlife Fund. *1988-1988 Annual Report on the Matching Grant for a Program in Wildlands and Human Needs*. Washington, DC: WWF, 1989. US AID Grant #OTR-0158-A-00-8160-00.

World Wildlife Fund. *The Africa and Madagascar Program* [pamphlet]. Washington DC: WWF, 1994.

World Wildlife Fund. *Project Folder* #6152.

World Wildlife Fund. *Project Folder* #6250.

Wright, Michael. *The Wildlands and Human Needs Program: Program Statement and Framework*. Washington, DC: World Wildlife Fund, April 1990.

Wright, Michael. "People-Centered Conservation: An Introduction." *Wildlands and Human Needs: A Program of World Wildlife Fund* [pamphlet]. Washington, DC: WWF, 1989).

Young, Oran. *Compliance and Public Authority: A Theory with International Applications*. Baltimore: Johns Hopkins University Press, 1979.

Young, Oran. *International Cooperation: Building Regimes for Natural Resources and the Environment*. Ithaca, NY: Cornell University Press, 1989.

Young, Oran. *Arctic Politics: Conflict and Cooperation in the Circumpolar North*. Hanover, NH: University Press of New England, 1992.

Young, Oran, George Demko and Kilaparti Rama Krishna. "Global Environmental Change and International Governance," pamphlet, Dartmouth College, 1991.

Yudelman, Montague. "The World Bank and Agricultural Development— An Insider's View." *World Resources Institute Papers*, no. 1 (December 1985).

Zacher, Mark W., and Richard A. Matthew. "Liberal International Theory: Common Threads, Divergent Strands." In *Controversies in International Relations Theory: Realism and the Neo-Liberal Challenge*, ed. Charles W. Kegley, Jr. New York: St. Martin's Press, 1995.

Zaelke, Durwood, Paul Orbuch, and Robert Housman, eds. *Trade and the Environment: Law, Economics and Policy*. Washington, DC: Island Press, 1993.

Index

A

accountability, 55, 119, 120, 144–146
Alliance for Responsible CFC Policy, 131
anarchism, 33–34
Antarctica, 54–55, 134–138, 141
Antarctic and Southern Ocean Coalition (ASOC), 134–138

B

"bearing witness," 50–51, 54
Benedick, Richard, 131
bioregionalism, 9, 35–36
Boyan, A. Stephen, 30, 31, 36
Brower, David, 121, 124, 126, 194n

C

Caldwell, Lynton, 22, 23
Charter 77, 5
Chemical Manufactures Association, 131
Chipko Movement, 2
chlorofluorocarbons (CFCs), 53,
    and interdependence, 127, 131–132
    and voluntary restrictions, 64–65, 182n
Cicero, 7, 168n

civil society, 4
    definition of, 4, 5, 158
    Gramsci's contribution to, 6, 143, 203
    Hegel's contribution to, 5, 158, 166n, 167n
    and the state, 5, 6
        strengthening of, 102, 104–112
    Tocqueville's contribution to, 5
    See also global civil society
Coalition for Environmentally Responsible Economies (CERES), 129–131, 132
Commission on Sustainable Development (CSD), 20
complex interdependence. See interdependence
Conservation International, 20
Convention on Climate Change, 22–23
Convention on International Trade in Endangered Species (CITES), 3, 8, 22
Convention on the Regulation of Antarctica Mineral Resources Activity (CRAMRA), 136–137

D

debt–for–nature swaps, 93–96, 98, 99, 108
    and debt-for-equity, 94–95,

233